Drug-Impaired Driving in Canada

DRUG-IMPAIRED DRIVING IN CANADA

Nathan Baker

IRWIN LAW

Drug-Impaired Driving in Canada

Published in 2018 by

Irwin Law Inc
Suite 206, 14 Duncan Street
Toronto, ON M5H 3G8
www.irwinlaw.com

ISBN: 978-1-55221-492-3 e-book ISBN: 978-1-55221-493-0

Library and Archives Canada Cataloguing in Publication

Baker, Nathan, author
Drug-impaired driving in Canada / Nathan Baker.

Includes bibliographical references and index.
Issued in print and electronic formats.
ISBN 978-1-55221-492-3 (softcover).—ISBN 978-1-55221-493-0 (PDF)

1. Drugged driving—Law and legislation—Canada. I. Title.

KE2114.B34 2018 345.71'0247 C2018-904410-1
KF2231.B34 2018 C2018-904411-X

Canada
Ontario
Ontario Media Development Corporation
Société de développement de l'industrie des médias de l'Ontario

Printed and bound by CPI Group (UK) Ltd, Croydon, CR0 4YY
1 2 3 4 5 22 21 20 19 18

Contents

Foreword

Drug Recognition Evaluations (DRE) and Standardized Field Sobriety Testing (SFST) still seem to be relatively new introductions to the Canadian criminal justice system. However, it has been almost ten years since they were statutorily approved. In acknowledging the changes brought into being by these amendments, the Quebec Court of Appeal stated it best, in *R v Gaulin*, 2017 QCCA 705 at para 28:

> [T]he objectives of the 2008 statutory amendments were numerous and included facilitating detection and investigation of cases involving driving while impaired by a drug and increasing minimum sentences for impaired driving. Specifically, the amendments authorize trained police officers to impose challenges and tests to determine whether a driver's ability is weakened by a drug or the combined effect of a drug and alcohol. One of the goals of the statutory addition was to toughen sentences for impaired driving and, in cases of driving while impaired by alcohol, to limit challenges of blood alcohol test results.

These goals—the identification and prosecution of individuals impaired by drug—were important to Parliament because of the growing evidence of the harm done by drug-impaired driving. This concern continues to grow as we enter a new stage in Canada with the legalization of another impairing substance, marijuana.

The law relating to driving under the influence of drugs is currently evolving. This is as a result of the impending legalization of marijuana, the ongoing "opioid crisis," and a rise in the use of prescription drugs for an aging population. Along with the impending legalization of marijuana comes companion legislation regarding impaired driving involving drugs. This will bring an enhanced focus on the DRE and SFST, as well as new technologies to confirm by chemical means the use of drugs, both illicit and prescribed, in drivers. New legal presumptions will also be required, and these will undoubtedly be the subject of significant litigation. It is important that Crown Attorneys, defence lawyers, and the judiciary all have a working knowledge of the strengths and weaknesses of this testing and how the *Charter of Rights and Freedoms* will apply.

ALCOHOL: JUST ANOTHER DRUG?

Drug is defined in *Black's Law Dictionary*, 7th ed, as:

1. A substance intended for use in the diagnosis, cure, treatment, or prevention of disease.
2. A natural or synthetic substance that alters one's perception or consciousness.

Drug is not defined in the *Criminal Code* or the *Controlled Drugs and Substances Act*. As a result, many things that might not otherwise be considered drugs are potentially included.

The one strange-seeming exception to this lack of definition is alcohol. Alcohol, while classified as a drug in most scientific opinions, is specifically dealt with separately from other drugs in the *Criminal Code*. It's important to note this, as other legal drugs are not. This classification originated from an early understanding of the impairing effects of alcohol and societal views on driving while impaired by this drug. However, the failure over successive revisions to the *Criminal Code* to include alcohol with other drugs shows a parliamentary intent to deal with it separately. That being said, although alcohol is treated separately, it is often useful to consider alcohol-impaired driving as a learning point for drug-impaired driving. Conceptually, they are no different.

Imagine an alcohol-impaired driving charge where, for some reason, there are no samples of breath or blood to test, or at least where no evidence of exceeding the *per se* limit is forthcoming. In this scenario, impaired driving can still be shown. The ability of civilian witnesses, police officers, and other lay witnesses to recognize the effects of alcohol has been well established. While impairment by other drugs is not necessarily something in the experience of every lay witness, with the legalization of marijuana forthcoming and its use in society having become so prevalent, caselaw may soon change to recognize that lay witnesses can speak to such impairment. Operating a motor vehicle is a complex task that requires the ability to perceive and react, often with attention divided among multiple tasks. Typically, the impairment of such abilities is evident through poor driving, lack of physical coordination, or other observed indicia. The true question for the trier-of-fact in most cases is whether that impairment rises to that which impairs the ability to operate a motor vehicle and whether that impairment is caused by a drug (alcohol or otherwise).

Assessing impairment to a criminal degree necessitates reference to the *Stellato* test of a constellation of factors. This must be more than any impairment but need not be a marked departure from the norm:

> In all criminal cases the trial judge must be satisfied as to the accused's guilt beyond a reasonable doubt before a conviction can be registered. Accordingly, before convicting an accused of impaired driving, the trial judge must be satisfied that the accused's ability to operate a motor vehicle was impaired by alcohol or a drug. If the evidence of impairment is so frail as to leave the trial judge with a reasonable doubt as to impairment, the accused must be acquitted. If the evidence of impairment establishes any degree of impairment ranging from slight to great, the offence has been made out.
>
> *R v Stellato*, 1993 ONCA 3375 at para 14, aff'd 1994 CanLII 94 (SCC)

Typically, this is a question of fact that a judge or jury can assess without significant help from experts, including officers designated as Drug Recognition Experts. The leap of faith that is typically in the way of conviction is determining whether the signs of impairment are the result of the effects of a drug or something else. This is particularly difficult where drugs have been consumed to deal with a medical issue and the impairment could be caused by there being too much drug and thus worthy of criminality, or not enough drug to treat the illness and therefore the impairment is caused by the illness and not to be criminalized.

DRE testing seeks to link the ability to perform certain divided-attention tasks and the ability to operate a motor vehicle while using the results of other physical tests to categorize to a class of drug. However, the link between these two sides of DRE testing is where a trier-of-fact is often left most concerned. Much of this book concerns itself with how and when that link is and is not made.

It is useful to refer to alcohol-impaired driving as a conceptual starting point. If the individual is unable to operate their motor vehicle properly, if they have clear signs of impairment, if witnesses provide credible and reliable evidence of that impairment, if there is proof of consumption, such as the odour of alcoholic beverage or admission, and if the signs of impairment are consistent with human experience with being impaired by alcohol (here an expert may be necessary in a drug-impaired driving case), then a *prima facie* case will be made out. The trier-of-fact may be left with an inescapable inference of impairment by alcohol, barring an effective defence counsel pointing out where the links are not made, where there are other inferences to be made, or where the Crown has otherwise not proven its case. Sometimes matters are overcomplicated needlessly and both Crown and defence need to simplify their thinking in order to obtain a conviction or an acquittal.

It is important to note that it is the *Criminal Code* that makes a distinction between alcohol and a drug, even though, medically, alcohol is a drug. Alcohol is a central nervous system depressant and should be noted as such during Drug Recognition Evaluations.

The penalties for impaired operation by alcohol and impaired operation by drug are different, and while everyone knows not to drink and drive, many people do not understand the effects that drugs, be they prescription, illicit, or otherwise, have on them.

The *Criminal Code* draws no differentiation between punishment for impaired driving by alcohol or a drug. The prescribed minimums are $1000 fine and one year no driving on a first offence, 30 days jail and two years no driving on a second offence, and 120 days jail and three years no driving for a third or subsequent offence.

If drug-impaired driving occurs on a vessel or railway equipment, then loss of driving privileges for motor vehicles may still be affected by consequential provincial legislation, whereas the inverse would not be true.

Early reinstatement of driving privileges exists in most provinces in concert with section 259(1.1) of the *Criminal Code* where an ignition interlock device, a device which does not allow the vehicle to start or run if a certain blood alcohol concentration is detected, is installed. However, similar technology for drug detection is not yet technologically advanced to the point of being useful. As a result, in some provinces individuals will be prohibited from driving for a longer period as a result of driving while impaired by drug than when compared to alcohol.

The law and the science in these sorts of cases are intrinsically linked. This book hopes to provide a better understanding of the science and how it should relate to the creation and interpretation of the law in Canada surrounding impaired operation by drugs, including the suggested *per se* limits that may be promulgated. Safer roads and a more efficient justice system can only be achieved when members of the justice system have the necessary tools to understand, interpret, and apply this area of law in a meaningful way.

Acknowledgements

This volume would not have been possible without the help I received from a number of people who are deserving of acknowledgement and thanks. From Tony Corroto, who first piqued my interest and kept me supplied with updates from the United States; to Richard Aitken, who took me to the courses that gave me the knowledge to write this book; to the police officers, who helped my learning from the prosecution side; to all the members of the DRE Netletter who shared their cases, experience, and encouragement. Specifically, I want to thank Katelyn Mangold and Sheldon Casey for their research assistance, as well as Lisa Thomson, for being able to unscramble my notes and dictation. Finally, I need to thank my editors who saw me through my revisions—Joleen Hiland; my mother, Connie Baker; and Alisa Posesorski, from Irwin Law. I hope that this book remains a living document, and anyone wishing to join the Netletter can email me to have their name added at nathanbakerlaw@gmail.com.

To Amy, Joshua, and Oliver, who have supported me throughout and given me the time and purpose to keep going.

CHAPTER 1

Sources of Information

Drug-impaired driving involves numerous sources of information that can help decide such a case. Some of the information will only be available to the accused whereas others are in the control of the Crown. Much of the information will be quite familiar to criminal practitioners. Police synopsis, notes, witness statements, and the like are all still of use. Overcomplicating matters where the facts are apparent on their face is a common mistake by all parties in drug-impaired driving. Where an accused is driving poorly, exhibiting motor control issues, and showing signs of drug consumption, by admission or toxicological tests, without other explanation as to why the symptoms of impairment are present, may lead to an inescapable inference of impaired driving by a trier-of-fact. For a list of possible disclosure materials that may be useful in assessing a case, see the appendix.

Where drug-impaired driving cases differ is in the information that can be garnered through the Drug Recognition Evaluations (DRE) and toxicological testing. A proper understanding of what is involved in the testing is reviewed later in this chapter. Two steps must also be completed: (1) seeing how the client performs on the evaluations as against expectations of a sober individual; and (2) seeing how the DRE officer conducted the evaluations as against their training.

The DRE officer is required to complete a number of different reports when testing a subject. The first, and arguably most important, of these is the face sheet. The face sheet is a standard form used by all DRE officers, with only minor changes from jurisdiction to jurisdiction, such as changing "Miranda Warning" on the American version to "Charter Caution" on the Canadian version. The face sheet provides the DRE officer with a ready reference tool that helps them recall the tests they are to complete and what to look for at what time. For many of the tests, graphical representations of the actual tests are portrayed on the face sheet to allow the officer to note exactly what is seen. Officers are trained to mark up their face sheet extensively, which encourages them to take better notes by making more notes rather than fewer. The face sheet includes questioning portions that may be refused by a subject and this can cause confusion among both DRE officers and subjects about which parts are mandatory and which are voluntary. Prior to testing, it's important for defence counsel to give clear instructions to an accused that they are not required to answer any of the questions but only to participate in the physical testing. This is often useful for officers to ensure voluntariness so that the answers can more easily be relied upon in court. The DRE officer should be filling out a face sheet while the subject actually performs the tests (see Figure 1).

As noted on the face sheet, the DRE officer's opinion is to be reviewed by another officer, typically a DRE instructor. Part of the process to ensure continued credentialing requires tests performed to be reviewed.

As well as the face sheet, the DRE officer will typically have handwritten notes. Some DRE officers use standard force-issued notepads to keep records while others take more complex notes elsewhere. These will often include times that may become important when assessing issues, such as whether the tests were taken as soon as practicable, what setup was required to prepare for the tests, and what grounds they received prior to obtaining custody of the subject.

DRE officers are expected in each case to prepare a typed synopsis of their testing as well. This traditionally follows immediately after the face sheet is filled in and is prepared very quickly after the tests are complete. It details the officer's observations throughout the different phases of the DRE officer's interactions, including what they are told by other officers, what they have been told witnesses may have said, and other information that can create grounds for cross-examination by defence counsel where differences occur. Although the face sheet will provide

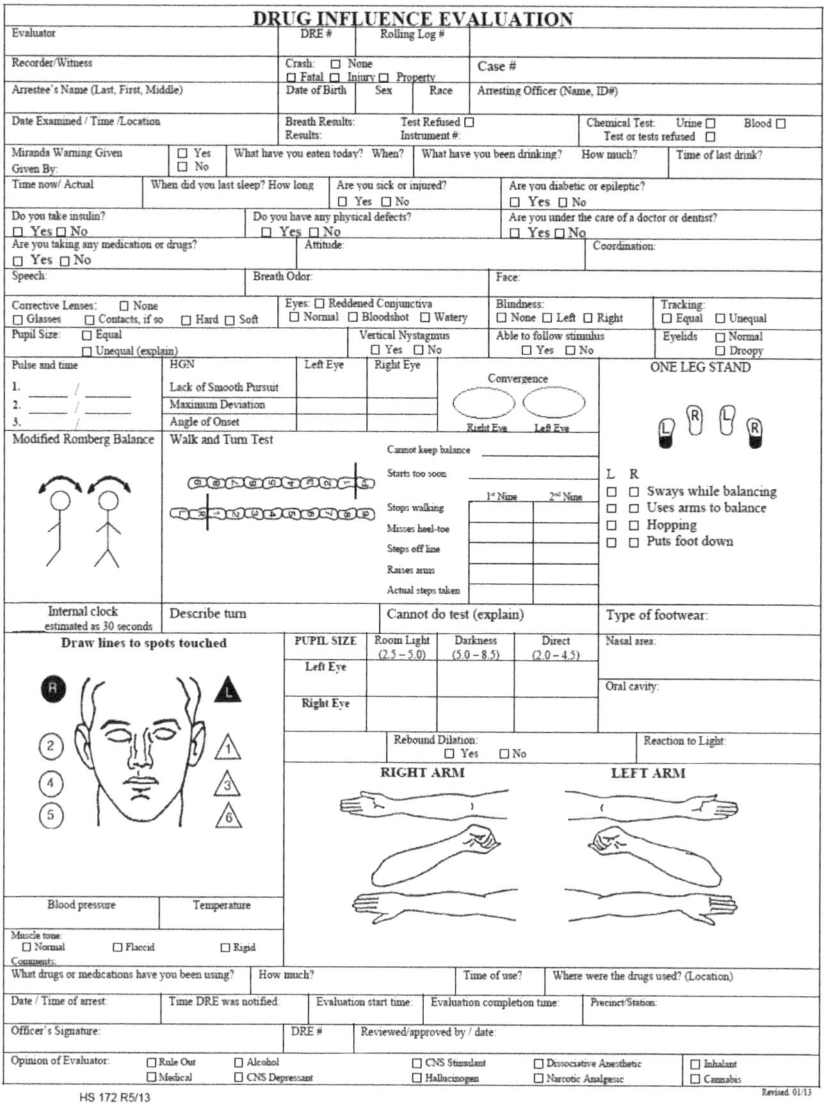

DRUG INFLUENCE EVALUATION

Evaluator | DRE # | Rolling Log #

Recorder/Witness | Crash: ☐ None ☐ Fatal ☐ Injury ☐ Property | Case #

Arrestee's Name (Last, First, Middle) | Date of Birth | Sex | Race | Arresting Officer (Name, ID#)

Date Examined / Time /Location | Breath Results: Results: | Test Refused ☐ Instrument #: | Chemical Test: Urine ☐ Blood ☐ Test or tests refused ☐

Miranda Warning Given Given By: | ☐ Yes ☐ No | What have you eaten today? When? | What have you been drinking? How much? | Time of last drink?

Time now/ Actual | When did you last sleep? How long | Are you sick or injured? ☐ Yes ☐ No | Are you diabetic or epileptic? ☐ Yes ☐ No

Do you take insulin? ☐ Yes ☐ No | Do you have any physical defects? ☐ Yes ☐ No | Are you under the care of a doctor or dentist? ☐ Yes ☐ No

Are you taking any medication or drugs? ☐ Yes ☐ No | Attitude: | Coordination:

Speech: | Breath Odor: | Face:

Corrective Lenses: ☐ None ☐ Glasses ☐ Contacts, if so ☐ Hard ☐ Soft | Eyes: ☐ Reddened Conjunctiva ☐ Normal ☐ Bloodshot ☐ Watery | Blindness: ☐ None ☐ Left ☐ Right | Tracking: ☐ Equal ☐ Unequal

Pupil Size: ☐ Equal ☐ Unequal (explain) | Vertical Nystagmus ☐ Yes ☐ No | Able to follow stimulus ☐ Yes ☐ No | Eyelids ☐ Normal ☐ Droopy

Pulse and time 1. / 2. / 3. / | HGN | Left Eye | Right Eye | Convergence Right Eye Left Eye | ONE LEG STAND

Lack of Smooth Pursuit

Maximum Deviation

Angle of Onset

Modified Romberg Balance | Walk and Turn Test | Cannot keep balance | Starts too soon | 1st Nine | 2nd Nine | Stops walking | Misses heel-toe | Steps off line | Raises arms | Actual steps taken

L R ☐ ☐ Sways while balancing ☐ ☐ Uses arms to balance ☐ ☐ Hopping ☐ ☐ Puts foot down

Internal clock estimated as 30 seconds | Describe turn | Cannot do test (explain) | Type of footwear:

Draw lines to spots touched

PUPIL SIZE | Room Light (2.5 – 5.0) | Darkness (5.0 – 8.5) | Direct (2.0 – 4.5)

Left Eye

Right Eye

Nasal area:

Oral cavity:

Rebound Dilation: ☐ Yes ☐ No | Reaction to Light:

RIGHT ARM | LEFT ARM

Blood pressure | Temperature

Muscle tone: ☐ Normal ☐ Flaccid ☐ Rigid

Comments:

What drugs or medications have you been using? | How much? | Time of use? | Where were the drugs used? (Location)

Date / Time of arrest: | Time DRE was notified: | Evaluation start time: | Evaluation completion time: | Precinct/Station:

Officer's Signature: | DRE # | Reviewed/approved by / date:

Opinion of Evaluator: ☐ Rule Out ☐ Medical ☐ Alcohol ☐ CNS Depressant ☐ CNS Stimulant ☐ Hallucinogen ☐ Dissociative Anesthetic ☐ Narcotic Analgesic ☐ Inhalant ☐ Cannabis

HS 172 R5/13 Revised 01/13

FIGURE 1 DRE Face Sheet Used in the US

graphical representation of how the accused performed on each test, the typed report should provide greater detail on each clue noted, including descriptions of each fail or clue.

Officers receive extensive training in order to be designated a DRE officer. That training is reviewed in Chapter 2 of this book. However, knowing the officer's background is important as well. Their credentialing as a DRE officer should be forthcoming upon request because it is an integral piece of evidence required to be proven in order to avoid a *Mohan* voir dire to establish their expertise. *Mohan* criteria for admission of expert opinion require that the opinion must be: (1) relevant; (2) necessary to assist the trier-of-fact; (3) not otherwise excluded; and (4) given by a properly qualified expert. Officers should be able to provide information about their training, including a curriculum vitae and an indication as to when they were trained as DRE officers and under which version of the training manual. This is important because a proper assessment of the officer's evidence will rely upon comparing their findings to the training they received. Further, being able to compare and contrast the training they have with the most recent manuals can occasionally reveal important differences. The manual(s) upon which the DRE or SFST officer relies is important to allow for a proper review of the tests. Officers should have ready access to their manuals so they can provide them to prosecution and defence. The DRE officer's opinion needs to be measured against their training to ensure that the conclusion reached relies on that training and is properly founded.

Further to the manual, which provides the objective basis against which the officer's actions can be measured, each DRE officer must maintain a rolling log of tests they have completed (see Figure 2). These logs reach back into their initial training and show the reliability of the officer's opinion. As with any witness, credibility and reliability are two separate heads that need to be measured individually. The officer may be following what they believe their training to be but not coming out with correct calls as to the nature of substances toxicologically confirmed in the subjects they test. As a result, the rolling log is hugely helpful in assessing the officer's reliability. The rolling log of the DRE officer confirms prior tests that the officer has undertaken, the date, their opinion, and the toxicological results to provide either confirmation or lack thereof of the opinion which the officer held. It should also contain information, such as subject names, which will need to be redacted to ensure privacy and confidentiality. These logs are kept by the individual officer but are typically also shared with the overseeing body, such as the RCMP or OPP coordinator for the DRE progam.

DRUG EVALUATION AND CLASSIFICATION PROGRAM

<u>LOG OF DRUG INFLUENCE EVALUATIONS</u>

Drug Recognition Expert ____________________ Page ______

IACP Certification Number ______________________________

CONTROL NUMBER	SUSPECT'S NAME	WITNESS	DATE	OPINION OF DRE	TOXICOLOGIAL RESULTS

FIGURE 2 A Rolling Log

Chapter 4 specifically reviews the matrix that is used systemically to determine the drug class that the DRE officer will call. It is often useful to request a copy of the matrix separately because officers will receive multiple copies of this across their training. Although it is contained in the officer's training materials, the matrix upon which the DRE officer relies may actually be external to the manuals so that they have easy access to it. Pre-printed laminated cards, clipboards with the matrix printed directly on them, or even handwritten versions have all been seen at different cases. As a result, it is important to see the matrix that was relied upon to compare it to the training manual to ensure no transcription issues have occurred. As well, these aids often contain other information as prompts or hints, including checklists, expected test results, descriptors to be used for each drug category, and more.

Copies of the exact demands made to an individual are important to determine whether the wording of any of the demands caused confusion regarding which tests were required, which statements were voluntary, and whether there was a change in circumstance sufficient to require a further opportunity to consult counsel.

Information regarding the type of instrumentation used by the DRE officer should also be obtained. For example, knowing the kind of light used will help determine whether it could be used properly, i.e., whether enough light could be blocked to be of use in dark-room testing. Knowing the kind of time-keeping mechanism, be it wristwatch or wall clock, may allow a better assessment of an officer's opinion as to pulse rate if the timepiece is difficult to read to the second or runs fast or slow. An examination of the **pupilometer** used to ensure that the sizing recorded is accurate as to the gradations it notes will allow a proper assessment of the weight that should be given to a DRE officer's opinion.

The type of **sphygmomanometer**, or blood pressure cuff, should be determined to ensure that it is of proper quality to do testing. Whether it is digital or analog, the gradation used (i.e., how does an officer indicate a blood pressure to the last digit if the measuring tool does not?), and an opportunity to know when and how it was calibrated and any maintenance which has been undertaken, either required or otherwise, will ensure its continued usefulness. Instrument drift is not unheard of, especially if the instrument is not properly taken care of or is thrown about or dropped, as can happen when dealing with confrontational or aggressive people in custody.

Video technology is so prevalent that it is the rare case where the DRE tests are not captured in both audio and video format. Following along with the officer's notes and face sheet while watching the video allows a thorough review of the officer's ability to observe from an objective standpoint as to whether the conclusions are evident. It is important, in assessing, to remember the officer may be able to observe things that are not readily apparent and visible on the video but may nonetheless be there. However, it is equally important to critically assess the officer's observations against the objective standard of the video. Obtaining video beyond the DRE test is also relevant as this can provide strong evidence as to how a subject is acting when not faced with the controlled situations of the DRE testing. Video is often very useful to the defence to provide to experts for review; explanations for signs of impairment are also observable in the video. However, it is often the strongest evidence of impairment when the gross inability of a subject to perform simple tasks, especially those not included in the DRE but regular actions like walking and talking, is visible. If no portion of the arrest, lodging, or testing of the subject is available then this needs to be critically assessed as to how it may affect the case. Testing, such as the Horizontal Gaze Nystagmus (HGN) test, relies on the officer's ability to perform the test in a particular way, including timing the passes of the stimulus properly at two seconds per pass. Without video, it will be exceptionally difficult to determine where, if at all, the officer failed to perform the testing as required by the standardization of same. Although there is typically no reason for an officer to exaggerate or improperly record what went on, the failure to video record tests such as the DRE, and especially the statements given during them, may be open to challenge where a defendant disagrees and provides positive evidence of a different result. Loss of or destruction of video is important in any impaired driving case but especially so in drug-impaired driving where the interpretation of tests is subjective. A breach of an accused's right is likely to be found in such a case.

An opportunity to examine the site of the testing when video evidence is not forthcoming is of importance. The need to determine lighting conditions, including the lack of light when undertaking the dark-room tests, is key. Additional light through a window or poorly closed door may unintentionally decrease the size of an accused's pupils. Unmaintained fluorescent lighting that flickers or strobes may unintentionally induce nystagmus. Uneven floor or obstructions on the floor, such as a divot or a drain, may cause issues with footing or balance on a number of the divided attention physical tests. The presence of other prisoners or individuals in the area where the testing is undertaken may unduly influence an individual and give rise to a form of *white-coat hypertension* whereby a person's blood pressure and/or pulse may elevate as a result of the individuals around them. The determination of the space needed to perform certain tests, such as the Walk-and-Turn, in often cramped spaces in police stations that were never intended for such testing or are filled with other items that may constitute obstacles, needs to be undertaken.

Toxicological testing is an important part of the DRE testing regime. This allows the DRE officer to confirm their opinion through objective scientific testing. The results are to be correlated to the opinion or call of the DRE officer and noted in the rolling log. Where the DRE officer's opinion is not confirmed by the toxicological sample, then the resulting weight that can be given to the opinion is necessarily reduced. Although there is an argument that forensic laboratories cannot and do not test for every substance, they are very detailed in their analysis. Forensic laboratories are not in the business of missing substances, be they illicit or prescription, when testing samples. It is important to query what substances the forensic laboratory did test for and to seek such a list from them. That list can then be put to the DRE officer if a drug in the category called was not present. As well, where drugs are toxicologically confirmed but do not fit the category called by the officer, it can be expected that the defence will cross-examine as to the reasons for the missed call. Most defence counsel will highlight the basis upon which the DRE officer relied to make the call and point out the results on tests upon which the DRE officer called that do not fit within the drug category found. It is important for the prosecution to be able to explain such variances, though there are times where they simply cannot.

Toxicological testing is dealt with further in Chapter 3. However, making sure that the disclosure received is more than just a report with a conclusory opinion, but also the raw data upon which that opinion is based so that it can be critically assessed is important to allow for the maintenance of integrity in the system of forensically testing bodily samples. This includes not merely the results of the **GCMS** (Gas Chromatography Mass Spectrometry) or **LCMS** (Liquid Chromatography Mass Spectrometry) testing of the bodily sample but also the raw data results, preferably in graphed form so it can be reviewed by an expert to determine the possibility of interfering chemicals providing false positives in such tests, as well as the range of drugs that such results might indicate. The possibility of a different drug, even of the same class, may clearly have an impact on the manner in which a defence of a charge is conducted.

The forensic testing report may also have limitations that are evident on its face. Issues with the weight and usefulness of urine samples as opposed to blood or oral fluids may be key for both sides to understand and be able to educate the trier-of-fact.

Further to forensic tests on bodily samples, should any drugs have been found on the person of the subject or in their vicinity, then the analysis of them will be important. Given the wide-ranging number of drugs available and the often similar manner in which they present (consider heroin vs. fentanyl or Tylenol vs. Tylenol Cold). The importance of testing the seized drug applies equally to illicit and legal drugs. Neither Crown nor defence should be content to rely upon an unknown substance to base its submissions. The method used to analyze substances should be examined along with quality assurance to make sure that any such analysis is properly conducted and reliable.

CHAPTER 2

SFST and DRE Testing

Physical testing for the presence and impairment of drugs in Canada is accomplished through the Standardized Field Sobriety Tests (**SFST**) and Drug Recognition Evaluations (**DRE**). The SFST forms an integral part of the DRE testing but is to be used only for screening in Canada whereas the DRE is to be used as evidence at a trial proper. A useful way of considering them is that the SFST acts like an Approved Screening Device (**ASD**), to provide grounds for an arrest, while the DRE is more akin evidentially to the Approved Instrument (**AI**), only justifiable if reasonable and probable grounds exist but then for the purpose of proving the charge before the court.

The total sum of the testing that is allowed to be statutorily compelled, and the only testing that has been approved for use, is enumerated in the regulation to the *Criminal Code*: Evaluation of Impaired Operation (Drugs and Alcohol) Regulations, SOR/2008-196. Item 2 allows for the use of physical screening tests to be undertaken pursuant to section 254(2)(a) as being those involved in the SFST:

> 2. The physical coordination tests to be conducted under paragraph 254(2)(a) of the *Criminal Code* are the following standard field sobriety tests:
> (a) the horizontal gaze nystagmus test;
> (b) the walk-and-turn test; and
> (c) the one-leg stand test.

The regulation goes on to state the tests to be completed in relation to a subsection 253(3.1) demand as being those that form the DRE:

> 3. The tests to be conducted and the procedures to be followed during an evaluation under subsection 254(3.1) of the *Criminal Code* are
>
> (a) a preliminary examination, which consists of measuring the pulse and determining that the pupils are the same size and that the eyes track an object equally;
>
> (b) eye examinations, which consist of
>
> (i) the horizontal gaze nystagmus test,
>
> (ii) the vertical gaze nystagmus test, and
>
> (iii) the lack-of-convergence test;
>
> (c) divided-attention tests, which consist of
>
> (i) the Romberg balance test,
>
> (ii) the walk-and-turn test referred to in paragraph 2(b),
>
> (iii) the one-leg-stand test referred to in paragraph 2(c), and
>
> (iv) the finger-to-nose test, which includes the test subject tilting the head back and touching the tip of their index finger to the tip of their nose in a specified manner while keeping their eyes closed;
>
> (d) an examination, which consists of measuring the blood pressure, temperature, and pulse;
>
> (e) an examination of pupil sizes under light levels of ambient light, near total darkness, and direct light and an examination of the nasal and oral cavities;
>
> (f) an examination, which consists of checking the muscle tone and pulse; and
>
> (g) a visual examination of the arms, neck, and, if exposed, the legs for evidence of injection sites.

What is meant by each of these tests is better defined in the training that an officer receives to undertake SFST or to be designated as a DRE officer. Officers are taught to break down their tests into twelve steps:

1. Breath Alcohol Test
   (Note that in Canada this is not authorized to be completed by a DRE officer unless so authorized by section 254(3.3), which allows for testing if a reasonable suspicion exists, no breath sample has been taken,

and a demand is made and the sample is taken as soon as practicable. Further, such a sample is not supported by the presumptions in section 258 as a section 254(3) demand would be.)

2. Interview of the Arresting Officer
3. Preliminary Examination
4. Examinations of the Eyes
5. Divided-Attention Tests
6. Examination of Vital Signs
7. Dark-Room Examinations
8. Examination of Muscle Tone
9. Examination for Injection Sites
10. Subject's Statements and Other Observations
11. Opinion of Evaluator
12. Toxicological Examination

While there are similarities between the enabling statute and the training, it is in the differences where the most litigation lies. As a warrantless search, the officers must ensure they are following the procedure and authorized practices as outlined in statute. Defence counsel also needs to understand what is and is not required and be able to communicate this effectively with a detained individual to best ensure the rights of the individual. Many patterns will emerge as a person examines the tests (such as always starting on the subject's left side) that will help with understanding the standardized portion of the testing and how important it is to the validity of the results.

Standardized Field Sobriety Testing was developed as a method of determining quickly whether an individual's blood alcohol concentration (**BAC**) was above the prescribed limit—namely, 100 mg of alcohol in 100 ml of blood. The validation studies conducted to confirm the efficacy of the testing regime work toward validating the test at these levels. Literature supporting the use of SFST in determining drug impairment is more fulsome. Although some studies have been undertaken, the inability of scientists to dose individuals with what typically are illegal narcotics affects the ability to properly validate these tests. Where the tests have been checked for validity in determining drug impairment, they have shown some indicators of usefulness.

However, there are limitations in each of the following three tests, depending on the drug category being tested. The most common of these is, of course, cannabis. It is important to note that while the Walk-and-Turn test and One-Leg-Stand test are generally good indicators when detecting cannabis use, the Horizontal Gaze Nystagmus test is specifically a poor indicator. As well, the SFST exist as a field sobriety testing regime, as indicated in its very title. The use of these tests to determine impairment is more difficult. The SFST were designed to note the presence of alcohol at a particular level but they have not been validated to detect drugs at any particular level. The validation studies that do exist relate to their ability to confirm the presence of drugs but not at any particular level. As a result, they will be of no use in determining a *per se* level in an individual and have somewhat limited use in determining impairment. They may be useful as psychophysical tests to test a person through divided attention to determine impairment but the validation test in this regard is thin. At best they are a screening device and should not be relied upon as proof beyond a reasonable doubt of impairment, and often signs noted by an officer or a lay witness as to impairment will be stronger than those noted through the SFST battery.

The proper name for the drug recognition expert program is the Drug Evaluation and Classification Program. The reason for this name reflects the fact that the system was designed truly to detect and classify the kind of drug in an individual system. While seeking to prove impairment has always been part of the goal, the validated studies typically focus upon the ability of the testing regime to determine a particular class of drug in an individual system. The validation studies rarely go to the steps of determining whether or not the drug was truly impairing the individual, because that would require some form of qualitative analysis of the individual's ability to operate a motor vehicle. Validation studies are very difficult because of this lack of qualitative analysis as it would typically involve the need for an individual to operate a motor vehicle both when sober and again when under the influence of a drug. Double-blind studies tend to control for the ability to drive by using a control group that has not been dosed with a particular drug which is being examined in the study. However, what this fails to control is the individual's ability to drive normally. Since the individual being tested is not compared with their own ability to drive, such validation studies are arguably of limited value. However, when a significant-sized sample group is tested, that can be a proper method of control. Further testing involving individuals in a double-blind method both dosed and not dosed with the medication would be the most useful sort of study to pursue. Alternatively, an exceptionally large sample base could effect the same results. The DRE classification program focuses largely on the classification of the drug category within which the individual is believed to be under the influence. The test in the matrix focuses on that.

The other tests are those that are supposed to be related to the ability to operate a motor vehicle. It is important for the prosecution to be able to relate how the divided-attention tests in the testing battery indicate an impaired ability to operate a motor vehicle. The inability to focus on divided-attention tests relates to the ability to operate a motor vehicle since it is itself an exercise in divided attention. The complex number of activities that must be managed when properly operating a motor vehicle can be in some ways related to the simpler divided-attention tests in the testing battery. However, certain of them may be overly complicated due to the individual's lack of experience with them. The greater an individual's experience with a particular task, the more confident they will be. The environment can also have such an effect on the individual's performance. Consider that an individual in custody already under arrest may be stressed to the point where their ability to properly perform divided-attention tests is affected not by the impairment of a drug but by the impact of the situation in which they find themselves. The goal for the prosecution must be to show that the control tests on the DRE battery are sufficiently simple with instructions clear enough that there can be no doubt of the impairment of the individual before the court. However, the role of the defence counsel will be to show an attempt to point out the unfamiliarity of such tests and the lack of direct evidence relating to the ability to perform them to the ability to operate a motor vehicle. As an example, the defence may seek to point out that the ability to stand on one leg or to stand steady with eyes closed and head tilted back is not easily relatable to the ability required to operate a motor vehicle. The prosecution must instead point out that such basic tasks and ability to control the physical human form show a lack of ability to perceive, respond, and interact with the environment to a sufficient degree to properly operate complex machinery, such as a motor vehicle. The prosecution will be best aided with driving evidence or evidence of the accused outside the testing regime to back up and support the conclusions made by drug recognition experts.

HORIZONTAL GAZE NYSTAGMUS TEST

The Horizontal Gaze Nystagmus (**HGN**) test is a procedure where an officer moves a stimulus, such as a pen or small light, in a horizontal fashion in front of a person's face. While generally it appears simple, an officer is expected to undertake a great deal of complex actions and observations during this test. **Nystagmus** is an involuntary repetitive movement of the eye. It is often compared to marbles rolling across a table. While one would expect normally that the eyes would move consistently like a marble rolling on a smooth table, a nystagmus is more like a rough table with stops and starts intermittently. Police are trained to give the example of windshield wipers on dry glass. An example of a very temporary nystagmus—namely, a rotational variety—can be induced in a person by having them spin a number of times in a circle then stop and try to focus on a spot across the room. This can be induced on even a sober individual and is not long lasting.

An important issue to keep in mind when this test is undertaken is the presence of any wind, dust, strobing or flashing lights, or any other irritants that may interfere with the efficacy of the tests because they may unintentionally induce the signs that the officer is looking for. For example, optokinetic nystagmus occurs when what the person was looking at moves suddenly out of sight as happens with strobe lighting. An officer is also required to be cognizant of other signs of impairment while doing these tests, such as swaying or inability to follow instructions and, while not a fail of the test itself, are still signs of impairment.

The first step of the HGN test is for the officer to check whether the person to be tested is wearing eyeglasses. It is important that this is observed, as eyeglasses may affect peripheral vision or impede an officer's ability to observe carefully the action of the eye, which is the key point of this test. Some contact lenses may also impact testing and an officer should be checking for them, especially coloured contacts, as they can affect the ability of an officer to compare pupil size. While an individual needs to be able to see the stimulus well enough to follow it, they do not need to be able to see it with any detail. This test is not meant to be a vision test but a test of involuntary eye movements.

The officer is then required to provide instructions to the individual being tested. These instructions must include that the individual:

- Put their feet together with their hands at their side;
- Keep their head still;
- Look at the stimulus;
- Follow the movement of the stimulus with their eyes only;
- Keep following and looking at the stimulus until they are told the test is over.

Officers are trained that these are major points that must be conveyed during the verbal instructions. Failure to properly instruct an individual will affect the utility of the testing procedure. As is stated in the very title of the testing, it is meant to be *standardized.*

While the individual is being tested, the officer is to be observing and recording whether the individual has any balance issues, including sway.

Once the individual being tested has been provided with the instructions, the officer is then to position the stimulus approximately 30 to 38 cm (12 to 15 in.) in front of the subject's nose and slightly above eye level to start the test. This is done to ensure that the individual's eyes are open wide to give the officer a better view of the eyes to observe nystagmus.

The officer's first observation in the actual test will be to determine whether nystagmus is present without moving the stimulus. This is referred to as *resting nystagmus.* The officer is also required to compare the size of the pupils in each eye. While resting nystagmus and unequal pupil size may be indicia of a medical concern, officers are trained that they may, nonetheless, continue with testing to see if any possible indicators of impairment are present.

The officer will then begin the actual testing, looking for clues of impairment, by passing the stimulus "rapidly" from centre to far right to far left and back to centre. Officers are generally instructed that "rapidly" generally means about 4 seconds from centre to an extreme, meaning 8 seconds to fully cross from one side to the other. The pass by the stimulus therefore should take about 16 seconds.

On the first set of passes of the stimulus, the officer is looking to determine if the eyes track equally, that is to say, whether one eye moves at a different pace than the other. This can be indicative of a lazy eye or other medical condition. During this test, the officer is looking at both eyes at once and comparing them.

After a "clear, distinguishable break" the officer is to then move on to check for smooth pursuit. This will involve passing the stimulus in a manner similar to the check for equal tracking, but this requires two complete passes, i.e., from centre to far right, to far left, to far right, to far left, then to centre. The officer is checking to see if the eyes move fluidly like marbles on a smooth table or if any involuntary jerking occurs. During this test, the officer focuses on one eye, then the other. So while moving the stimulus to one side they are to check for smooth pursuit on that eye, and after crossing the centre position they are to focus on the other eye. If either eye, while being observed on that side, jerks while moving, then that is one clue. "Clue" relates to an observation that does not meet what is expected but suggests the possibility or likelihood of impairment. Two eyes means up to two clues but if only one eye jerks, even if multiple times, then it is only one clue.

The next step of the test involves passing the stimulus from centre rapidly to the point of "maximum deviation." This is the point where all the white portion of the eye on one side is buried. It is at that maximum deviation where the officer is then looking for "definite, distinct and sustained" nystagmus. This means that the officer must note the jerking of the eye, be sure of it, and that it must continue for some time, at least 4 seconds. Nystagmus should continue if the officer holds the stimulus steady, even well after 4 seconds. The time taken to observe the nystagmus is important because nystagmus can be induced by improper actions by the officer in the manipulation of the stimulus. The eyes require time to recover from movement to stop. Nystagmus that is noted but that does not remain may be indicative of nothing. The way a smooth marble rolls across the table into a wall and briefly rebounds but then comes to a rest, an eye may similarly rebound then settle in a second or two and the benefit of the doubt must be given; hence the requirement for distinct *and* sustained nystagmus to be present to be a clue. It is also important to know how long the officer held the stimulus before noting the jerking being present. Fatigue nystagmus can occur if the stimulus is held for longer than 30 seconds.

Each eye is to be checked independently and twice per eye for a total of four checks. If distinct and sustained nystagmus is present in either eye on either test then that is a clue. Again, two eyes means up to two clues but multiple jerks from one eye mean only one clue.

Finally, the officer is to check for onset of nystagmus prior to 45 degrees. This involves moving the stimulus in the same manner as the prior test but instead of continuing until there is no white of the eye visible in the corner of the eye, the officer is to check whether any jerking of the eye occurs prior to 45 degrees. If any jerking occurs prior to 45 degrees then that is one clue. Each eye is to be tested separately at least two times per eye. Each eye can give up to one clue.

At the end of this, the officer is to total the number of clues, recognizing that the maximum number of clues is six, being three per eye. Four or more clues being present is considered a fail. It is important to note that the training links such a failure to a BAC and not directly to impairment. Therefore, use as a screening test for drug impairment without the rest of the DRE protocol can be limited. HGN is expected with alcohol, Central Nervous System Depressants, Inhalants and Dissociative Anesthetics, but not so with other classes of drugs.

Officers are instructed that a subject's performance may not be the same for each eye but that generally, as impairment increases, at least by alcohol, typically a person will first show inability of smooth pursuit, then nystagmus at maximum deviation, and finally onset prior to 45 degrees, though this is not always true.

Issues that may cause nystagmus are numerous but tend not to be common without other, more serious neurological issues being present. Some of these have been recognized by US courts.

WALK-AND-TURN TEST

It is important to take note of certain things when assessing the use to be made of the results of the Walk-and-Turn (**W&T**) test. When used as a screening tool in SFST, the value needed to be made will be lower than when used in DRE testing as proof of impairment. Wind and weather can affect an individual's ability to perform the tests. As well, people over sixty-five years or with back, leg, or inner ear problems may have difficulty. Initially, validation tests did not deal with individuals with these issues. Further, the training provides that individuals wearing shoes with heels of 2 inches or more should be allowed to remove them or any other odd footwear, such as flip-flops.

The testing itself has two stages: instructions and walking. The tests are to be conducted on a dry, hard, level, non-slippery surface with sufficient space to allow for room for the nine steps out and nine steps back that will be required.

The instructions to be given are as follows:

1. "Place your left foot on the line." The officer is to demonstrate.
2. "Place your right foot on the line ahead of the left foot with the heel of your right foot against the toe of the left foot." The officer is then to demonstrate.
3. "Place your arms at your side." The officer demonstrates.
4. "Maintain this position until the instructions are completed. Do not start to walk until told to do so." The officer is then to ask, "Do you understand the instructions so far?" and an affirmative answer is required before continuing.
5. "When I tell you to start, take nine heel-to-toe steps on the line, turn, and take nine heel-to-toe steps on the line back." The officer is then to demonstrate at least three steps.
6. "When you turn, keep the front foot on the line, and turn by taking a series of small steps with the foot either like this." The officer then demonstrates the turn and a minimum of three of the heel-to-toe return steps.
7. "When walking, keep your arms at your side, watch your feet, and count your steps out loud. Once you start walking, don't stop until you've completed this task. Do you understand?" The officer then instructs the person to begin.

The officer is looking for a number of clues:

- Inability to keep balance while being instructed. Note that the person's feet must actually break apart or come off the line. Swaying or use of arms to balance is okay at this point.
- The person starts walking too soon, i.e., before instructed to.
- The person stops walking. This must be clear and deliberate and not just slowness.

- The person does not touch heel-to-toe. A miss requires a space of more than half an inch between heel and toe on any step.
- The person steps off the line. This means one foot is completely off the line, not merely a part of it.
- The person uses their arms to balance. This means the arm is lifted more than 6 inches from the side.
- Improper turn. The person does not turn as demonstrated. This would include such things as removing the front foot from the line or performing a pivot similar to a military turn rather than the small steps demonstrated.
- Incorrect number of steps. This means something other than nine steps each way.

If a person makes a mistake then the officer is to instruct them to continue from that point and not start over. The test loses sensitivity if it is repeated. Even a single failure in one of the above eight categories is considered a clue. However, it is important to note that multiple instances of failure in one category is considered only one clue (i.e., stepping off the line multiple times is still only one clue).

Two or more clues observed are considered a failure on this test for screening purposes.

ONE-LEG-STAND TEST

The One-Leg-Stand (**OLS**) test consists of two stages: the instructions stage and then the balance and counting stage.

Officers are instructed that they need a dry, hard, level, non-slippery surface. People over sixty-five years of age or with back, leg, or inner ear problems or who are overweight by 50 or more pounds may have difficulty on this test. Individuals wearing shoes with heels of 2 inches or more will be given the opportunity to remove them. An individual should be afforded the opportunity to remove any unusual footwear as well.

The instructions to be given are:

- "Please stand with your feet together and your arms down your sides like this." The officer is then to demonstrate.

- "Do not start to perform the task until I tell you to do so. Do you understand the instructions so far?" An affirmative answer is required before proceeding.
- "When I tell you to start, raise either leg with the foot approximately 6 inches off the ground, keeping your foot parallel to the ground." The officer is then to demonstrate.
- "Keep both legs straight and your arms at your side. While holding that position, count out loud in the following manner: 1001, 1002, 1003, and so on until told to stop." Again, the officer is to demonstrate.
- "Keep your arms at your side at all times and keep watching your raised foot" (note that officers are instructed not to look at their foot when demonstrating in case the client becomes violent). "Do you understand?" The officer is then to answer any questions or, if the person has no questions, then proceed.
- "Go ahead and perform the test."
- The officer should time 30 seconds and discontinue the tests at that point. If the person puts their foot down, then they are to be instructed to pick the foot up again and continue counting from the point they left off.
- The clues which the officer is looking for are:
- Swaying that is distinct and noticeable, including from side to side or front to back. Slight tremors of the foot or the body are NOT swaying.
- Use of arms to balance. This means moving the arm 6 inches or more from the body.
- Hopping.
- Putting the raised foot down.

Any single incident of a clue is sufficient but multiple instances of each clue are still only considered a single clue (i.e., putting the raised foot down multiple times is only one clue). Two or more clues constitute a failure.

PRELIMINARY EXAMINATION

The portions of the preliminary examination are set out in the top portion of a DRE officer's worksheet. The preliminary examination involves obtaining biographical, medical, and other data from the subject. The

DRE is to take place in a controlled environment, such as a police station. As such, the subject should have already been arrested, provided rights to counsel, and cautioned. This means that further evidence statements by the accused are likely to be admissible.

The regulations provide for a preliminary examination to check pulse and determine equality of pupil size and the eyes' ability to track a stimulus. The check for pulse can be conducted on any artery. The most common are:

- the radial artery located on the side of the wrist by the thumb;
- the brachial artery located in the crook of the arm, near the centre; or
- the carotid artery on the neck on either side of the voice box.

Officers are trained to use any or all of these three arteries. They are trained to check for 30 seconds and then double their count to assess against the average or normal rate of 60 to 90 beats per minute (**bpm**). As well, it is important to use fingers and not the thumb in checking or else the officer may be counting their own pulse through the thumb. Any variation in any of the three pulse checks can properly be used as a clue by the officer, i.e., high pulse rate on any one of the three may be relied on as indicative of a fast pulse. However, the trier-of-fact will have to determine whether the totality of the circumstances support the officer's opinion. It is for that reason that a good DRE officer will rely on more than a single sign to indicate a particular drug class or impairment and will instead rely on multiple pieces of evidence taken in their totality.

The tests regarding equal tracking and equal pupil size are taught to officers as part of the HGN test which is thoroughly reviewed earlier in this chapter. These are checked to ensure that medical issues are not present which could be improperly interpreted as impairment.

EYE EXAMINATIONS

The Horizontal Gaze Nystagmus (HGN) test was reviewed in depth earlier in this chapter. The Vertical Gaze Nystagmus (**VGN**) test is to check whether there is involuntary movement in the eyes in an up-and-down motion. This is somewhat similar to the HGN test. The officer begins the test with the stimulus 30 to 38 cm (12 to 15 in.) in front of the subject just above eye level. The subject is instructed to focus on the stimulus and to keep their head steady. The officer is then to raise the stimulus until the subject's eyes are raised as high as possible. If the eyes jerk noticeably, then VGN is present. If the eyes do not jerk, then it is said to not be present. VGN should not occur in people who do not also exhibit HGN as a result of drug consumption.

The Lack-of-Convergence (**LOC**) test sees whether a subject can cross their eyes. The officer instructs the accused to focus on a stimulus. The officer passes the stimulus in a circular motion to ensure that the eyes are tracking it. The stimulus is then moved toward the bridge of the subject's nose and held there, approximately 2 inches from the nose, for 1 second. The officer is looking to see if the eyes can cross. This is often referred to as the least reliable portion of the DRE protocol because a significant portion of the general population lacks the ability to converge their eyes under normal conditions. As well, the ability to see and focus is necessary for this test, so glasses, contact lenses, or other corrective aids may be needed to allow for convergence. Officers typically note the path which they observe the eyes to follow with arrows on their face sheet.

DIVIDED-ATTENTION TESTS

It is important to remember that these tests do not all have pass or fail criteria but that all the observations are to be considered in their totality when assessing impairment.

1) *Romberg Balance Test*

The modified Romberg Balance Test is one which has not been scientifically scrutinized but is often used as a reliable indicator of impairment. The subject is instructed to stand with feet together and with arms at their side. They are told to hold that position until they are instructed to begin. The subject is instructed that, when told to, they are to tilt their head back and close their eyes. The subject is instructed to keep their eyes closed and their head tilted back until they think 30 seconds has passed. The subject is instructed that when they believe 30 seconds has elapsed, to open their eyes, tilt their head forward, and say "stop." Subjects may count out loud if they wish, but no instruction to do so or not to do so is to be given. The subject is to be asked if they understand and if they do, they are told to start. If the subject has not stopped the test themselves at 90 seconds, then the DRE officer is to terminate the test and note this.

The clues which the officer is looking for are whether and by how much the subject sways and the actual amount of time they kept their eyes closed.

2) Walk-and-Turn Test and One-Leg-Stand Test

Both these tests are described in detail earlier in this chapter as they also form part of the SFST battery of tests. However, it should be noted that for SFST purposes, the One-Leg-Stand test is done once and using the foot of the subject's choosing. For DRE purposes, the subject is required to perform the test twice, once with each foot.

3) Finger-to-Nose Test

In the Finger-to-Nose (**FtN**) test the subject is informed that they will be instructed throughout the test to indicate which fingertip is to be brought up to touch the nose. The subject is told to stand with feet together and arms at the side, facing the officer. The officer is to demonstrate the pose. The subject is then to be instructed to close their hands (form a fist), rotate palm out toward the officer, and extend both index fingers. The subject is to be told that they are expected to touch the tip of the finger to the tip of the nose each time they are instructed. The officer is to demonstrate this but stop short of actually touching their own nose. This is significant as many individuals will use the pad of their finger when touching their nose which is considered improper but arguably confusing given the lack of actual demonstration by the officer.

The officer is to instruct the subject, "When I say left, touch the tip of your left index finger to the tip of your nose." The subject is to be instructed that after touching the nose they are to return the arm to their side. The officer should perform their demonstrations from an angle so that the subject can see the proper method for touching the nose.

The subject is to be instructed to tip their head back slightly and close their eyes. The officer is to demonstrate but without closing their eyes for safety reasons. The officer will then instruct the person that the test is beginning. The subject should close their eyes and tilt their head back. The officer is to instruct left, right, left, right, right, left. The officer is to wait until the subject has returned their arm to their side before proceeding to the next direction.

The officer is to note where the subject did touch. There is no sharp line of pass/fail for ease of interpretation and both Crown and defence may argue different interpretations in a close case.

EXAMINATION TO MEASURE BLOOD PRESSURE, TEMPERATURE, AND PULSE

Officers are instructed on the use of a sphygmomanometer, commonly known as a blood pressure cuff. The officer places the cuff around the upper arm of the subject and pumps it until it cuts off the blood flow. The officer then slowly releases the pressure until they can hear the flow of blood through the stethoscope attached to the sphygmomanometer, typically as a pulse or heartbeat. This is the **systolic** pressure. Pressure should continually be released until blood flows continuously. This will be when the pulse or heartbeat is no longer heard. This is the **diastolic** pressure.

Blood pressure is expected to be in a normal or average range of 120 to 140 for systolic and 70 to 90 for diastolic. If the officer faces any issues while performing the test, they are required to wait at least 3 minutes before retrying. This includes the fact that it is not appropriate to re-inflate the cuff once pressure begins to be released.

It is useful to have a working knowledge of blood pressure equipment to get the best evidence from a DRE officer. Knowledge of the range of error, the ability of the officer's hearing, and proper maintenance and calibration of the instrument used will be important to prove to rely on the symptoms observed.

Temperature is measured using an oral digital thermometer. Fresh, disposable mouthpieces are to be available for each test. The sanitary nature of the mouthpiece is of similar concern as that involving breath testing mouthpieces. Similar to blood pressure testing, knowledge of the calibration and maintenance of the thermometer will be important to ensure accurate results.

Pulse rates are reviewed in preceding material and are checked in the same method this second time.

EXAMINATION OF PUPIL SIZES UNDER LIGHT LEVELS OF AMBIENT LIGHT, NEAR TOTAL DARKNESS, AND DIRECT LIGHT AND EXAMINATION OF NASAL AND ORAL CAVITIES

DRE officers examine the pupil size of subjects by turning to a pupilometer. In essence, this is a piece of paper with different-sized circles, and/or half-circles, printed on it, typically ranging from 1 to 9.5 millimetres in diameter in half-millimetre increments. Officers hold the paper beside the subject's head and compare the circle to the pupil and choose which circle most closely matches the same size as the pupil. A common error to be on guard against here is the determination of whether the sizes of the circles match the size noted, because something as simple as a photocopying error could produce an improperly sized pupilometer. Darker eyes tend to make comparisons more difficult and an officer's ability to determine to the half-millimetre needs to be shown in some cases where pupil size is close to or within the normal or average range. This test is to be done in three different lighting conditions.

The expected results are 2.5 to 5.0 mm in ambient or room light, 5.0 to 8.5 mm in darkness or near darkness, and 2.0 to 4.5 mm in direct light. Because of the pupil's natural reaction to being exposed to light, it is important, especially in the dark-room test, that the amount of light being used by the officer is minimal or else the reaction may be induced by the light rather than observed as an actual sign of impairment. Pupils are generally considered normal, dilated (enlarged), or constricted (smaller) based on the size seen. The DRE officer is to wait 90 seconds between lighting changes to allow the pupil to adapt to the new lighting conditions.

It should be noted that any measurement outside of the normal or average range can be considered indicative of that clue. For example, if the pupils are of expected size in room light and direct light but enlarged in the dark, this can be used as a clue that the pupils were, in fact, dilated, even though they were within normal ranges on the other tests.

After the sizing of the pupils, officers are to examine the nasal and oral cavities of the individual. The officer is looking for any signs of drug use or concealment. This includes looking for injection sites, presence of the drug, or residue (as in cocaine found in the nose), redness, runny nose, or any other indicia of consumption or concealment.

EXAMINATION TO CHECK MUSCLE TONE AND PULSE

Different drug categories affect muscle tone differently. As well, individual use, experience, and exposure to the drug or drugs can impact tone differently over time. Normal, flaccid, or rigid are the three options for a DRE to note, though they are encouraged to comment further. Although the officer is encouraged to note muscle tone throughout their interaction with a subject, during the actual testing phase, they are to firmly grasp the upper arm and slowly move down the arm toward the hand to determine tone. They are to first test the subject's left arm, then right. Again, a pulse is taken at this point.

VISUAL EXAMINATION OF THE ARMS, NECK, AND, IF EXPOSED, THE LEGS FOR INJECTION SITES

Officers are trained to look for injection sites. They are taught to recognize that sometimes observation will be easy while in other cases individuals are better at hiding such signs of ingestion. It is important to recognize the limitations on where the officer is allowed to examine as set out in the regulation—namely, a visual examination of arms and neck. The legs may only be examined if exposed.

Officers are encouraged to use a magnifying glass or tactile methods for checking. This would include running the hands over the areas on the body to see if any sites can be noted by the bumps they often leave.

OTHER TESTS/QUESTIONING

While this ends the approved and codified testing, there are times when other tests are utilized. Should an officer do so, then an explanation as to the reasons why should be forthcoming. As well, officers are trained to ask questions after the physical testing has been completed, such as what drugs or medications the subject has used, how much, when and where.

These questions are not part of the enumerated tests codified by statute and regulation in Canada. They are, however, pre-printed on the forms that the DRE officers use and part of the process they are taught. It is for this reason that proper advice to a detained individual is so important so that they realize which questions they must answer and which are permissive. It is important as well for officers to ensure that proper rights to counsel and cautions are provided prior to the testing in order that they can rely upon the answers as voluntary and provided in accordance with *Charter* rights as this is often some of the strongest evidence in such a case.

THE DRE OFFICER OR DRUG RECOGNITION EXPERT

An officer need only receive training in order to conduct the SFST. No formal credentialing or approval is needed. Once an officer has received this training, they are entitled to use it forever without any form of further education. This is usually justified, given the screening nature for which these tests are expected to be used.

However, the Evaluation of Impaired Operation Regulations, SOR/2008-196 requires at section 1: "An evaluating officer must be a certified drug recognition expert accredited by the International Association of Chiefs of Police [IACP]." While qualifications may be admitted upon receipt of documents showing such a certification, this is often a part of the officer's evidence that is not well rehearsed. It is important to recognize that while there are no "magic words," the officer must nonetheless show two things: first, that they are a certified DRE, and second, that they are accredited by the IACP. Canadian officers have typically also been certified or accredited through national governing bodies, but it is the IACP designation that is required.

In order to become a certified DRE officer, the officer must attend numerous courses. Typically, they are first trained as to how to administer the SFST or else complete a pre-course known as the Advanced Roadside Impaired Driving Enforcement (ARIDE) program, which typically takes 16 hours of instruction. From there, the DRE school requires an additional 56 hours of study which include written tests. The officer is then required to progress to a field certification which will take another 40 to 60 hours. During the certification stage, the officer is required to complete a minimum of twelve DRE tests. The officer must be faced with individuals under the influence of at least three different drug categories to ensure sufficient exposure. In these certification tests, the officer must obtain a minimum of 75 percent toxicological confirmation rate. This means that the officer must have at least nine tests where the toxicology results confirmed the drug category called before being accredited. During and after the certification training, DRE officers are required to maintain a rolling log of the tests they administer, including the date of the test, the opinion they came to, and the toxicological results that were returned. Further, the face sheet of each test should also include a "reviewed/approved by/date" section where another DRE officer or instructor should review the decision of the DRE to confirm that such a call could be made on the evidence on the face sheet.

Officers are required to recertify every two years following original certification by completing the following:

- Performing a minimum of four acceptable evaluations since the date of last certification, all of which must be reviewed then approved by a DRE instructor with at least one of them witnessed by a certified DRE instructor. These may be done during classroom simulations rather than on actually impaired individuals.
- Performing a minimum of eight hours of recertification training, consistent with IACP standards and must be completed either in one section or two sections of no less than 4 hours each.
- Presenting an updated CV and rolling log to their program coordinator.

As a result, DRE officers have significant training and experience in their specialized field. It is of little surprise then that courts no longer require a *Mohan*-style qualification for such officers but instead look toward what weight should be afforded to the opinion.

In addition to the above-noted and statutorily recognized testing, there are many other physical tests that some enforcement agencies or officers sometimes seek to rely upon. These can include reciting the alphabet, picking a correct coin out of an officer's hand, or really anything that comes to the imagination. What is important is to recognize that only the SFST and DRE testing have been standardized, tested, and approved. Any other tests cannot be demanded, only requested. As well, the results, and use of such results, of such ad hoc testing is limited at best. Only officers properly trained on the SFST or designated as DRE officers have the training to perform the tests and only those tests which have been scientifically researched and validated. Anything else would not be reasonable and the results would be of minimal usefulness.

CHAPTER 3

Chemical Testing for Drugs: What It Is, How It Works

Section 254(3.4) of the *Criminal Code* of Canada provides:

> (3.4) If, on completion of the evaluation, the evaluating officer has reasonable grounds to believe, based on the evaluation, that the person's ability to operate a motor vehicle, a vessel, an aircraft or railway equipment is impaired by a drug or by a combination of alcohol and a drug, the evaluating officer may, by demand made as soon as practicable, require the person to provide, as soon as practicable,
>
> (a) a sample of either oral fluid or urine that, in the evaluating officer's opinion, will enable a proper analysis to be made to determine whether the person has a drug in their body; or
>
> (b) samples of blood that, in the opinion of the qualified medical practitioner or qualified technician taking the samples, will enable a proper analysis to be made to determine whether the person has a drug in their body.

There are three bodily samples, oral fluid (saliva), urine, and blood, which can be taken from a person under investigation. They will each be examined in this chapter. Each of these can be taken in different methods and then tested in different ways. The manner in which they are taken and the method used for testing will affect the reasonableness of the search undertaken, the probative value of the tests, and the weight that a trier-of-fact can give to the tests.

Chain of custody relating to bodily samples is important for the Crown, not only in ensuring that the expert opinion relating to testing can be relied upon, but also in ensuring the privacy interest of an accused. Determining who took the sample, how, when, and under what conditions will ensure that the sample can be relied upon forensically to provide probative information. Eliminating issues surrounding contamination, proper storage, time to testing, and proper transportation to the testing laboratory will be important to ensuring conviction.

ORAL FLUID TESTING

Oral fluid means saliva. Saliva testing is one of the less intrusive methods to enable testing for drugs in an individual. Although it does require the close monitoring similar to urine sampling to ensure an unadulterated sample, it does not invade the privacy in the same way that observing a person urinating does, nor does it interfere with the bodily integrity of the individual in the same way as blood testing. While certainly more intrusive than a breath sample, it has many hallmarks of concern in common with breath testing, such as the sanitary method in which samples are taken. The issue of saliva testing comes down to limits on the technology available to police.

The most common form of saliva testing is to use an immunoassay screening process. This uses a form of enzyme that reacts to the drug compound in the saliva to create a reaction. This is often seen through a strip that changes colour, or in new testing methods through a machine that provides a digital reading. This form of testing is prone to false positives, which is an obvious concern when using such tests as evidence in a criminal matter. Most oral fluid testing can only detect a class of drug and not a particular drug; for example, it will indicate opioids but not the kind, such as oxycodone, morphine, or some other particular drug. The advantage of saliva or oral fluid testing is that it can show present exposure to a drug, because drug compounds in blood are also seen in the saliva. In addition to this, there is no need for the drug to be processed through the body to waste as in the case of urine testing. Oral consumption, including smoking, can lead to false positives due to samples of the drug being left in the oral cavity, but for only a short time after consumption. Given the allowance to wait a reasonable time to test at roadside where alcohol contamination in the mouth may affect a sample, and the significantly more time-consuming manner in which drug recognition testing is done, the risks of false positives can be easily handled both from a *Charter of Rights and Freedoms* standpoint, and a practical one. The disadvantages of oral fluid testing relate to the fact that immunoassay testing can lead to false positives and more in-depth practices, such as spectrography and chromatography, take a more significant amount of time to perform. Currently, the Centre for Forensic Sciences in Ontario does not have analytical methods in place for the detection of drugs in oral fluid. There are no approved containers for its collection. However, roadside immunoassay testing for drugs has been used in other jurisdictions, most notably Australia, for a significant period of time.

New technologies being developed and tested in Canada for roadside oral fluid screening were reviewed from late 2016 until early 2017 through the Oral Fluid Drug Screening Device Pilot Project. In that project, two different types of devices, the Securetec DrugRead and the Alere DDS-2, were piloted. While these devices provided positive experiences for screening, certain concerns were highlighted with such oral fluid screening. The most significant identified issues related to the time taken to process the tests (9.3 minutes on average) and "noteworthy, two of the Alere devices and one Securetec device began registering exclusively drug-positive results, including when tested on the police officers." Officer training and familiarity with the devices decreased errors and highlighted the importance of officer training and the birthing pains that may occur should such a testing regime be instituted. Changes to legislation and more reliable technology will be required to ensure public confidence and long-term viability of a roadside oral fluid screening regime. Standards will be required to be set by the scientific community to determine what will be needed in such screening devices related to **precision**, **accuracy**, and **specificity**. Screening for such drugs will detect exposure to the drug but will include some people using valid medically prescribed drugs in a therapeutic level that may or may not cause an impairing effect, such as prescription opioids at certain levels. The grounds upon which an officer will need to rely to make such a screening demand remain to be seen and will be very important in assessing its concordance with the *Charter*.

Roadside oral fluid screening device technology is relatively new. The technology is still in its infancy but grows every day. A recent study confirms that when comparing the two previously mentioned drug screening devices along with a third, the Dräger DrugTest 5000, the **sensitivity** was noted as 87 percent, meaning that in that percentage of cases, the reading on the screening device could be confirmed through Gas Chromatography Mass Spectrometry (GCMS) testing; 93.2 percent of individuals who had no drugs in their system were confirmed as such. However, this means that 6.8 percent of cases indicated false positives, which are some of the most worrisome cases when considering the limits imposed for reasonable searches and the grounds required for same. On a positive note, the false alarm rate varied based on substance from 1 percent with cocaine to just under 7 percent with opioids.

While false positives are concerning from a rights and freedoms standpoint, what was also concerning were the false negatives, whereby an individual may have drugs in their system but not detected by the oral fluid testing. Although generally the devices worked well and had strong sensitivity and specificity with most drug categories in the 80 to 90+ percent range, benzodiazepine (**benzo**) and amphetamine registered a sensitivity value of only 59.2 and 77.1 percent, respectively. This means that such screening would miss a potentially significant subset of drivers who are possible dangers to the community. Work in this area will need to continue. False negatives should be of little concern from a *Charter* standpoint because the individual will not be detained or searched any further. However, from a public interest standpoint this is important.

SECURETEC DRUGREAD

Securetec DrugRead uses opto-electronical photometer analysis. This complicated-sounding term means that it uses a light source and a sensor (called a photometer) to measure the intensity or other properties of reflection of the light. The Securetec DrugRead relies upon the company's DrugWipe Saliva test. The DrugRead, in essence, reads the results from the DrugWipe that does the actual testing. DrugRead is basically an interpretive tool so that improper readings are not interpreted from the DrugWipe test. The advantage of the DrugRead system is that it takes human error out of the reading of the lines on the DrugWipe test and also provides the ability to save and print results. The DrugWipe test appears to work similarly to a pregnancy test. A sample of saliva is collected into the collector. From there, the collector is placed inside a testing cassette. An ampoule inside the cassette is then broken which releases a chemical that reacts with the saliva sample to produce a test result that produces a series of lines. Depending on the lines that show up, the individual is confirmed as having or not having consumed a particular class of drug. The classes it is designed to test for are cannabis, cocaine, ecstasy/amphetamines or heroin/opiates. A weakness for use in Canadian climates is that the temperature range for measurements is from 5 to 40 degrees Celsius. This will require officers to conduct tests inside their cruisers or another warm place in winter months to properly rely on the results. The test will result in a present/not present outcome at a particular measuring limit, typically 5 **ng**/100 ml (nanograms per millilitres) of blood. The use of this test for lower limits will need to be investigated further. In essence, this system uses an immunoassay test backed up by an automated reader to eliminate human error in reading the results.

The Securetec DrugRead system, rather than only the DrugWipe test, enhances the usefulness of the testing. It does three things: (1) eliminates differences between officers seeing or not seeing a line; (2) makes sure officers are not making a call based on bad lighting; and (3) standardizes what is a fail or not in such testing. Where any doubt exists between an officer reviewing the DrugWipe test and the decision or call made by the DrugRead, the DrugRead result is to be deemed authoritative.

The Securetec DrugRead manual is instructive with regard to a number of issues that will need to be properly taught to officers or adapted to Canadian use. Clarification of the impact of instructions in the manual will be needed in order to develop support for such a system. For example, regarding safety and maintenance, it is recommended that the system and its batteries not be stored at temperatures lower than 0 degrees Celsius. Whether this will simply impact on battery life or testing ability is the kind of thing that is often important in developing training manuals. Regarding maintenance and cleaning, all such work must be done by "authorized, qualified personnel."

Quality control tests are expected to be performed regularly. It is anticipated that such testing will be completed by qualified technicians similar to the manner in which approved screening devices for alcohol are calibrated by qualified instrument technicians on a regular basis. The Securetec DrugRead system uses quality control test cassettes. One indicates all positive test results whereas the other indicates all negative test results. The manual recommends using both in sequence before each test series and allows them to be used prior to each test if deemed appropriate.

The requirement built into the device provides a reminder to perform the quality control tests at least every sixty days though the device can be configured to turn this reminder off. Dirt, dust, moisture, or other particulate matter on the test strips can affect the quality control tests. Thus, proper maintenance and cleanliness of the test strips will also be important. Fading as a result of prolonged exposure to sunlight may also affect their efficacy. Further, the correct positioning of the DrugWipe cassette must be ensured to endorse the accuracy of the DrugRead result. Simply put, a cassette that is not fully inserted may be misread by the device.

The manufacturer acknowledges that the DrugWipe technology is susceptible to certain substances that may cross-react with the testing method used. This acknowledges that there are substances that could result in a false positive result. This helps explain why such testing is best used for screening purposes and not authoritatively as positive proof of the presence of a particular substance.

The device is designed for mobile screening or in police stations but the DrugWipe test cassettes must be protected from exposure to moisture to ensure their continued utility. Transportation temperatures for the DrugRead device are suggested by the manufacturer to be between –10 and 60 degrees Celsius. Testing is to occur between 5 and 40 degrees Celsius. The device allows for a system reset should problems recur with use. This will reset the device to factory settings, necessitating inputting date and time data again.

Two methods of operation are prescribed in the manual. The recommended procedure is to collect a sample from the driver, then insert the cassette into the device and press the button which breaks the ampoule. The second procedural option is to collect a sample from the driver, then hold the cassette upside down and press the button breaking the ampoule. After 10 seconds of holding the cassette upside down, it should be placed on a horizontal surface. In 5 to 8 minutes, the cassette can be inserted into the DrugRead device but this procedure requires testing within only 10 minutes, thus leaving a somewhat narrow window.

Issues regarding expiry date, damage to the packaging, moisture penetrating the packaging, or control lines that have already changed colour can invalidate the test. The device allows for the input, saving, and printing of data including name, ID, officer information, location, and other comments should the agency operating the device request this option and the officer utilize it. This data can be saved on the device and later printed or downloaded to a computer, though this will delete the data from the device.

Testing using this system requires 3 to 8 minutes for measurement, time for collection of the sample, manual processing time, data entry if so desired, and human interaction with the device. All told, most interactions will take 8 to 15 minutes, assuming results are obtained in the first test and a retest is not required. This takes significantly longer than current breath alcohol screening tests, and the application and interaction of other rights, such as the right to consult counsel, may play an important role as devices like this come into their own.

DrugWipe cassettes that are utilized in the procedure also have their own requirements which must be met to ensure validity. They require storage at temperatures between 2 and 25 degrees Celsius and use between 5 and 40 degrees Celsius. It is important to note that temperature levels in motor vehicles such as the trunk on a hot summer day or a cold winter day may lead to temperatures outside this range. Use at temperatures above 40 degrees Celsius is not advisable due to damage that may occur to the cassette. Use below that temperature requires the cassette to be brought up to the operating temperature.

ALERE DDS-2

Alere DDS-2 uses similar technology. The system consists of a testing cartridge and a device. The method of use is to insert a fresh cartridge into the device, then use the oral fluid collection device to collect saliva.

The collection device is then inserted into the cartridge in the device and the device analyzes the interaction between the oral fluid and drug protein conjugate. Again, this is somewhat similar to a pregnancy test in terms of what happens visually—namely, the application of a bodily fluid to a test to provide a visual clue by colour change. The Alere DDS-2 does not allow for viewing of results by eye but instead requires the use of the device to determine results. The advantage to this is that it can discourage officers from using their observations of the test strip to influence what they believe the results should be. In effect, this elimination of the possibility of human error, similar to what the DrugRead system does, is a requirement rather than an option and will enhance the objectivity of such a device. The device itself uses "advanced image processing algorithms to accurately determine the line intensity on the test cartridge."

The Alere DDS-2 system leads off its instructions by reminding that this device is intended for screening purposes and that any positive test result "should be confirmed by a second test method such as GCMS or LCMS." The test works by gathering the oral fluid with the collection device and bringing it into contact with a reagent (a reactive chemical that produces a known reaction when exposed to a particular chemical, i.e., a drug). The saliva flows into the testing cartridge by means of capillary action. Simply put, this means that the sides of the piping that go from the collection device to the testing cartridge are sufficiently close together that the walls themselves pull the oral fluid to the testing area without need of a pump or gravity. The reagent reacts, or does not, with the oral fluid, producing either no change or change. If the change is sufficient (i.e., the colour is dark enough) then a positive result is registered with the device itself.

A number of precautions are required to be followed to ensure proper results are obtained. The first is regarding storage of the device and the cartridges. The cartridges must be stored between 15 and 25 degrees Celsius in order to ensure stability of the reagents. The test cartridges must not be at or below −5 degrees Celsius for more than 10 minutes. Cartridges are not to be used past their expiry date and are not even to be opened past the expiry date. The device is to automatically detect the expiry date through a bar code and reject any expired test cartridge, thus eliminating accidental use of an expired cartridge. Further, the device heats the test cartridge to an optimal temperature for testing.

To deal with concerns regarding moisture contaminating the tests, each cartridge is packed with a silica gel pack (similar to packets seen in many forms of packing as a desiccant). The operator is to confirm that the crystals in the silica patch are yellow. If they are green, then moisture has invaded the cartridge and it should not be used. An issue that affects operability but not necessarily reliability is the requirement to keep the device level and to still allow the capillary action to bring the oral fluid in contact with the reagent. Persistent movement may stop the two coming into contact.

Operating temperatures for running a test are between 5 and 35 degrees Celsius. The system can be stored at temperatures between −20 and 45 degrees Celsius. It is important to note that temperature levels in motor vehicles (such as the trunk) on a hot summer day or a cold winter day may lead to temperatures outside this range. Humidity levels must be non-condensing and only then between 20 and 80 percent. The manufacturer's instructions require that the device be allowed to reach ambient temperature before use and notes that "this may take at least 30 minutes" but acknowledges even longer times may be required depending on "climatic differences."

Quality control testing is performed by way of a positive and negative test cartridge. These tests are recommended to be performed at least once on each day of testing. The test cartridges also have a best before date and cannot be used after expiry as the device will automatically reject it. Testing can be undertaken before each drug test if required. Annual servicing is required to be carried out by a qualified service engineer.

The Alere DDS-2 system acknowledges issues with cross-reactivity in its instruction guide. However, most of the cross-reactions noted occur as a result of other known drugs being falsely identified. While this may affect the exact nature of the substance for which an individual is being tested, they are generally in the same category (i.e., codeine, heroin, and morphine all test positive as "opiates"). This will have little effect where the screening device is used in a larger way just to confirm the presence of "a drug." However, this can be of greater concern when a particular level or *per se* limit is being looked for because a lower level of a different drug may actually be detected and improperly classified. For this reason, the screening device will not be able to confirm a level beyond a reasonable doubt with existing technology.

The area of concern with the cross-reactivity is most acute when dealing with marijuana and its active ingredient **THC**. Specifically, a small amount of the inactive **metabolite** of THC, carboxy-THC (11-Nor-9 Carboxy Δ9-THC) can produce a positive reading for Δ9-THC, the active ingredient that is specifically targeted in *per se* legislation. This will be worrisome given that detection of drivers impaired by the consumption of marijuana will be one of the main focuses of the use of such devices; the false positive possibility will need to be explored in litigation. As an inactive metabolite, carboxy-THC is indicative of prior exposure, but to rely on such a test to justify a significantly intrusive test such as blood testing, will surely be an area of litigation with regard to the intrusion into the personal integrity and liberty of the individual. That the manufacturer has provided this information publicly is commendable.

Of note is that the system allows for the storing and downloading of data to generate useful reports including identification of trends with storage of up to ten thousand results. The use by police forces in identifying common drugs being used in drivers will allow for better law to be made and the best allocation of resources to help deal with the problem of drug-impaired drivers. Unfortunately, tests where an error occurred and no analysis or result took place will not be saved in the data.

The device is not to be used in proximity to a pacemaker as it may affect its operation. As well, antivirus support for the computer used to download data is recommended, raising the concern of hacking of such devices.

DRÄGER DRUGTEST 5000

The test system for the Dräger DrugTest 5000 works by bringing the test strip in contact with the oral fluid sample at the required temperature. It can operate in ambient temperature of between 5 and 40 degrees Celsius and humidity between 5 and 95 percent. Concerns where the system is moved from a cold environment to a hot environment raise issues of moisture contamination. As a result, it is suggested that a wait of about 1.5 hours is appropriate in a change from 0 to 20 degrees Celsius. Cartridges are also to be at similar temperatures though they can reach same in 15 minutes. Storage of the system can be from –20 to 60 degrees Celsius.

Tilt of 10 degrees along any axis is the maximum allowable, thus requiring a reasonably level location to conduct the testing procedure. An adequacy indicator on the sampler changes colour to indicate sufficient oral fluid has been collected, allowing the officer to know when to begin the analysis by the device. The unit is recommended to be serviced once every twelve months.

Quality control recommended by the manufacturer is the testing of a known drug-free sample. While positive controls for tests are available, they must be purchased separately and are not discussed at length in the device's manual. The system works to detect drugs at or above a certain level, similar to the other discussed devices.

The manufacturer acknowledges that false results can occur as a result of similar chemical structures from similar drugs, or in rare cases non-specific interactions, such as physiological variation, state of health, and contamination with food or other substances.

URINE TESTING

Urine testing detects tests past exposure to a drug and not a present level. This is a part of every report relating to urinalysis that counsel are likely to see. Urine is, of course, a waste product of the body and chemicals detected are there as a result of being metabolized through the body. Urine testing is typically done through Gas Chromatography and Mass Spectrometry (GCMS). This is a complex scientific process by which the sample is vaporized, typically in concert with a carrier gas, and then passes through a column that separates the constituent chemicals in the compound, identifies the chemicals, and ionizes each substance. Then the instrument is able to determine, based on the type of electrical charge, the quantity of the chemical along with again confirming the type of chemical. Using two methods together increases the reliability. Proper understanding of the limitations and analytical methods used in GCMS testing is beyond most lawyers, but education is important to ensure that lawyers know the proper questions to ask and for experts to have to properly interpret such tests. Raw data including the chromatographs produced, these being graphed results from the GCMS, can be interpreted by a proper expert to ensure that proper procedures were followed, especially when determining substances that are less traditional forms of drugs (i.e., certain synthetic cannabinoids). Even the most alert forensic laboratory can be overwhelmed by the variety of drugs being ingested by the population. As well, determining which compounds were tested for may also reveal substances that were not tested for, that may have caused some of the effects of impairment noted, whether the effect noticed was impairing or not (i.e., issues that may appear impairing on the DRE tests but not actually impairing a person's ability to operate a motor vehicle). Liquid Chromatography Mass Spectrometry (LCMS) is a more acute process that involves similar theory in testing but utilizes a liquid carrier agent rather than a gaseous one. This allows a different range of substances to be tested than in GCMS because there is no need to vaporize the sample being tested.

Urine testing is generally not seen to be as intrusive as blood testing but is more invasive than breath testing. Because of the risk of adulteration of the sample (i.e., an accused scooping water out of the toilet at the police station), an accused should be monitored while providing the sample. This issue must be balanced with an accused's privacy interests. Generally, an accused, even when detained at the police station, maintains a degree of privacy interest while using the bathroom. The proper balancing including respect towards a person's gender identity, sexual preferences, and cultural or religious beliefs will need to be struck when ensuring that the accused is monitored but not unduly so.

While a person under investigation who is not breathing would be of especial concern to a police officer, the person who cannot urinate is a different issue. A person can be charged with refusing to provide a sample if they do not urinate on demand; yet certain drugs, the person's impairment, or simple performance anxiety all may interfere with the ability to provide a sample. *Mens rea* issues and the intent to refuse have not been greatly tested in urine samples to this date but one can see such an issue arising in the future.

Given that urine is a waste by-product of the body and testing can only indicate prior exposure, the issue of **elimination** rate and half-life of a drug is important for counsel to understand. Different substances remain in the body for different amounts of time. These can range from mere minutes to months, depending on the substance. The probative value of urinalysis is limited, depending on the type of drug and what other evidence can be shown to indicate a time of last consumption. The lack of read-back or presumption of identity is something that has troubled courts for years. Bill C-46, currently before the Senate, seeks to deal with such issues though it remains to be seen what changes may occur in the legislative future. It is often useful to consider a drug-impaired driving case in a manner similar to that of an alcohol-impaired case. Alcohol is a drug, and like other drugs, can be detected in the urine for a significant time after an impairing blood concentration has gone. Unlike alcohol, no other drug currently has a presumption of identity.

Urine testing is further limited as by-products of the chemical reactions that take place in the body may be indicative of prior consumption of a particular drug or may occur as a result of something else. Particular drugs may not show up in urine tests but instead show metabolites such as is the case with marijuana's active ingredient THC. THC is less likely to be detected than its active metabolite hydroxy-THC or its inactive metabolite carboxy-THC. Active metabolites still have impairing effects but inactive metabolites do not. That being said, presence of carboxy-THC is good evidence of prior consumption though not necessarily of when. In heavy users carboxy-THC may be evident for days or longer after heavy usage. However, it is evidence of consumption. Other drugs break down into their metabolites which may be inactive or non-impairing versions of other drugs. Chemical testing may only give an either/or answer that the person either took the non-impairing drug or has metabolized the impairing drug. Of course, the weight which a trier-of-fact can give to such evidence is impacted as a result.

BLOOD TESTING

Generally speaking, blood is the gold standard for drug testing. It provides the most probative evidence but with some of the greatest interference to the bodily integrity of an individual. Often, it is useful to provide an image of a blood draw (see Figure 3), or even better video, to aid the trier-of-fact in recognizing the interference with liberty that a blood draw entails and the impact on the bodily integrity, and thus *Charter* rights, of an accused.

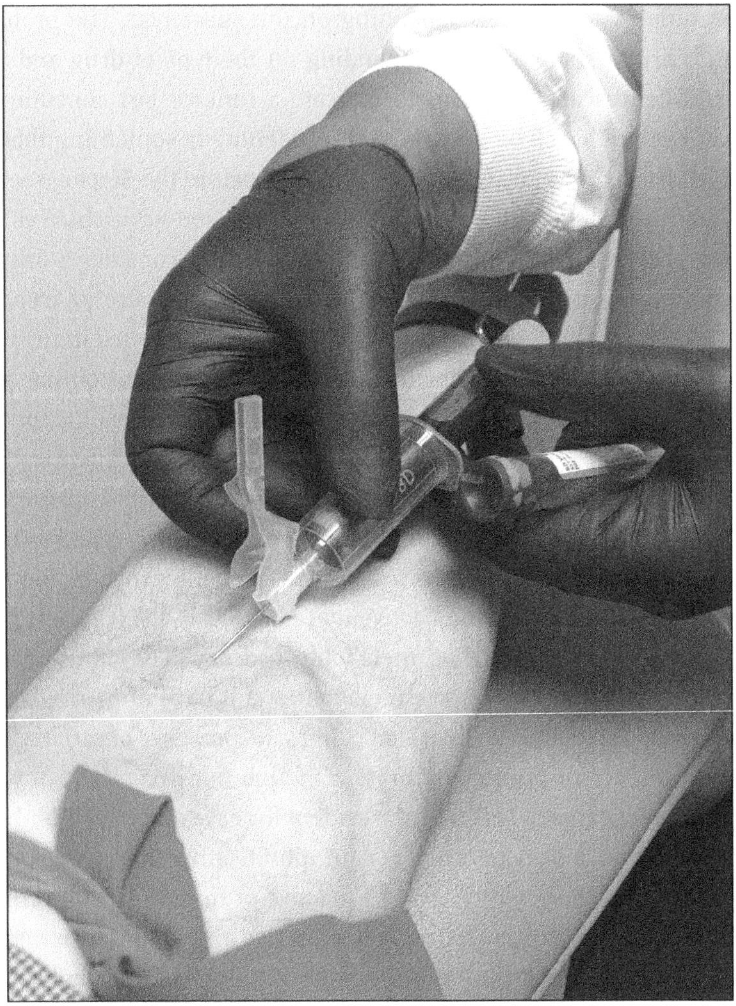

FIGURE 3 Blood Draw in Testing for Drugs

There is a high privacy interest in a person's blood. It is important to note the different requirements for a blood draw between alcohol and other drugs in the *Criminal Code*. Although blood testing for alcohol requires that an officer have a belief that "because of their physical condition" a person cannot provide a breath sample, there is no such requirement when demanding blood in a drug-impaired driving case, only a requirement that the person taking the blood believes it will provide a sample capable of analysis. Blood is currently the only method that allows for a *per se* limit to be tested. As new technologies are developed, this is expected to change, but for now there is no equivalent to a breath test for alcohol in determining limits for drugs.

There are two main methods for drug testing in blood: immunoassay and chromatography/spectrometry. Immunoassay testing is the first. It can be used to determine drug concentrations in the blood. This testing is done by enzymes creating a measurable reaction to a chemical found in the blood. This testing uses up a portion of the chemical found during the reaction. Similar to immunoassay testing in oral fluid, this method can produce false positives. For this reason it is imperative that where the evidentiary foundation will be proven through hospital records, the type of testing be examined and proper education on the method, reliability, and specificity of such testing is examined by all parties. The defence should determine what common compounds could act as interferents. The defence must concern itself with false positives, reliability, and specificity. The Crown needs to satisfy itself that it can properly rely on such testing to prove the case beyond a reasonable doubt. Both sides would be wise to remember the old adage from the Trojan War about being wary of enemies bearing gifts as a concession regarding hospital blood records that can be perilous to both sides. Immunoassay testing is most commonly seen in hospital blood tests rather than in forensic laboratory testing due to its speed of testing and relatively good reliability. Also of concern with immunoassay testing is the fact that since the testing uses up a portion of the substance being tested for, in the test itself, through a reaction, the ability to replicate the test on a particular sample is not available, making the forensic use of such a test of limited value.

Another issue with hospital-drawn blood is that often it is taken as serum rather than whole blood. This type of blood requires a conversion factor, most commonly 1.1:1, to convert the drug quantity found in it to that found in whole blood. This matters less in drug cases as there is currently no *per se* limits set for any drug. But it will become more important as such limits get set or while interpreting whether the quantity found in an individual's system is in a range from mere detection through therapeutic level to beyond therapeutic/impairing level. Of note is that some drugs are impairing even in the therapeutic level, though many are not. Beyond the type of blood sample taken is that hospitals use various different containers to collect blood. Under the *Criminal Code* there are only six approved containers for taking blood. Proper testing typically involves using a grey-topped Vacutainer brand container. This looks like a small glass vial with a grey auto-sealing rubber/plastic top through which a needle pierces and the vacuum environment inside the container sucks in an appropriate amount of venial blood. The colour of the top of the Vacutainer will let you know what chemicals are already in the vial. These differ based on the tests intended to be performed. Hospital tests are often different from those that would be forensically preferred in order to provide the best evidence. Determining what impact the particular type of container used will have on the sample and the ability to test it for drugs will be important in determining whether the sample can provide proof beyond a reasonable doubt of the drug found. Technique matters and ensuring that blood drawn and the chemicals in the vial mix properly is one of the most common mistakes made when drawing blood (look for the phlebotomist tipping the sample back and forth). Some vials do not contain any substances so will not need mixing. However, such vials require testing quickly (generally within 2 hours) due to the lack of preservatives and the possibility of the blood breaking down or undergoing chemical changes. Given the high standards of proof beyond a reasonable doubt, it would be useful for police officers to be trained as Qualified Technicians so that they can take blood samples when necessary without seeking a medical practitioner to ensure forensically viable samples.

Forensic laboratories prefer to use GCMS and LCMS testing. As discussed earlier in this chapter under Urine Testing, GCMS and LCMS are complex scientific processes by which the blood sample is vaporized in concert with a carrier gas or liquid, passes through a column that separates the constituent chemicals in the compound, identifies the chemicals, and ionizes each substance. The instrument then is able to determine, based on the type of electrical charge, the quantity of the chemical along with again confirming the type of chemical. By using two methods together, the reliability is increased. Proper understanding of the limitations and analytical methods used in GCMS testing is beyond most lawyers, but education is important to ensure that lawyers know the proper questions to ask and experts have to attend to properly interpret such tests. Raw data including graphed results from the GCMS can be interpreted by a proper expert to ensure that proper procedures were followed, especially when determining substances that are less traditional forms of drugs (i.e., certain synthetic cannabinoids). Even the most alert forensic laboratory can be overwhelmed by the variety of drugs being ingested by the population. As well, determining which compounds were tested for may also reveal: a) substances that were not tested for and which may have caused some of the effects of impairment noted; and b) whether the effect noticed was impairing or not (i.e., issues that may appear impairing on the DRE tests but are not actually impairing a person's ability to operate a motor vehicle).

GCMS testing in blood is more useful than with urine testing because urine results will vary depending on when a person has last urinated and how long they have been metabolizing the drug. Simply put, a particular amount found in urine only indicates prior exposure and not current levels. Blood eliminates this issue and shows the current level of the drug in a person's system, often expressed as a mass per volume, such as nanograms per decilitre (ng/100ml or ng/dl). That being said, different expressions can be used and an ability to find useful conversions, often through speaking to an expert, will help determine whether the amount found is significant of not.

Issues with blood testing which can arise relate in a number of different ways. First is with ensuring that the equipment used for sampling is correct. While typically not an issue with hospital blood draws, determining whether or not a police blood sampling kit is beyond its best before date is imperative. The manner in which the blood is drawn to ensure no contamination, especially if an individual uses injectable drugs, is important. With testing through GCMS and LCMS it is important to make sure that the internal standard—i.e., the sample run through the machine to determine accuracy—used was stable and pure because this has a significantly different **retention time** than that of the drug being tested for. Proper maintenance of auto-injectors, where used, proper carrier gas for the specific detector, and significance of the retention time for the reagent used must all be examined to ensure that no problems arise with the testing of the actual substance. Determining whether venous or arterial blood was tested may also be relevant as certain drugs can have differing levels in these two types of blood based on the phase (absorption or elimination phase). As the law makes no differentiation of these with regard to *per se* limits, it may be important to determine if some portion of the blood exceeds the limit if that is enough or if it must be throughout the body. Further, with regard to impairment, determining which phase the individual was in at the time of driving may give useful evidence as to impairment or lack thereof by the drug. By the time testing is completed this may no longer be testable, similar to bolus drinking in alcohol cases. Determining if the tests on the accused were done individually or as a batch can also be important. Where batch testing is undertaken, a review of the results for the batch may help determine whether there are any problems in the testing of the batch or, conversely, if the results are supported by proper procedures. Before a sample is tested on a GCMS or LCMS device, standards are run through the machine to determine accuracy. These are typically run at different levels to check the "**linearity**" of the instrument. Typically, these will include standards both above and below the result in the bodily sample tested to ensure proper calibration. With the Intoxilyzer 8000C semi-annual testing at 50, 100, and 350 mgs of alcohol/100 ml of blood is done in a similar way. GCMS and LCMS testing is similar in this procedural regard.

Counsel should also consider issues of continuity. In the case of a hospital draw, was the sample sealed after taking? While the container self-seals after the sample is taken, intentional contamination via another needle inserted into the same hole is possible. Police typically affix a seal overtop; examination of the seal prior to its breaking for testing should be undertaken by the testing facility. The manner in which the sample was stored, transported, and taken care of should be easily provided.

PER SE LIMITS

Bill C-46 suggests to implement a *per se* limit with respect to driving with tetrahydrocannabinol (THC), the active drug chemical in marijuana, in a person's system. It would impose fines for individuals caught with between over 2 ng THC/ml of blood to a limit of 5 ng THC/ml of blood. Individuals over 5 ng THC/ml of blood would face penalties similar to impaired driving or driving with over 80 mg alcohol/100 ml of blood. In cases where a person has greater than 50 mg alcohol/100 ml of blood and greater than 2.5 ng THC/ml of blood, a person would face the same consequences as those over 5 ng THC/100 ml of blood, the combination of alcohol and THC being of concern. Provincial legislation such as Ontario's *Highway Traffic Act* has not seen proposed amendments to keep pace with this, so while the *Criminal Code* would not see individuals in the lower ranges lose their licence, the provincial companion legislation in most provinces currently would.

Additional *per se* limits are being suggested for Gammahydroxybutyrate (GHB). Originally an absolute ban (i.e., a limit of zero) was suggested. However, this substance can be produced naturally in the body. Given this, the proper testing procedure and explanations for its natural occurrence at or above the limit will be integral to forming a proper defence.

Absolute zero limits are being proposed for LSD, psilocybin (magic mushrooms), ketamine, cocaine, methamphetamine and 6-monoacetylmorphine (metabolite of heroin). As some of these are drugs available with a prescription or otherwise used in valid medical treatment, the public will be in a situation where the impact of their actions will need to be explained in-depth to them prior to surgery or administration of the drug, lest the person become impaired by the drug and unable to understand the warning. An emphasis on looking for recent medical treatment and what warnings were provided by medical professionals will become more common for defence to seek and prosecutors to rebut.

Per se limits relating to other drugs have not been proposed. The concern regarding marijuana is taking the fore due to its impending legalization. Set limits provide direct guidance to law enforcement as to acceptable limits. There is concern that the limits proposed may catch too many individuals not impaired while others show concern that it may allow too many guilty to go free. This sort of concern was raised when *per se* limits were introduced regarding alcohol and the 80 mgs alcohol/100 ml of blood recognizes a compromise that left neither side fully happy. It is not uncommon to see toxicologists talk of how significant impairment actually starts with alcohol as low as 50 mgs alcohol/100 ml of blood and some individuals are impaired as low as 15 mgs alcohol/100 ml of blood though it is generally accepted that virtually everyone is impaired to operate by 100 mgs alcohol/100 ml of blood.

Per se limits for drugs are in their infancy and will require fine tuning as scientific review reaches a consensus on the appropriate limits. Once imposed, it will be up to the average citizen to determine whether they exceed such limits, though with no experience or education that has existed with regards to alcohol. Parliament seems to be attempting to strike a balance with the two levels being proposed with regard to THC but the criminal culpability being attached to both levels leads to concerns from a moralist sense in imposing criminal sanction on what may or may not be a morally blameworthy act (i.e., without the danger of impairment proven through scientific study). The question to be reviewed is whether the criminal limits being proposed equate to the moral reprehensibility deserving of a criminal record. Differing tolerance from individual to individual means that any *per se* limit will necessarily either catch innocents, miss the guilty or both.

MEASUREMENT UNCERTAINTY

Measurement Uncertainty (MU) is an area of science that deals with the ability of the technology conducting the measurement to be correct. Science deals with hard numbers. Organizations such as the Centre of Forensic Sciences (CFS) in Ontario provide their MU in reports. Triers-of-fact deserve to know MU but also need to be educated with regard to it. MU is typically reported with a percentage confidence. A lawyer with numbers subject to interpretation can be a dangerous thing. Proof beyond a reasonable doubt in a criminal matter is not easily quantifiable. Some would say it requires certainty nearing 99 percent; others would point out that 11/12 jurors cannot lead to a conviction so 91.6 percent is not sufficient. MU is a concept that does not easily transfer into one of reasonable doubt. Having an expert explain what the MU involved in a particular analysis is, is important as the MU may also connote uncertainty that increases the likelihood of guilt as much as the kind of uncertainty that suggests acquittal.

Competent lawyers should be well versed in concepts such as accuracy and precision, the ability or instrumentation reliability, the importance of statistical analysis in assessing false positives, false negatives, and measures of standard deviation in determining the actual risk of inadvertently convicting an innocent party when relying on measurements made with scientific instrumentation. Utilization of proper experts to explain such concepts to the trier-of-fact is invaluable, often both to the trier-of-fact and the lawyer.

ACCURACY VS. PRECISION

A very precise measuring tool may be inaccurate while a very accurate tool may be imprecise. For testing that will be relied upon to the criminal standard of proof beyond a reasonable doubt, the testing must be both accurate and precise. Accuracy is the ability of a test to determine the number of correct calls, both positive and negative. Precision is the ability of the test to produce results in a test that are close to those expected through testing with an outside source or standard. As Figure 4 shows, either accuracy or precision is not enough, and instead both need to be present to reach the high standard necessary in criminal prosecutions.

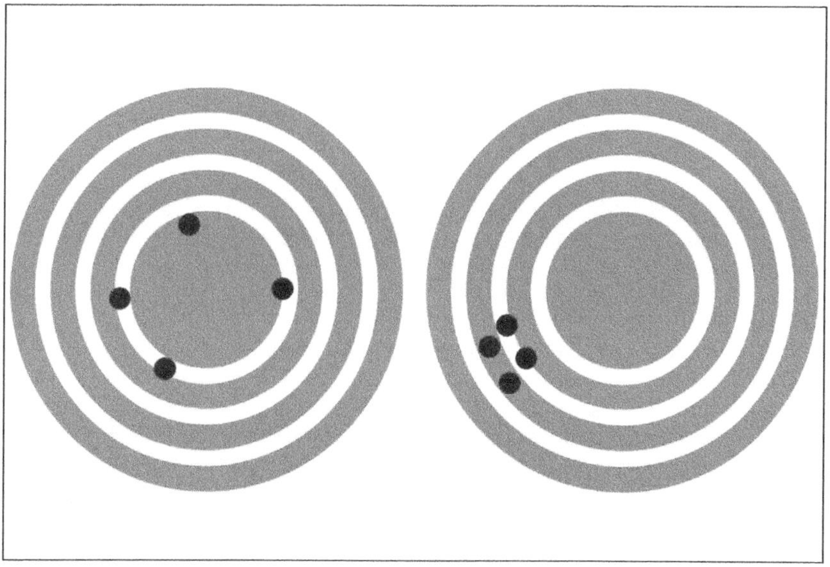

FIGURE 4 Accuracy (on the left) and Precision (on the right) Both Need to Be Present

It is important therefore to understand these concepts. When considering the evidence of an expert who performed a form of testing, be it DRE or chemical analysis, it is also important to understand both the nature of the test and also its assessment in relation to prior tests. Forensic laboratories subscribe to a set of minimum quality standards. The CFS in Ontario, for example, is an ASCLD/LAB-*International* accredited testing laboratory and conforms with ISO/IEC 17025-2005. This means that it follows a particular quality management system including having a proper scope, using proper references for testing, conforming to particular terms and definitions, as well as meeting certain management and technical requirements.

CHAPTER 4

The Matrix

The drug category **matrix** is at the centre of the classification system in the Drug Recognition Evaluations. This matrix, shown in Figure 5, provides a method of classification, based on symptoms and reactions, to test to determine the kind of drug or rather the drug category by which a person is impaired. While this matrix appears straightforward, it is often anything but. This is due to the fact that officers are to consider the totality of circumstances and also recognize that an individual may be affected by more than one drug along with pre-existing medical conditions. Couple with this the fact that, depending on the dosage of particular drugs, the impact on a particular test may change. Take, as an example, the issue of cannabis. Depending on the dosage and tolerance of an individual, the person's pupils may either be dilated or normal. Discrimination becomes even more complicated with inhalants in body temperature where the temperature may rise, fall, or remain normal. In essence, regardless of the result, it may be counted on as an indicator.

Explanation as to why particular results of the test do not conform with the matrix is an area ripe for cross-examination. DRE officers are trained to give a response and in testing any particular individual, the results may vary. The standard response will typically indicate something such as, "I took into account the totality of my training and testing." This highlights the subjective nature of DRE testing, which was confirmed in *Bingley*. Quite often, the results of the testing do not match any category

THE MATRIX

	CNS Depressants	*CNS Stimulants*	*Hallucinogens*	*Dissociative Anesthetic*	*Narcotic Analgesics*	*Inhalants*	*Cannabis*
Horizontal Gaze Nystagmus	Present	None	None	Present	None	Present	None
Vertical Nystagmus	(High Dose)* Present	None	None	Present	None	(High Dose) Present	None
Lack of Convergence	Present	None	None	Present	None	Present	Present
Pupil Size	(1) Normal	Dilated	Dilated	Normal	Constricted	(4) Normal	(6) Dilated
Reaction to Light	Slow	Slow	(3) Normal	Normal	Little or None Visible	Slow	Normal
Pulse	(2) Down	Up	Up	Up	Down	Up	Up
Blood Pressure	Down	Up	Up	Up	Down	(5) Up/Down	Up
Body Temperature	Normal	Up	Up	Up	Down	Up/Down Normal	Normal
Muscle Tone	Flaccid	Rigid	Rigid	Rigid	Flaccid	Normal/Flaccid	Normal

(1) Soma, Quaaludes, and some antidepressants usually dilate
(2) Quaaludes, alcohol, and some antidepressants may elevate
(3) Certain psychedelic amphetamines may cause slowing
(4) Normal but may be dilated
(5) Down with anesthetic gases; up with volatile solvents & aerosols
(6) Possibly normal
* High dose for that individual

FIGURE 5 Drug Symptomatology Matrix Used by DRE Officer to Determine Class of Impairing Drug

perfectly. It is important in the review of each file to compare the results received by the officer to the matrix to determine whether their call most accurately reflects the indicators on the matrix. Specifically, it is important to know whether or not there are other drug categories that more closely match the symptoms and signs noted. Specifically, officers often rely upon an individual self-report of what medications or drugs they have taken in determining what class to call. It is important to know that self-reporting is not a portion of the matrix but instead, in many ways, goes against the objective nature of the system.

Subjectivity in testing is often best illustrated through an officer ignoring the proper call via the matrix and instead relying upon the self-report of the accused person. Cross-examination on the issue of why an officer made or did not make a particular drug category call, with specific reference to why particular test results do not match the expected result for that category on the matrix, is something that police and Crowns need to anticipate.

The matrix is the portion of the testing which is, in some ways, the most objective, in that certain results are expected to correlate with certain drugs. However, the subjective nature of some of the tests involved is the portion more likely to be challenged rather than the matrix itself. As with other experts, it is often not the knowledge on which the expert relies but the underpinning facts that cause difficulty in having expert evidence accepted.

It is also important to understand the rebound or negative effect of a drug. While drugs of a certain class generally produce one sort of reaction, the rebound effect, which is basically a form of withdrawal, is when the body seeks to return to equilibrium and overcorrects. As a result, the effects of a drug category may change based on the stage of drug effect a person is in. The question at law will be whether any impact as a result is truly affected "by the drug" or if it is a physiological reaction and thus not to be criminalized.

Qualification of drug category through use of the matrix is intended to indicate the type of drug but not the impact. Thus, testimony relating to the degree of impairment based on the interpretation of the matrix is fraught with issues. A good DRE officer recognizes the difference between the tests listed on the matrix and other tests such as divided-attention tests.

Counsel should note carefully that even partial fails such as dilated or constricted pupils on one test (i.e., direct light), means that this can be considered a positive call for the indicator, even if in room light and near total darkness the individual performs within the baselines.

For these reasons, the use of the matrix, while central to the standardization of the procedures, is nonetheless open to interpretation by the DRE officer. The weight to be given to a particular opinion must be assessed in view of the subjective component of the interpretation, where not all results categorize perfectly to a single drug category. Multi-drug use, prior existing conditions, or variation in individual physiology may allow for an officer to make a "correct call" even where the results do not neatly match the expectations of the matrix. While the officer cannot be faulted for this, due to the nature of the criminal justice system, the weight which a trier-of-fact may attach to such calls may be limited. For the prosecution, it will be imperative to educate the trier as to the reasons why the results may not match perfectly, while for the defence, it will be an exercise in attaching the proper weight to such an opinion. Strengths and weaknesses in both sides will need to be examined and assigned their importance in each case.

CHAPTER 5

Drug Categories and Their Expected Symptoms

There are seven drug categories which the DRE program considers. These are not the same as pharmacological categories of similar names and although knowledge of pharmacology can be very beneficial, it is important to not strictly limit the category in pharmacological terms.

The seven categories are:

- Central Nervous System (**CNS**) Depressants
- CNS Stimulants
- Hallucinogens
- Dissociative Anesthetics
- Narcotic Analgesics
- Inhalants
- Cannabis

The matrix, reviewed in Chapter 4, provides the expected results on each of the nine classification tests. However, beyond those tests, each category of drug is likely to produce other typical signs of impairment associated with each class of drug.

A sometimes useful way of considering each class is by way of a drug which the lawyer may have come into contact with in other prosecutions or popular culture and will be reviewed with each drug category.

Common signs and effect of a drug category are useful tools in assessing the kind of drug present in a person's system. However, the presence or absence of any singular sign or clue should not be correlated to any particular conclusion. Following are the "usual" signs and symptoms that DRE officers are taught to note. That being said, it is important to recognize that DRE officers are provided with these signs in their training and may become result focussed and subject to tunnel vision when an accused purports to have taken a certain kind of drug. The best experts avoid tunnel vision and focus on their observations rather than fitting the observations to the expected call.

Consumption is something that is ever evolving. Any mode of administration is subject to change by an inventive user. Some drugs do not fit well within any particular category of drug and as a result, the effects observed may be different than those expected. With all that being said, it is important when examining a DRE officer's conclusions to assess why a particular call may have been made in the absence of expected symptoms. As in other cases, absence of or lack of a particular sign on its own may not provide a defence, but collectively there must still be a sufficient constellation of factors upon which the officer bases their opinion to support said opinion.

The DRE officer, as an expert, should allow for other possibilities when reviewing their opinion. However, they should be able to discount such other possibilities and inferences with reference to the observations they made, the experience and training they have and the assessment in the particular case, to justify their opinion.

Often, the best evidence in an impaired by drug case comes from the video. The DRE officer should be able to control the situation so as to allow them to maximize observations of impairment. The video, when properly set up, should allow review by the trier-of-fact to determine exactly which signs of impairment are present and to what degree. While impairment need only be proven to a slight degree based on a constellation of factors, it is nonetheless important for the DRE officer to be able to present what they observed in a way in which the trier-of-fact can easily digest.

Proving impairment is one thing, but being able to prove that impairment is caused by a drug or drugs and not some other factor is equally important in a case involving impairment by drug. Often, signifiers of impairment, such as drowsiness, lack of coordination, and certain physical factors, may be as a result of the stress of an arrest. As a result, it is imperative that the DRE officer explain why this is something more than an effect of being arrested. The video provides the best evidence in the circumstances as to what happened, and where the video is of sufficient quality, it can be relied upon to show each observed sign of impairment or clue in the DRE tests. A thorough review of the video to determine the performance of the subject on each of the tests as well as their actions otherwise in the police station while not subject to the DRE tests will provide strong evidence. While an individual may not be able to perform well on certain tests, their actions otherwise may be indicative of sobriety or impairment as the case may be. As the tests that form the DRE protocol are unfamiliar to most individuals, performance otherwise in a controlled environment may provide both signs of effect or sobriety.

CENTRAL NERVOUS SYSTEM (CNS) DEPRESSANTS

The most commonly encountered form of CNS depressant is alcohol, though this category includes harder drugs such as barbiturates, tranquilizers, and Quaaludes. CNS depressants will usually lead to a lack of coordination, often bordering on disorientation. Reactions tend to be sluggish with thick or slurred speech. Behaviour is often noted to be similar to that of a drunk person affected by alcohol. Drowsiness, including droopy eyes, is fairly common. Officers may refer to gait **ataxia** or **dyskinesia** which is, more simply put, staggering or poor balance. Fumbling and other issues indicative of a lack of coordination are to be expected.

Most individuals consume these drugs orally though some are taken by injection. Shallow breathing, cold clammy skin, dilated pupils (**mydriasis**), and a rapid weak pulse are all indicative of overdose. A coma is also possible at higher levels. The duration of effects for these kinds of drugs are some of the widest ranging and can affect an individual for over 16 hours in some cases.

CNS STIMULANTS

Cocaine, amphetamine, and methamphetamine are the most common kinds of drugs in the CNS stimulant category. This category of drugs leads to restlessness, tremors, and often excited or even euphoric subjects.

They tend to be talkative, show anxiety, and suffer from insomnia. They will sometimes grind their teeth, have exaggerated reflexes, and show irritability. An increased alertness can be noted at times but does not necessarily connote a lack of impairment. Signs of consumption include dry mouth, runny nose, or redness in the nasal area.

These drugs are taken in a variety of ways from snorting (**insufflation**), smoking, injecting, or orally. High doses lead to agitation, increased body temperature, and eventually hallucination and convulsions. They can impact an individual for as little as 5 minutes or many hours depending on the dose, experience of the user, and other factors.

HALLUCINOGENS

Common drugs that fall under the head of hallucinogens are lysergic acid diethylamide (LSD), psilocybin (magic mushrooms), and 3,4-Methylenedioxymethamphetamine (**MDMA**). Users will often have a dazed appearance, have difficulty perceiving time or distance, be disoriented, or even suffer from flashbacks. They have difficulty with speech, are uncoordinated, and often suffer from nausea. Paranoia, **malaise**, memory loss, hallucinations, and synesthesia (perceiving one sense as another, i.e., seeing the music) are common.

They may be administered in virtually any way including orally, by injection snorting, smoking, or even trans-dermally. The effect duration varies widely from one drug to another but often lasts for hours. Long, intense "trips" are indicative of over consumption.

DISSOCIATIVE ANESTHETICS

Phencyclidine (PCP) and ketamine are examples of dissociative anesthetics. They tend to distort perceptions, somewhat similar to a hallucinogen but with more impact on the ability to perceive and react to the environment and one's self. A feeling of detachment or dissociation is the purpose of these drugs. They can cause perspiring (**diaphoresis**). Problems with speech, including incomplete responses and repetitiveness, are signs. Confusion, **malaise**, agitation, hallucination, and even violent or combative behaviour can occur. The subject is often non-communicative. They may be disoriented and exhibit a blank stare. An increased pain threshold is also typical. Sensory distortion is one of the main impacts of this category of drug.

Again, a wide variety of administration is available. Smoking, snorting, injecting, taking orally, or even using eye-drops can be used for these sorts of drugs. Onset of effect can be very brief or longer, but effects typically last for hours once they are exhibited. This can be especially dangerous for drivers who ingest and then begin driving before effects are evident but continue to drive having entered a disconnected state. Again, a long intense "trip" is indicative of overconsumption.

NARCOTIC ANALGESICS

Heroin, methadone, and many other opioids are the most commonly seen drugs in the narcotic analgesic category. Often prescribed as painkillers, these drugs are ripe for overuse and abuse, both illicitly and by many members of the general populace. Drowsiness, droopy eyelids (**ptosis**), depressed reflexes, and slowed breathing are not uncommon. Nodding to the point of falling asleep (**somnolence**) can be seen in some doses. Experiences can range from nausea to euphoria. Facial itching, dry mouth, low raspy slow speech, and constricted pupils (**miosis**) may all be signs. Puncture marks and track marks are usually evident where injection is the preferred mode of administration.

While injection is one of the most common methods of ingestion, oral, smoking, and snorting are not uncommon either. The effect length can vary but some drugs have an impact on the individual for up to 24 hours, especially dosed methods of administration, such as methadone. Overdose may result in slow, shallow breathing, clammy skin, coma, or even convulsions.

INHALANTS

One of the most readily available and cheapest drugs to produce a high is inhalants. Often, legal substances such as gasoline or glue are the drug of choice in this category. Signs of consumption include residue of the substance around the nose and/or mouth, the odour of the substance inhaled, and a flushed face. Nausea, slow slurred speech, disorientation, and confusion are not uncommon. Lack of muscle control and non-communication from the subject can be seen at times. Bloodshot, watery eyes, constricted pupils, and often intense headaches are commonplace. The type of gas will often be evident based on the effect on blood pressure with solvents tending to rise, and anesthetic gases tending to lower, the pressure.

As the name suggests, these drugs are insufflated (inhaled). They tend to be fast acting and of short duration. Often this leads to problems with chemical or toxicological confirmation. It is not uncommon for a person taking inhalants to have come down from their high even before reaching the police station, thereby making DRE testing and toxicological testing of little value. In these cases, observations of the accused at the scene and while driving will be key in proving a case. High doses can lead to coma.

CANNABIS

Cannabis, in its many forms, from smoking marijuana, to vaping, to oral consumption through candy, to derivatives such as butter or raw consumption can have an impact on a person's ability to operate a motor vehicle. The active ingredient, THC, is being specifically targeted. While not quite as well known as alcohol, the signs and effects of marijuana consumption are becoming better known each day. It may only take time until courts recognize a layperson's ability to recognize signs of marijuana impairment and give a resulting opinion as they are currently allowed to do in alcohol-impaired cases. Red, bloodshot eyes (reddened **conjunctiva**) are very common. Odour of marijuana, marijuana debris on the person or in their vicinity is regularly seen. Body and eyelid tremors, relaxed inhibitions, and an increased appetite are routinely observed. Impaired perception of time or distance, disorientation, **malaise**, paranoia, and even **psychosis** are common with higher doses or particular strains.

Typically smoked or eaten, marijuana is one of the most common drugs seen in the general population. Impairment will typically be evident for two to three hours but actual impairment which is not as easily observed may occur for much longer. Observation in toxicological samples may be evident beyond any impairing time due to the presence of metabolites both active and inactive. With the onset of *per se* limits nearing, blood and oral sampling will be required to show quantities of THC in the blood either directly or in proportion to an oral sample. Urine sampling will be of no use in determining *per se* limits given its lack of a rational correlation to quantities in the blood. Further, the detection of active and inactive metabolites in the urine can cause issues for *per se* measurement.

DRE OFFICER'S OPINION

In the end, the DRE officer authors an opinion. That opinion should aid the trier-of-fact with their job of determining what happened but must be recognized as an opinion and not substituted for the trier-of-fact's own determination of the case on its merits. Just as certain signs of impairment are more or less likely with each category of drug, the DRE officer must do their best to explain what they see and why it is indicative of both impairment and impairment caused by a drug. The goal of a properly used DRE officer is to leave the trier-of-fact with no other reasonable inference than impairment by drug. Officers are trained that signs and symptoms, in some detail, are the best evidence upon which to base a conviction. It is for this reason that they are trained to note everything and explain with detail. Rather than merely stating that an accused was unsteady on their feet, they are trained to use words like *gait ataxia*. A good DRE will explain exactly what they saw, how the person's walking was affected, and for what duration. Rather than merely indicate standard indicia that sound repetitive, they are trained to explain that the person stepped to their left or right, leaned on particular things for balance, tripped on their own feet, or other more descriptive examples.

However, the DRE officer must also limit their opinion to that which is within their sphere of expertise. They are trained to recognize signs of impairment, conduct particular tests, and then synthesize an opinion based on their observations and analysis. DRE officers are not medical doctors. They do not have a wide knowledge of pharmacology. They do not typically know the subject outside of the testing they are undertaking. They are limited by the science involved in the confirmation of the tests. As a result, even where a DRE officer expresses an opinion in strong terms, it is essential to evaluate the basis for such an opinion as well as any other explanations for such signs of impairment.

The weight to be attached to the DRE officer's opinion is for the trier-of-fact to determine. The experience, knowledge, and possibility of bias for each DRE officer must be examined. The evidence must be examined beyond the conclusory nature of the DRE officer's opinion. Assessing all the evidence, including roadside actions, witness statements, actions while not performing the tests, and the DRE opinion will form the proper basis for assessment of the case on its merits. Anything less does a disservice to the concept of criminal justice and the presumption of innocence.

CHAPTER 6

Experts

There are a plethora of experts to consult in a case involving impairment by drug. Cost and expertise are the two items most commonly affecting defence access to advice. Crown prosecutors face resource strains as well and are likely to face even more such limitations with the imminent legalization of marijuana. Accessing appropriate expert advice will help in the best possible review of a file of this sort. Because of the infancy of this area of law in Canada, a search further afield may be required. Our neighbours to the South have a great deal more experience with DRE, and both expert advice and Continuing Professional Development on these matters are often easier to access there.

DRE OFFICERS

The first type of expert that is commonly overlooked in this sort of case is a DRE officer. In cases where DRE tests are undertaken, it is useful to have such results reviewed by another similarly trained officer. As a result of the protocols involved in DRE testing, the officer should be seeing their results reviewed as part of the testing process. For the defence, finding a retired officer with DRE training is a relatively easy way to have the report reviewed. An interesting question will be whether the retention of a retired DRE officer who maintains their qualifications and can point out the frailties in the tests themselves and the manner in which they are undertaken, will become more and more common. As the DRE training remains in place for a longer time, more officers with this training will age out of the system and retire, making themselves available for private review for either the Crown or defence. If a DRE officer is an expert only by way of their certification by the IACP, and a retiring officer does not necessarily lose this certification simply because they are retired, then this officer may be classified as an expert without resort to a *Mohan*-style qualification, just the same as when they were acting prior to retirement. Given that DRE officers are, by their very designation, experts able to provide opinion evidence, it would seem open to the defence to call such officers without needing to resort to anything more than pointing to the individual's designation.

Getting into the mind of an officer conducting the evaluation, to understand what they are looking for and how they assess things, becomes key in a case involving DRE testing. Having a trained DRE officer, on behalf of the defence, review the face sheet, the rolling log of prior tests, and the rest of the disclosure allows review of the actual officer who performed the DRE tests to confirm the efficacy of the performing officer. What disclosure is available for review will also affect the review of the officer performing the DRE tests. If face sheets from prior tests are available, a review to determine if this is an officer who regularly calls the right drug category based on admissions by the accused but does not follow their training and matrix may warrant further examination.

TOXICOLOGY AND PHARMACOLOGY

Toxicology and pharmacology are very similar areas of science. Both require an active knowledge of chemistry, biology, and scientific principles. However, whereas pharmacology focusses on the therapeutic effects of drugs (chemicals) on the human body, toxicology focusses more on the adverse effects of drugs (chemicals) and risk assessment. Understanding the difference between these two disciplines will help with how to decide which is the best expert to use. While most practitioners of each discipline have a strong knowledge of the other, there are times when one may be preferred over the other.

When reviewing a case, a pharmacologist may have the stronger knowledge of the therapeutic effect of the drug and of the positive role it can play in an individual. The pharmacologist should be able to provide strong information on the absorption, distribution, and effect of a drug on the human body. They should also be able to provide evidence useful in determining things such as the therapeutic dose and effect alongside the negative consequences or side effects.

A toxicologist, on the other hand, has a more detailed knowledge of the negative interactions of drugs and chemicals on the human body. As well, toxicologists tend to have more information regarding the kinds of testing done to determine exposure to drugs, including the chemical testing reviewed in Chapter 3. Government lab scientists, such as those from the Centre of Forensic Sciences in Toronto, tend to be toxicologists rather than pharmacologists. As a result, they have detailed knowledge of the impairing impact that different kinds of drugs can have on the human body. However, their knowledge is often limited in areas such as the therapeutic use of medications, the underlying conditions for which such medications may be prescribed, or the drug-drug interactions that may occur with a poly-substance user.

In general, toxicology is a required science to determine the concentration, if any, of a drug in the human body, its possible impairing effects, and whether that drug is present or metabolized. A pharmacologist, on the other hand, will be able to advise as to why the drug might have been used, what positive effects it may have had, including helping with the ability to drive. As well, the pharmacologist can, if a particular level of a drug is found in a person's system by a toxicologist, opine as to the likely effects to the person at that level of exposure.

Pharmacologists are particularly useful when dealing with medically prescribed medications, where the effect may be beneficial rather than detrimental, depending on the quantity ingested and over what period of time. Using both a pharmacologist as well as a treating physician can often provide the combined evidence that explains why an individual may show signs of impairment, but also why that impairment may not be caused by a drug and therefore not meet the criminal standard. Having a strong understanding of the different sorts of drugs found in a person is often the foundation of a strong defence and where the lawyer lacks this understanding, an expert in this field can be invaluable.

For a defence perspective of the usefulness of such an expert, see *Biagi*.

MEDICAL EXPERTS

The use of a medical expert can serve many functions in evaluating a drug-impaired driving file. Most of the uses benefit the defence since this sort of evidence tends to provide other reasons for the signs of impairment noted by police (other than drugs). There are many medical conditions that can mimic impairment through their symptoms. Often, a disease can cause impairment. However, the requirement that the impairment be caused by a drug rather than being symptomatic of a disease eliminates the criminality of the act in Canada. The plethora of illnesses and diseases that mimic impairment by certain drugs is almost impossible to list. However, some concrete examples will be reviewed later in this chapter. It is important to review with a client any problems that they have had with their health in the past in order to determine whether such existing factors may provide an innocent explanation for all or some of the noted signs of impairment. The use of medical practitioners by the prosecution is often of limited value because they will not have the ability for a fulsome review of the accused in person by the medical expert, which is typically required to render properly the kind of opinion necessary to aid in seeking a conviction. While broad statements about disease symptoms can often aid the defence in raising a reasonable doubt, the same is not to be said about the prosecution's onus of proving matters beyond a reasonable doubt.

Although seeking out experts in a particular field of medicine is often a beneficial step in assessing the viability of a medically induced impairment theory, the best first step is often to consult with the family physician for the client. As the front line of medical care for the client, a family physician or nurse practitioner can provide insight of great value. This can provide an overview of what must be reviewed in determining impact on the case.

Determining which medications the accused was prescribed, in what dosage, and at what times is important in preparing a case. Medications may be noted via chemical testing performed by the state though this is not always the case. As the chemical testing performed is often seeking to clarify the presence or absence of certain substances, there are other substances that may not be detected. It can become important to both prosecution and defence to determine whether certain substances were tested for in the chemical testing procedure. For the defence, it may allow a better explanation for the trier-of-fact to determine whether an accused was following the regime of medications prescribed by the medical practitioners whose care they are under, whereas for the prosecution the opposite may be true. As well, the prosecution may wish to know what drugs were tested for in order to be ready for whether an individual suffering from a particular disease may be taking medications not found as present in the chemical testing but that may be nonetheless impairing.

A family doctor will typically be able to provide the best evidence of any ongoing medical issues from which a person may suffer. A prosecutor should always be alive to the question of why the defence may be calling a person other than a primary care physician to provide the background of medical issues for an accused. While there may be innocent explanations, such as a lack of primary care available to the accused, the use of a medical expert who does not have an ongoing plan of care for the individual and an ongoing knowledge of the comorbidities (the combination of health issues) for which a person is being treated may only present part of the picture of the person.

A family physician will usually have the longest relationship with the accused and have the best knowledge of the medications and diseases affecting the accused, including knowledge of issues treated by specialists from a wide range of areas, depending on the particular accused.

Specialists are doctors who treat an individual in regard to one particular area of practice. Cardiologists treat the heart, dermatologists the skin, and so on. Just as a real estate lawyer may not be as proficient at defending criminal cases, a pain management physician may not know the intricacies or symptoms of the disease from which the accused suffers.

It is important then to make sure that the specialist has knowledge of the patient specifically where necessary, and also of the disease. It can be quite useful to have an expert who can opine only in a certain area for defence. It is for this reason that prosecutors must be vigilant in reviewing notice provided under section 657.3 of the *Criminal Code* in order to determine whether or not some other form of expert should be readied for reply evidence. It is also for this reason that the defence should be careful to use the proper expert for the proper issue, prepare the expert, and ensure that both prosecution and defence remain within the boundaries of the expert's knowledge.

With the current state of chemical testing for drugs in drug-impaired driving, many times the prosecution is left with the unenviable position of only being able to prove prior exposure to the drug rather than a current level in the blood. As a result, the quantification of the drug in the system is often absent. Without this, the prosecution will often ask the trier-of-fact to draw the inference that the signs of impairment noted are as a result of the ingestion of the drug found. However, a proper defence will utilize medical evidence where the drug or drugs may have been used to treat an illness to sow doubt as to whether the signs of impairment noted are as a result of the drug or the illness. As well, medications typically have different effects on a person depending on the dosage used, the individual's tolerance to the medication, and the weight of the individual.

Some medications are vastly impairing when taken at the wrong dosage or early on in the course of taking them, but these effects taper over time and exposure. As a result, it will be important to know how long the accused was on the medication, at what dose, and whether any signs of impairment have been noted by the medical professional testifying.

Issues surrounding *mens rea* may also arise through the calling of medical evidence. For individuals who are prescribed medications, the question of whether or not they knew or ought to have known about the impairing consequences of their medication regime may be hugely affected by the medical evidence called. While it is rarely the case where a medical professional will have forgotten to inform the individual of the side effects of a medication, it is not unheard of. Questions surrounding dosage and explanation given to a patient will be important to determine whether the accused had the requisite *mens rea* or not and whether they were reckless as to the state of affairs having taken the medication. For example, the client who is prescribed a short-term dose of a particular medication may have confusion regarding the dosage and take more or less than intended because of the way in which it is provided, packaged, or dispensed.

Beyond explaining the proper dosage and use of medications by an accused, medical professionals may be able to provide cogent evidence of medical conditions that afflict a person. This is especially important with issues that may affect balance or coordination. While a defendant may not appreciate the effect of an ongoing affliction sufficiently to report it during the drug influence evaluation, it may nonetheless be cogent to the eventual assessment of guilt. The most common underreported issue is lingering injuries. Sports injuries from an individual's past may not seem like a sickness or physical defect that should be reported to police during testing but may be extremely important. Joint and muscle injuries may have long-lasting effect on an individual's ability to balance. Similarly, obesity can affect coordination. All of this may affect an individual's ability to perform as required on the tests involved in the Drug Recognition Evaluation. As a result, the noted signs of impairment may have an innocent explanation that resulted from a physical condition rather than the impact of a drug.

As a result, it may be important to canvass issues such as this with a client specifically since they may not realize the importance of them. Further, while the primary care physician may have knowledge of the issues, there may be others (such as physiotherapists) in the circle of care who may be in the best place to provide the evidence needed.

The rebound effect of a drug is the result of the body seeking equilibrium. What this means is that a drug intended to have a particular effect on the body may actually cause the opposite effect. This could be something as simple as raising blood pressure and/or heart rate, or affecting the mood. This can be a result that upon exposure to a drug, the body will seek to return to a state of equilibrium. On a longer-term scale, this is why it is sometimes necessary to use an increasing amount of a drug to accomplish the same effect. Experience and exposure to a drug changes the effectiveness of the drug as a result of the body building up a tolerance to it. Each individual taking the drug has a particular effect. The importance of this to the defence is that the reaction noted by an officer may, in fact, be the body's attempt to negate the effects of the drug. Because the body continues to react to the effect of the drug, even after the drug has worn off, the body may continue to seek equilibrium and actually result in the opposite effect of the drug action. For example, cocaine would typically increase pulse rate but the body's reaction to the administration of it may lower pulse rate as it continues to react to the drug even after it is no longer causing the effect. It is the body overreacting to the presence of the drug that is no longer in the system. The interesting point in law is whether or not this rebound effect, which is caused by the body's natural reaction to the drug, is impairment by drug or not, because it is not the drug directly causing the impairing signs but rather the body's reaction. While medical issues are not criminalized by operation of Canadian law, impairment by a drug is. The rebound effect is as a result of the drug administration, but indirectly. Caselaw on this issue has yet to develop from its infancy.

Another issue that often arises is the overprescription of certain drugs especially in the medical sphere. Professionals do not want to overprescribe but it cannot always be helped. This often occurs at the time of initial diagnosis as medical professionals are initially trying to determine what effect a medication will have on a patient as treatment. As well, depending on the severity of an illness at particular points in time the amount of a drug required to treat the symptoms may differ. Certain cases occur where an individual has built up a tolerance to a drug or where an illness increases in severity in a short period of time. Many mental illnesses that are treated by medication can have their severity of symptoms affected by increasing stress. Anxiety, depression, and other mental health diseases can be worsened by the introduction of stressors in an individual's life. As a result, an individual may show symptoms of their disease while having a present quantity of drugs in their system; however, the impairment shown on the DRE is not a result of a drug or chemical but in fact a lack of a sufficient quantity of a drug to treat the disease. Consider an individual who suffers from schizophrenia who stops taking their medication. A quantity of a drug may be found in their system from prior exposure but the amount still present may not be sufficient to treat the symptoms of their disease, resulting in symptoms that mimic impairment. This is the danger of a false positive being confirmed by chemical analysis when it is in fact a lack of treatment or sufficient drug being in a person's system. It is for that reason that it is important to review both with the accused and their medical professional what illnesses they suffer from, what diseases they have, what treatment they are undertaking, what the anticipated outcome of those are, and what would happen if an individual failed to properly follow the treatment to its fullest. This sort of issue is often less important where illicit drugs are found because these cannot be in an individual's system to treat symptoms. That being said, individuals with concurrent disorders may seek to self-medicate and medical issues may be masked by the consumption of a drug even though the signs of impairment noted are still as a result of a health concern rather than the consumption of a drug. This is most common with painkillers classified under the heading of narcotic analgesics where the pain an individual suffers may impair their ability to operate a motor vehicle to a greater degree than the side effects of the medication, legal or illicit, that they are taking. However, any impairment caused by a drug is sufficient to ground a conviction and the impact of the drug and pain together to cause impairment cannot easily be ruled out. The question to be asked is whether the drug exceeds what is necessary to treat the symptoms and causes some portion of impairment.

Use of an ophthalmologist may also be helpful if nystagmus or other eye issues are key pieces of evidence that are relied upon to prove impairment. A review of issues which can cause nystagmus in an unimpaired individual can help explain some of these issues. Ophthalmologists typically use very complex machines in order to do testing which an officer does with more crude tools. This may also help explain to a trier-of-fact the issues surrounding such testing. For the prosecution, an ophthalmologist may be able to point out the general unlikelihood of nystagmus in an otherwise healthy individual. Individualized testing of the accused will be the strongest evidence in this sort of a case and should it be lacking, the ophthalmologist can only speak in general terms and the evidence will be that much weaker.

STATISTICIANS

Drug Recognition Evaluations and Standardized Field Sobriety Testing rely on scientific support to prove their validity and their ability to be used in legal cases. Studies that support their use rely on a noted correlation between performance on the tasks involved and the impairment of the ability to operate a motor vehicle. It is important to note the difference between correlation and causation. Correlation is the coincident nature of two things whereas causation is one factor impacting on the likelihood of another occurring. Causative factors will always be correlated; correlated factors will not always be causative. Repetitive study of the battery of tests used in DRE and SFST seek to prove causation through the elimination of other causes, leaving only the impairment of the ability to operate a motor vehicle as a possible result. Although the results of scientific studies relied upon by experts in the field indicate a strong correlation between poor performance on the DRE and SFST and impairment of the ability to operate a motor vehicle, this is not necessarily the only inference that can be drawn. Other factors can lead to poor performance on the testing batteries and different interpretations of the scientific studies that underpin these procedures. As a result, statistical analysis of the studies upon which the prosecution rely can provide some defence to an accused person. It is important that prosecutors understand on some level the kind of test used, scientific validation study that underpins the testing, and how this impacts the usefulness of the DRE tests. Similarly, defence counsel who do not understand the issues of cause-and-effect versus correlation when explaining to a trier-of-fact how an opinion is gained from the evaluation will be at a loss. As the DREs seek to categorize the class of drug that the individual has ingested as part of an opinion, it is important to understand the expected results of the symptoms of each category of drug. For the defence, it will be a ripe area of cross-examination where results on the test are different from the anticipated results on the matrix. Similarly, it is important for a prosecutor to understand and be able to explain through their expert why the results may differ from the expected results. Given the number of different tasks performed in categorizing the drug that is expected to be found in the individual's system, it is not uncommon to see at least some of the tests providing results that do not match exactly the drug category that the DRE officer identifies. There are many different reasons for this to occur. Some may be as simple as the dosage which a person has taken or maybe, more importantly, issues such as the misunderstanding of the officer as to whether certain signs will be present in a particular drug category. This is even more important when assessing results on the SFST. This is because the officer will tend not to have as much training. They will not be qualified experts and they are less likely to be able to understand or explain why the failure may not actually indicate presence of a particular drug or drug class.

A good example of this is where cannabis is involved. Officers often state that there is a failure on the Horizontal Gaze Nystagmus test with cannabis. Cannabis does not cause any issues with nystagmus. However, drug use where a combination of alcohol and marijuana are taken can cause nystagmus. Of interest, the use of a statistician can help educate either side to improve the understanding of the literature surrounding DRE and SFST. An understanding of accuracy, precision, and reliability will help the Crown show how reliable the tests are or conversely allow the defence to raise issues to the point of a reasonable doubt. A survey of some of the most commonly used studies in DRE and SFST will be reviewed later, in Chapter 13, for many lawyers who do not seek the statistician in interpreting the results. Although a DRE officer will be classified as an expert as a result of their designation through the International Association of Chiefs of Police, that does not mean they are above challenge. Having a scientist or statistician available to interpret the studies and scientific literature may sway the trier-of-fact regarding the weight that can be given to the evidence. Simply put, the prosecution needs to be able to explain what is good about the test and the defence needs to understand where the frailties lie. Beyond that, counsel needs to be able to explain to the trier-of-fact why their position should be accepted. Further, it is important to realize that much of the study surrounding DRE and SFST seeks to test for the presence or absence of a particular class of drug. The tests noted on the matrix exist to aid in classification of the drug that is expected to be present in the person's system. However, impairment by the drug is better borne out by the other tests, the divided-attention and physical tests, that are part of the battery of tests. A DRE officer is expected to provide an opinion from their tally of observations in their training. Of particular note are the gaps in the literature relating the ability to perform certain psychophysical divided-attention tasks to the ability to operate a motor vehicle. This tends to be covered by an explanation that driving is a divided-attention task that requires division of attention over a number of tasks, and individuals who are unable to divide their attention are unable to operate a motor vehicle.

OTHER SCIENCE

The possibilities when assessing drug-impaired driving are virtually endless, and determining the expert who can best help your client is often difficult. Further, the use of experts quickly becomes expensive to the point of being prohibitively so. Having a general knowledge as a criminal defence practitioner and being able to quickly leverage relationships for preliminary reviews will aid in the defence.

For the prosecution, resource management can be almost as tough. While government laboratories often offer expertise of the desired kind, the demands on such experts are often high. Once an expert is considered and consulted, this must be disclosed and the steps required may outweigh doing so.

Accident reconstructionists can sometimes explain why a driver performed the way they did and provide explanation for exceptional driving, including swerving, crashes, or strange actions. Forensic mechanical investigation may also be of use to determine whether the fitness of the vehicle played any part in the actions of an accused. An assessment of this sort can sometimes aid the prosecution in determining whether a conviction may be well founded for dangerous driving where proof of impairment by drug is difficult. The combination of factors of an unsafe vehicle, issues with reacting to the conditions of the roadway, and the consumption of impairing substances can combine to prove a marked departure from the standard expected of a reasonable driver.

The impact of the weather on a driver, from temperature to icing to the location of the sun and its impact on the driver, can all be relevant touchstones in explaining uncommon behaviour on the road.

Assessment of an individual at a particular dose of a drug, provided it is safe to bring a person to that level as well as legal to do so, may be helpful in determining whether the impairment classified and signs noted correspond with that particular individual's reaction to a drug. Obviously, there are particular controls that may have to be matched to the time of driving and they may make such testing difficult or even impossible. Certainly, this is something only open for the defence to undertake.

The examination of possible sources of accidental or unintentional ingesting of drugs must also be undertaken. Where certain drugs, both prescription and illicit, are consumed by a population, certain amounts of these drugs or their active metabolites will enter into the wastewater system and eventually discharge into the environment. Certain of these may even survive drinking water treatment and be detectable in the drinking water of a municipality. Although the chances of an impairing quantity of these drugs to be later found in the blood of an individual are virtually impossible, the investigation into whether such substances could be present in detectable quantities in a urine sample sufficient to register positively is something that a well-funded accused may do.

CHAPTER 7

Charter Considerations

Many *Charter of Rights and Freedoms* considerations in drug-impaired driving cases mirror those of alcohol-impaired driving. There is no need to repeat here what is well stated in the works of other authors on the topics that are so similar. However, courts have recognized many differences in interpreting drug-impaired driving cases, and these are highlighted in this chapter.

THE CALL IN THE MIDDLE OF THE NIGHT

Many of the truisms applicable to any other call to a lawyer from an arrested individual apply in the same way in impaired by drug cases. Inquiring if privacy has been given, whether the police officers are watching, if any recording devices or cameras are present, and whether the individual is in custody at a police station or mobile command post will all be important first inquiries.

What flows differently is the ability to advise and inform the client about what does and does not have to be complied with. The starting point for this needs to be an inquiry to the arresting or booking officer to determine what the accused was arrested for, what their grounds were, and what tests are expected to take place. Given the limited availability of DRE officers, in some jurisdictions SFST tests are, improperly, demanded of individuals already arrested. It is important to know what the officers are intending to do, properly or improperly. It may be one of the few times advice to refuse a demand to participate in testing would be appropriate.

Understanding the officer's grounds is important, especially whether any particular drug or class of drugs is already suspect. Having a copy of the matrix on hand to determine what the police may be looking for will help you question the client to properly protect them.

Most important is stressing to the client the requirement that they do not provide any further statement—specifically, that questioning during the testing does not require an answer. Questions such as asking what a person ate or drank, what time it is right now, how much sleep the person has had, whether the person is sick or injured, diabetic, epileptic, taking insulin, has physical defects or disabilities, whether the person is under the care of a doctor, whether any drugs or medications are prescribed or being taken, what drugs, how much, when, and where, are all going to be asked and DRE officers are trained to ask these in every case; yet they are not part of the testing required by statute. As such, counsel should be advising clients to exercise their right to silence. Asking the client some of the questions likely to be asked of them and having them practice their response, "I am not answering" or something similarly simple is a useful exercise to get clients in the habit of exercising their right.

A client who denies being sick or injured may not realize that a long-standing sports injury or issue caused by age is significant. Answers during the DRE test limit defences available later. It is certainly good practice by police to ask questions post-counsel talk, but individuals should know that they do not need to answer them since they do not form part of the testing. An officer who insists or demands such answers on penalty of a refuse charge will quickly see voluntariness affected, but if no threat, promise, or other compulsion arises, then such answers are likely to be admissible.

It is important to review with the client that two types of tests will be undertaken, physical testing and divided-attention tasks, and that both must be completed. This is your opportunity to try to calm your client so that the physical tests are not artificially affected by things like nervousness, though this can be difficult to achieve.

Counsel must explain that, after these tests are completed, a bodily sample demand is likely, typically urine or blood. Explain that such tests are mandatory if demanded. However, it is important to alert the client that in some cases officers request rather than demand and the client should ask for clarification from the officer if there is any doubt about whether it is a request or a demand and if it cannot be clarified easily, to request a second call to counsel.

The DRE tests require an individual to complete specific tasks in a specific way. These are known as divided-attention tests. Individuals must listen closely to the instructions before beginning the tests. Failure to turn as directed, use of the improper part of the finger to touch the nose, counting improperly, or lifting an arm at the wrong time can all lead to a failure on a specific test. Telling the client to listen carefully, not to start before they are told to, follow instructions to the letter, and request clarification if confused are all important things to stress. In a perfect world, explaining what constitutes failure on each test will help a client avoid accidentally showing a clue that is not truly present.

The issues therefore to be stressed most with a client are: 1) do not answer the questions during the test; 2) listen closely to instructions and do not begin until told to; 3) seek clarification from the officer when in doubt; and 4) be very careful when performing tasks.

DISCLOSURE

R v Khemraj, 2010 ONCJ 36

Arresting officer found Khemraj driving at excessive speeds, drifting within his lane, and running a red light. The officer pulled Khemraj over and the smell of an alcoholic beverage came from the car when the window was rolled down. Khemraj had difficulty finding his documents, yelled at the officer to deny running the light and, when asked, told the officer he had had two drinks. The officer said Khemraj's eyes were slightly red and unfocussed and that his speech was slurred. After being asked several times, Khemraj said he had consumed "two, or three, or four" drinks. The officer asked him to get out of the car and Khemraj was swaying from side to side as they walked to the back of the car. The officer decided to initiate SFST (his training was in 2008) and completed the Horizontal Gaze Nystagmus test, the Walk-and-Turn test, and the One-Legged-Stand test. Khemraj fell forward at one point during the test. After failing a breath screening, a breath demand was read, right to counsel was provided, and after blowing at the station his reading was 230 mg alcohol per 100 ml of blood.

The issues involve whether the officer formed a reasonable suspicion that Khemraj had alcohol in his body before administering the SFST such that the screening demand and test were not administered forthwith and whether the administration of the SFST alone violated his sections 8 and 9 rights. The SFSTs were administered five weeks before section 254(2) was amended to provide for them. The judge made a finding of fact that the officer did not have a reasonable suspicion that Khemraj had alcohol in his body prior to administering the SFSTs but that the objective basis for suspicion was present before administering the tests. The finding that subjective belief had not been formed was based on the officer's contention that he did not have reasonable suspicion before administering the tests, but was mostly based on the timing of events. There were only two minutes between the time at which Khemraj pulled over and when he was asked to submit to the SFSTs. Five minutes later the tests were over and the screening demand had been read. The judge explained that if he had determined that the officer did form suspicion before administering the tests, he would have found that the demand was administered forthwith based on the requirements from *Woods*, *Torsney*, and *George* of "immediacy" and "without delay." The judge found that Khemraj's rights would not have been violated even if the judge had found that the officer had reasonable suspicion before administering the SFSTs. Further, he found that the administration of the SFSTs did not violate Khemraj's sections 8 and 9 *Charter* rights because the officer had more than a sufficient basis for the screening demand and the conditions under which the tests were administered were acceptable. The judge found that Khemraj was driving while impaired and dismissed the *Charter* motions (see also *R v Peers* (26 March 2010), Peterborough, Information No 3311-0900647-00 (Ont Ct J), Taillon J).

R v Gardashnik, 2011 ONCJ 256

Gardashnik was charged with operating a motor vehicle while impaired by marijuana. He was stopped at a RIDE check and detained after he admitted to consuming marijuana. Sgt McCormack, a DRE, performed an evaluation of Gardashnik and determined his ability to operate a motor vehicle was impaired by a drug. The DRE found that the results gave her reasonable grounds to believe that Gardashnik's ability was impaired. After forming the opinion that he was impaired, the DRE made a demand for a urine sample. At the time of the evaluation the DRE had been certified for five to six weeks and Gardashnik was the second person that she had tested after receiving her certificate. The defence requested an order that the Crown disclose the DRE officer's training records, the toxicological corroboration of the officer's training examinations, and the officer's log of in-field evaluations after being certified. The defence submitted that the Crown intended to call the officer at trial to give her opinion based upon her evaluation and to ask that she be accepted as an expert on the issue of impairment by drug. The defence requested the documents mentioned in order to challenge the DRE's competence to give expert testimony and to challenge the drug evaluation tests as novel science. The Crown submitted that Parliament has determined that DREs can give testimony in this regard without having to be qualified as an expert under the *Mohan* criteria and that the section 254(3.1) evaluation is not a novel science because Parliament has recognized it as valid and reliable.

The DRE testified that the toxicological corroboration of her training evaluations, test scores, and training records was not available. The judge did not decide the issue (because it was not before the court in this case) but noted that the techniques from section 254(3.1) are "sufficiently new and debateable to make them appropriate subjects of scrutiny as to their efficacy and validity in the scientific community." Relying on the definition of "evaluating officer" in section 254(1) and Regulation 2008-296, the Crown argued that an evaluating officer, once accredited, is an expert and can testify without being qualified under *Mohan*. The judge did not accept the Crown's analogy between a DRE and a qualified breath technician, based on *Wakewich* and the fact that techniques used by a DRE have significant subjective components. The judge found nothing that would exempt a DRE from having to be qualified under *Mohan* and therefore found that the defence has the right to disclosure in the Crown's possession regarding the DRE's qualifications for full answer and defence. He also supported this finding by noting that Sgt McCormack is a new

DRE and the defence can use her logs to test her accuracy and ability to give opinion evidence. The judge found that the information the defence requested is relevant, "reasonably capable of affecting the accused's ability to make full answer and defence," and should be disclosed.

R v Stipo, 2017 ONSC 5208

Stipo was involved in a motor vehicle collision and an officer at the scene demanded a breath sample after noting indicia of impairment. The approved screening device did not detect alcohol so the officer concluded that Stipo was impaired by a drug and arrested her. A DRE performed an evaluation, concluded she was impaired by a central nervous system depressant, and made a demand for a urine sample. The Crown intends to rely on the DRE's testimony at trial. Stipo requested disclosure of the DRE's rolling logs but the Crown and the OPP submit that the logs are third-party records and disclosure is prohibited by section 258.1. Rolling logs contain every test that is administered by the DRE with the date, name of individual tested, DRE's opinion, and whether the opinion was confirmed by toxicological tests. The trial judge found that the logs were not third-party records and ordered that they be disclosed. The Crown and OPP applied to the Superior Court for *certiorari* with prohibition in aid and pursuant to section 37 of *Canada Evidence Act* (*CEA*) to quash the order of the trial judge.

The judge cited the holding in *Bingley* that a voir dire regarding admissibility is not required for a DRE but that the weight given to the evidence is for the trier-of-fact to determine. It discussed this in order to recognize that a toxicological analysis may not be able to determine the impact of a drug on a particular individual or when it was ingested, and that often the Crown has to rely on the DRE's opinion for this. The judge explained that if the rolling logs are relevant and in the possession of officers involved in the investigation then the Crown should obtain and disclose them. The judge found that, although the rolling logs were not "created, produced or even located during the investigation" as in *Jackson*, they are important to the DRE's qualification to give an opinion. He further explained that the DRE training manual notes that a rolling log is important to whether a court will qualify a DRE as an expert in a drug impairment case and that the rolling log should be taken to court when a DRE is testifying. While the judge agreed with the Crown's argument that the trial judge was incorrect in relying on the manual, the judge found that the trial judge was correct in using it to assess the relevance of rolling logs. The judge therefore concluded that the DRE is bound to provide the Crown with the rolling log and the Crown has a duty to disclose them as they are potentially relevant. The judge found that disclosure is permissible under section 258.1 and that such disclosure would not be contrary to public interest as noted by section 37 of the *CEA*. The application was dismissed.

R v Branson, 2018 ONCJ 163
In this case, the court recognizes that the admissibility of DRE officers' evidence is based on their being certified by the International Association of Chiefs of Police (IACP). The required training to meet this certification is defined by the IACP's International Standards. The court recognizes that "adherence to them (the standards) is what gives credibility to the DRE program" (para 7). The IACP International Standards "stress the importance of rolling logs .... [*T*]*he records may prove beneficial in establishing program validity for court purposes*" (para 9 [emphasis in original]). Further, no prohibition from disclosure was created in section 258.1 as identifying information of other individuals tested could be redacted. Thus, the rolling log of the DRE officer was ordered disclosed.

R v Mansour (30 April 2018), Ottawa (Ct J), Dorval J
This case adopts *Stipo* and *Branson* while additionally considering the French version of section 258.1 and similarly holding that section 258.1 does not prohibit disclosure. The rolling log was held to be a third-party record and required service on the police as well as the Crown Attorney. It recognized testimony from the DRE officer that "too many inaccurate calls on the category of drug causing impairment ... could lead to withholding the recertification" (para 8).

NOTES/RECORDINGS

R v Snelgrove, 2012 BCPC 218
Snelgrove was charged with having care or control while impaired and having a blood alcohol concentration (BAC) over 80. At the time of the

investigation Cst Nanton, the investigating officer, was an experienced impaired-driving investigator, having performed at least twenty investigations. He was a qualified breath technician and was qualified to conduct SFSTs. Nanton was on duty training another officer when they saw Snelgrove's vehicle accelerate to 100 km/h in a 60 km/h zone. After pulling him over, Nanton saw that Snelgrove's eyes were red, his face was flushed, and there was a smell of alcohol on his breath. Nanton formed the suspicion that he had alcohol in his system and read a breath demand. He did not have an alcohol screening device (ASD) in his car and was not in a position to readily receive one, so Nanton read a demand for physical coordination tests. This was the first time Nanton applied physical coordination tests in an investigation in the field. He did not make note of all steps/observations and he did not work from a checklist when testing Snelgrove, both of which are directed by his training. He conducted the Horizontal Gaze Nystagmus test, the Walk-and-Turn test, and the One-Leg-Stand test. Without having notes, Nanton was unable to recall many aspects of the tests, such as whether he asked Snelgrove if he had any medical conditions or disabilities, whether he checked each eye separately, or whether Snelgrove was wearing glasses. The judge found that Snelgrove was facing the police vehicle and the emergency lights were on during the Horizontal Gaze Nystagmus test. Staff Sgt Peat, qualified as an expert in the administration of SFSTs, was present during the tests but did not communicate observations to the investigating officer. He was called by the Crown for his expertise but the defence argued that the investigating officer who performs the tests must have the proper expertise. Peat testified that he saw Nanton properly conduct the tests.

Snelgrove applied to have evidence of the results of his breath sample excluded under section 24(2) due to a breach of his section 8 *Charter* right. Cst Nanton made a demand for physical coordination tests after developing the required suspicion and on the basis of the results of the tests formed reasonable grounds to make a breath demand. The judge found that Nanton's evidence regarding the administration of the tests was unreliable because he did not follow proper procedure in carrying out the tests to ensure accuracy. He also noted that the presence and training of Staff Sgt Peat did not make up for this and therefore the degree of care and precision required to apply the Horizontal Gaze Nystagmus test was not present in this case. Nanton formed subjective belief after the test but because of the judge's findings surrounding the test, Nanton's subjective belief was not objectively supported. Therefore, Snelgrove's section 8 *Charter* right was breached. The judge found that the certificate should be excluded under section 24(2), considering the lack of objective support for the subjective belief, the lack of proper procedure, and the suggestion that allowing the evidence under these circumstances would bring the administration of justice into disrepute.

R v Smith, [2012] OJ No 514 (Ct J)
Smith was observed inhaling cannabis from a bong in a conservation area parking lot. Officers arrived and arrested the accused. He was taken to the police station and performed poorly on the DRE examination. There was evidence of the peak effects of THC being some time after its consumption. The decision not to video record "because it is a drug" was noted as being poor practice though being not of import in the particular case given other findings.

RIGHT TO COUNSEL/VOLUNTARINESS

R v Bourdon, 2011 MBPC 83
Further demand for urine after DRE typically can be a change of jeopardy. However, the ability to speak to counsel prior to the DRE tests themselves suggests that the impact on an accused is lessened significantly. While a breach was found in this case, no exclusion was warranted.

R v Pedersen, 2015 ABQB 128
The starting point for voluntariness is, of course, that the Crown must prove voluntariness beyond a reasonable doubt. Where there are significant gaps with regard to what occurred during a particular time, the court may be left unable to determine the question of voluntariness. As a result, video- and audio-recording capabilities at a police station may be of especial importance. In this case, statements made to the DRE officer during the exam and prior were deemed voluntary while later statements where there was a gap in time and explanation were not.

R v Walsh, [2016] NJ No 63 (Prov Ct)

Right to counsel must still be given upon detention as in any other case, both the informational component and the ability to exercise the right. Constables Thompson and Burry responded to a call regarding a vehicle collision with a fence and a suspected impaired driver. They pulled the vehicle over as it was leaving the parking lot. Cst Thompson told Walsh the reason for the stop and requested that Walsh provide a sample for the ASD. When Walsh got out of the vehicle Cst Thompson noted Walsh had droopy eyes, slurred speech, and poor balance. Walsh was carrying two bottles of prescription medication (Clonazepam and Ritalin) as well as a syringe. At 11:10 am Walsh's sample was negative and Cst Thompson informed Walsh that he had passed. At 11:40 am Walsh was read his rights, caution, *Charter* warning, and DRE demand.

The Crown conceded that Walsh's section 10(a) and (b) rights were violated. The defence requested that the evidence from the drug testing be excluded under section 24(2). The judge found that there was no bad faith on the part of Cst Thompson regarding the delay in reading the rights and caution because he was an inexperienced officer and unsure about how to proceed with an impaired by drug investigation. Cst Thompson was negligent, however, in not asking a more experienced officer for assistance and detaining Walsh for 30 minutes without providing his right to counsel. The judge found that this was a serious breach of Walsh's rights, as was subjecting him to the DRE testing. The judge held that the evidence should be excluded under section 24(2) because of the seriousness of the *Charter* breaches.

R v Dunlop, 2011 NSPC 30

DRE testing includes questioning. However, questioning in these matters must be done post-rights to counsel and must be voluntary. The confusion where a demand is made to comply with mandatory testing, which seems to include questioning, can give rise to voluntariness issues: "Demanding that a person comply with a process or be charged with refusal, and then including an interrogation in that process, renders replies to the interrogation involuntary and contrary to the right against self incrimination. Use of the results of such an interrogation to advance criminal proceedings against an accused is akin to using a statutorily compelled report as evidence on a criminal charge, against the person who gave the report" (para 9).

Cst Galloway pulled Dunlop over for a motor vehicle infraction and noticed the smell of marijuana coming from the vehicle as he approached it. There was a roach in the ashtray of the vehicle and Dunlop admitted to smoking marijuana earlier. Cst Galloway arrested Dunlop for possession. Cst Galloway read a field sobriety test demand and, after the test was completed, made a DRE demand. Dunlop spoke to duty counsel and complied with the demand. Cst Galloway said he would be charged with refusal if he did not comply. As a trained DRE, Cst Galloway conducted the evaluation, during which Dunlop admitted to smoking marijuana earlier that day in the interrogation portion of the evaluation. Cst Galloway collected a urine sample from Dunlop upon completion of the evaluation.

The defence argued that the process of the DRE in the *Criminal Code* does not include interrogation and that Dunlop was forced to admit to using marijuana under the threat of a charge of refusal. Further, the defence argued that because this statement was part of the basis upon which Cst Galloway formed the belief that Dunlop was impaired, the urine sample should be excluded under section 24(2). The judge found that Dunlop's section 8 right had been violated because Cst Thompson was relying on the statement from the interrogation after telling Dunlop that refusal would result in a different charge, and such an interrogation is not an aspect of the evaluation approved by Parliament. In discussing the *Grant* analysis [which is a three-step test whereby a court should weigh the following factors to decide whether evidence should be excluded pursuant to section 24(2) of the *Charter*: (1) what is the seriousness of the *Charter*-infringing conduct?; (2) what is the impact on the accused?; and (3) what is society's interest in the adjudication of the case on its merits?], the judge noted that Cst Galloway was not acting maliciously or in bad faith and that the *Charter* breach had little significance because Dunlop had already told Cst Galloway similar information regarding drug use before the evaluation. The judge found that the evidence was admissible.

R v Fogarty, 2015 NSCA 6

Fogarty was charged with impaired driving causing death and dangerous driving causing death. Fogarty was driving west on Highway 4 towards

Antigonish, NS, when his vehicle collided with an eastbound vehicle. Both occupants of the eastbound vehicle died from the collision. An hour before the crash, RCMP Cpl Meisner heard a report of erratic driving from a vehicle matching the description of Fogarty's and that another corporal knew the driver to be a methadone patient. At the scene of the accident Fogarty told Cpl Meisner and Cst MacPherson that he was the driver of the vehicle, that he was a recovering drug addict, that his licence was scheduled for suspension, and that he had taken methadone that day at 8 am. The officers observed that Fogarty's eyes were glassy but didn't smell alcohol on him. Cpl Meisner was in an ambulance with Fogarty, had formed the opinion that his ability to operate a motor vehicle had been impaired by a drug, and demanded Fogarty submit to a DRE. Meisner read the demand and Fogarty indicated that he understood. Meisner arrested Fogarty for impaired driving after he was cleared by medical staff in the emergency room. Fogarty indicated that he understood the demand, wanted to talk to a lawyer, wanted more information about legal aid, and asked for Meisner to call any legal aid lawyer. Meisner conducted the DRE assessment when Fogarty was finished speaking with a lawyer. Meisner observed: poor coordination, fast and slightly slurred speech, flushed face, runny nose, droopy eyelids. His opinion was that Fogarty's ability to operate a motor vehicle was impaired by a drug that functioned as a central nervous system depressant and he demanded a blood sample. Fogarty said he understood the demand. When the doctor asked Fogarty if he consented to blood being drawn, Fogarty looked quizzically at Meisner, who said, "If you don't, you can be charged with refusal." After blood samples were taken, Fogarty was informed that he was being charged with impaired driving causing death and was given access to counsel. When Meisner learned that the second occupant of the other vehicle had died he was arrested for dangerous driving causing death.

The trial judge found that there was no *Charter* violation in not providing Fogarty the opportunity to consult counsel after the blood demand. The blood sample taken from Fogarty had been analyzed and found to contain Valium, mirtazapine, and methadone. On appeal, Fogarty argued that his section 10(b) right had been violated and that the blood sample and toxicology report should have been excluded under section 24(2). The court cited *R v Sinclair* for the general principle regarding the right to re-consult with counsel (where change of circumstances makes it necessary for detainee to re-consult in order to satisfy purpose of 10b). The trial judge found that Fogarty was aware of and understood his situation along with the demand for a DRE and that it was reasonable to infer that competent counsel would have advised of the procedure and possibility of a demand for bodily sample. On appeal, the court did not accept Fogarty's argument because "the DRE and blood demand are not disjunctive investigative techniques" (para 48). The court noted that there was no challenge to counsel's competency and that Fogarty had confirmed that he understood the blood demand. The court dismissed Fogarty's appeal.

R v Budarick, 2016 ONSC 3841

Constables Kolodziechuk and Crowhurst observed Budarick's car travelling at speeds of 157, 133, and 121 km/h in an 80 km/h zone. They pulled the vehicle over and found two men in the front seats. Budarick's eyes were watery and glassy and they detected a strong odour of alcoholic beverage. The passenger said that he had been drinking and Cst Crowhurst separated Budarick from his passenger. Cst Crowhurst smelled an odour of alcoholic beverage on Budarick's breath when he got out of the vehicle. His speech was slow and deliberate, he was unsteady on his feet, and the fly of his pants was open. Cst Crowhurst arrested Budarick for impaired driving. Budarick complained of chest pain as Cst Crowhurst was searching him, and he was put in the back of the police cruiser to wait for an ambulance to arrive. After the ambulance was called, Budarick was given his right to counsel and, having had it read to him twice, said that he understood. Budarick told the constables that he did not have a lawyer but was content with duty counsel as it was explained to him by the officers at 9:36 pm. Cst Crowhurst read the breath demand and he consented but continued to complain of chest pain. At 11:26 pm Cst Crowhurst called duty counsel. Budarick spoke to duty counsel at 11:44 pm. While at the hospital Budarick was shaking and gasping for breath, still complaining of chest pain. Cst Crowhurst believed he was faking but Cst Kolodziechuk, having not come to a conclusion about whether Budarick was faking, did not think it reasonably practical for him to provide a breath sample. Cst Kolodziechuk is a qualified breath technician. Cst Crowhurst made a blood demand after Budarick finished speaking with duty counsel. He was not re-provided with his rights to counsel. Budarick consented to blood being drawn but did not consent to them seizing the blood that had already been taken. New blood samples were taken. Budarick was found guilty of impaired driving at trial. He alleged breaches of his sections 8, 9, and 10(b) rights but the trial judge found that the blood demand was proper, the sample admissible, and Budarick's rights not violated.

The issue was whether Cst Crowhurst subjectively had reasonable grounds to believe that Budarick would be incapable of providing a breath sample because of his physical condition. The trial judge found that Cst Crowhurst's belief that Budarick was faking was simply a suspicion and that she was not required to get a medical opinion before making the blood demand. The court found that the trial judge did not err in concluding that Cst Crowhurst subjectively had the requisite belief to make the blood demand. Cst Crowhurst was clear that the opinion that Budarick was faking was a personal one and also relied on Cst Kolodziechuk's opinion that Budarick would not be able to provide a sample. The trial judge held that the officers were not required to allow Budarick to re-consult counsel after deciding to make a blood demand. The court found that the trial judge based this decision on two analogous cases and did not err in his conclusion. The court agreed that there is a fair comparison between Budarick's situation and the one in *Fogarty*, and that competent counsel, aware of Budarick's health concern, would have explained the possibility of a blood demand if he could not or would not provide a breath sample. The court held that the blood demand did not constitute a change in circumstances that would have required Budarick to re-consult duty counsel. The appeal was dismissed.

R v Bourdon, 2011 MBPC 83 (Breach but no exclusion)

Bourdon was charged with impaired driving and alleged that his sections 8 and 10 rights were violated. He was driving at approximately half the speed limit. Within a few minutes of stopping the vehicle, Cst Gordon told Bourdon that he would be required to undergo an SFST. Bourdon was taken to the police cruiser to wait for Sergeant Turner to conduct the test. Bourdon was trembling, sweating, had difficulty retrieving his identification, and smelled slightly of liquor. Cst Gordon suspected Bourdon was under the influence of a drug. Bourdon was in police custody from 2 am to 2:16–2:19 am and then placed under arrest and given his right to counsel. Bourdon contacted a lawyer at 3:08 am and the DRE continued by 3:21 am. Bourdon was released by 4:10 am.

The court found that the time period between the stop and the arrest was reasonable and that Bourdon's section 10 rights were not violated. The court then considered whether Sgt Turner had reasonable grounds to suspect that Bourdon had a drug in his body. Based on Bourdon's actions and the traits he was exhibiting at the time, the court found that there were objectively reasonable grounds to suspect that he had alcohol or a drug in his body when asked to perform the SFST. Bourdon's performance of the tests, along with the observations and conversation with Sgt Turner, led to Turner's belief that Bourdon was impaired by alcohol or drugs. The court found that Sgt Turner had the necessary and reasonable grounds to make a DRE demand because his belief was objectively reasonable. Further, Bourdon's section 8 rights were not breached by the taking of the breath sample because it was authorized by law and the testing procedure was done as soon as practicable. The court noted that Bourdon's evidence regarding the alleged breach of his section 10(b) rights is confusing as he maintains he was told once in custody that there would be more tests but also that there was never a formal DRE demand made. Cst Gordon testified that he made the DRE demand at 2:18 am and that Bourdon had said "yes" in response to the demand. The court found that Bourdon did not establish that his section 10(b) rights were breached in this respect. Regarding the request for a urine sample, the court noted that this is more invasive than a breathalyzer and that Bourdon should have been made aware of the potential for criminal charges upon refusal at the time of the original DRE demand or when the demand for urine was made. The court found a breach of section 10 on this basis. In the section 24(2) analysis, the court noted that the officers did not act in bad faith and that taking the urine sample was more intrusive than a breath sample but not as invasive as a blood sample or cavity search. The court found that the evidence should be admitted.

R v Smith, [2012] OJ No 514 (Ct J)

The Court found: "Statements of the accused while under detention and under test are not, in my view, admissible on the issue of impairment. At the scene, statements only go to reasonable and probable grounds for the demand, not to the merits of the matter. And while under test at the station, these tests essentially are compelled tests and during that time of compulsion as a result of the process, statements made by the accused, in my view, are inadmissible and I exclude them" (para 19).

REASONABLE SUSPICION

R v Tucker, [2014] NJ No 133 (Prov Ct)

Tucker was charged with impaired and "over 80" and was seeking an exclusion of breathalyzer evidence under section 24(2) based on an alleged breach of his sections 8, 9, and 10(b) *Charter* rights. Cst Abbott observed Tucker's vehicle at a high rate of speed almost collide with another vehicle and subsequently pulled the vehicle over. He saw two people in the vehicle with a flat front tire and noted a smell of alcohol coming from the vehicle. Tucker's speech was slurred but Cst Abbott could not be sure where the smell of alcohol was coming from because the passenger was intoxicated. Cst Abbott observed that Tucker "stood pretty fine at the time" when he had to walk to the trunk of the car to get his licence but noted that his eyes were watery. Abbott suspected he was under the influence of a drug and SFST specialist Cst Power was called to the scene to perform the test. Power informed Abbott that Tucker was impaired by alcohol and Abbott read a breath demand, caution, and right to counsel. Tucker did not want to contact a lawyer so Abbott took Tucker to the Royal Newfoundland Constabulary office where two samples of breath were taken by a qualified technician.

Cst Abbott's notes contained the speeding, flat tire, potentially attempting to evade the police, and watery eyes, but did not include slurred speech or an odour of alcohol in the report. Cst Power testified that Tucker failed the three tests, said that he had had "a few," and that there was a smell of alcohol coming from his breath. In determining whether there was a violation of Tucker's section 9 rights the judge considered whether Cst Power had a subjective reasonable suspicion of alcohol or a drug in Tucker's body because it was Power who made the SFST demand. Power had been informed of Abbott's observations before making the SFST demand. The judge found that there was not an objective basis for reasonable suspicion because something more than watery eyes and slurred speech is required.

Therefore, the judge found that Tucker's section 9 rights had been violated. The results from the SFSTs provided the ground for demanding a breath sample and as there were insufficient grounds for making this demand, the seizure was in violation of section 8. The judge found that Tucker's section 10(b) rights had not been violated because the SFST demand was made forthwith and there was no requirement of right to counsel at that stage. He further found that admitting the evidence against Tucker would bring the administration of justice into disrepute. The results of the breath tests were excluded based on section 24(2).

REASONABLE GROUNDS

The following cases deal with issues surrounding the lack of a generally accepted list of indicia for drug impairment and the impact of this on the ability of an officer to form grounds for arrest and demand.

R v Antosh, 2013 SKPC 81

Grounds can be affected by a number of different things. Where an officer begins an investigation in one vein but switches to a different focus, i.e., possession of controlled substances to impaired operation, then the court may scrutinize the grounds and whether any of said grounds should be excluded due to *Charter*-infringing conduct by the state.

R v Biagi, 2014 ONCJ 153

Where an officer does not have grounds to believe an accused is impaired but has suspicion of alcohol in the body, a lesser than expected breath reading does not give grounds to make a demand for physical testing such as the DRE.

R v Pedersen, 2015 ABQB 128

Police officers are often in an unenviable position with regard to drug-impaired driving. Currently, there is no screening device for drug impairment. Instead, SFST tests must be used and an officer who lacks this training is left at a loss. As a result, the officer must decide whether reasonable grounds to believe the accused is impaired exist. The difficulty in this case, as in many, is that while there were signs of impairment "that in the absence of some identifiable sign of drug consumption, the indicia of impairment observed by Cst. Adair could have been consistent with a medical condition or possibly extreme fatigue" (para 76).

ASAP (AS SOON AS PRACTICABLE)

R v Vanderbruggen, 2006 CanLII 9039 (Ont CA)

The definition of *as soon as practicable* in the alcohol-testing manner has come to mean "within a reasonably prompt time under the circumstances" (para 12):

> In deciding whether the tests were taken as soon as practicable, the trial judge should look at the whole chain of events, bearing in mind that the *Criminal Code* permits an outside limit of two hours from the time of the offence to the taking of the first test. The "as soon as practicable" requirement must be applied with reason. In particular, while the Crown is obligated to demonstrate that—in all the circumstances—the breath samples were taken within a reasonably prompt time, there is no requirement that the Crown provide a detailed explanation of what occurred during every minute that the accused is in custody. See *R. v. Letford* (2000), 2000 CanLII 17024 (ON CA), 150 C.C.C (3d) 225 (Ont. C.A.) at para 20; *R. v. Carter, supra; R. v. Cambrin* (1982), 1982 CanLII 353 (BC CA), 1 C.C.C. (3d) 59 (B.C.C.A.) at 61–3, and *R. v. Seed* at para. 7 (para. 13)."

There is a recognition of the accuracy that breath tests afford and the weight such testing should be given. Nevertheless, in the drug-impaired driving testing, this may be of somewhat less applicability:

> To conclude, these provisions, which are designed to expedite trials and aid in proof of the suspect's blood alcohol level, should not be interpreted so as to require an exact accounting of every moment in the chronology. We are now far removed from the days when the breathalyser was first introduced into Canada and there may have been some suspicion and scepticism about its accuracy and value and about the science underlying the presumption of identity. These provisions must be interpreted reasonably in a manner that is consistent with Parliament's purpose in facilitating the use of this reliable evidence (para 16).

Given the possibility of suspicion or scepticism about the accuracy and value involved in DRE testing, the definition may be more narrowly construed.

R v Tonelli, 2011 ONCJ 542

Tonelli represented himself at trial for a charge of impaired operation of a motor vehicle. PC Babin observed a vehicle swerving in its lane and called PC MacGillivray to help stop the vehicle. PC Babin stopped the vehicle, smelled cannabis marijuana coming from it, and arrested the passenger after he provided PC Babin with a bag of marijuana. PC Vienneau arrested Tonelli as the driver for driving while impaired by a drug based on grounds of slow and deliberate speech and movements, small pupils, watery eyes, and an odour of marijuana on Tonelli's breath. Tonelli refused counsel after being read his right and PC Vienneau read the caution and demand for an evaluation pursuant to section 254(3.1). After searching the vehicle and releasing the passenger on a promise to appear, PC Vienneau and PC Babin took Tonelli to the detachment to meet the evaluating officer, which was one and a half hours away. The evaluating officer arrived 20 minutes after Tonelli and the officers arrived at the detachment. The evaluating officer made the demand and Tonelli spoke to duty counsel. Following the evaluation, the evaluating officer made a demand for a urine sample that confirmed the presence of cannabis.

There was a delay of 2 hours and 4 minutes from making the demand to turning Tonelli over to the evaluating officer, resulting in a total delay of 2 hours and 20 minutes from the demand to the beginning of the test. Much of the delay can be attributed to the fact that the only evaluating officer had to travel approximately 200 kilometres to the detachment. The judge found that this did not constitute "as soon as practicable" and therefore was a breach of Tonelli's section 9 right. While the judge recognized that the officers did everything they could to connect Tonelli with the evaluating officer, he found that the delay was very serious due to a limited number of evaluating officers in the area and that there should be mechanisms in place to avoid this. He also found that the impact of the breach was very serious due to the length of the detention. The Crown did not attempt to have the evaluating officer qualified as an expert under *Mohan* but argued that his evidence should be treated as opinion evidence as would that of a breathalyzer technician. The judge found that the evidence given by the evaluating officer was not expert evidence and that without expert evidence the test results could not establish beyond a reasonable doubt that Tonelli was impaired by a drug while operating the vehicle. While impaired driving is a serious offence, the judge determined that the seriousness of the state conduct and the impact on Tonelli's rights favoured the exclusion of the evidence obtained as a result of the section 9 breach and Tonelli was found not guilty.

R v Pedersen, 2015 ABQB 128

The court should look at the entire chain of events. Where a demand is not made for a significant time or where the officer does not seek out a DRE officer quickly after grounds are formed, then the demand or tests are not taken as soon as practicable as required. Unless impractical or impossible, then requests for a DRE officer should be made immediately so that attendance and set up of the DRE officer may occur while other matters are being dealt with. Systemic issues or limitations on resources and numbers of DRE officers should play into such an assessment (see especially paras 93–95).

Cst Adair was dispatched to a call made by a civilian regarding an impaired driver. Cst Adair noted the vehicle appeared to be exceeding the speed limit and was swerving through the lanes of traffic. Adair pulled the vehicle over for public safety reasons after observing the pattern of driving and noticed an unconscious female passenger lying with her head in the driver's lap. When Pedersen got out of the vehicle, Cst Adair noticed the front of his pants were wet and a liquid was running down his leg. Pedersen told Cst Adair that he had not had anything to drink. Adair concluded that Pedersen was impaired by drugs based on his slurred speech, mannerisms, extreme driving pattern, and the fact that he was slumped to the right in the driver's seat of the vehicle. Cst Adair arrested Pedersen within 1 minute of Pedersen being outside the vehicle. Adair read Pedersen his section 10(b) right and caution and Pedersen replied "sure" when asked if he understood. Pedersen then admitted to smoking "one gram of meth plus two caps of G and maybe something else." Cst Adair put Pedersen in a jail cell and read the DRE demand. There was no response to Cst Adair's request for a DRE through Communications so he called Cst Shelrud, who advised that he would not be able to attend for an hour. Cst Green then called to advise Cst Adair that he would be able to perform the evaluation before Cst Shelrud. Cst Green and Cst Adair were having a discussion about the case outside of Pedersen's cell and Pedersen joined the conversation through the cell door regarding the drugs that he had taken. Cst Green read Pedersen the standard caution, to which Pedersen replied that he understood, and the tests were performed in the hallway. Cst Green obtained a urine sample from Pedersen.

The judge found Cst Adair to be a credible and reliable witness. Cst Adair did not require Pedersen to accompany him to perform physical coordination tests, but believed he already had reasonable and probable grounds and was going to find a DRE to perform an evaluation. The judge noted that when an officer suspects drug impairment but does not conduct physical coordination tests the officer must have other grounds to find a reasonable belief of impairment. The judge found that it was not sufficient to conclude that Pedersen's behaviour resulted from drug use simply because there were no indications of alcohol consumption. The judge found that the arrest and DRE demand violated sections 8 and 9 of the *Charter*. The defence argued that the DRE demand was not made as soon as practicable and therefore evidence of drug consumption resulting from the evaluation was obtained unlawfully. The Crown conceded that the demand was not made as soon as practicable but argued that this means "within a reasonably prompt time under the circumstances" and that the demand was reasonable in the circumstances of this case. The judge found that the conduct was reasonably prompt in the circumstances and that the delay from DRE demand to evaluation was satisfactorily explained; however, the total delay was unreasonable because Cst Adair could have made earlier efforts to contact a DRE. The defence further argued that the Crown had a duty to disclose the cell block videos taken during Pedersen's DRE evaluation, while the Crown argued that the video was not made for the purpose of aiding the investigation and that there was no obligation to disclose it. The video recording was destroyed in accordance with the thirty-day retention policy before the impaired driving charge was laid against Pedersen, and the judge found that this destruction violated Pedersen's section 7 rights. The judge found that the statement made by Pedersen through his cell door was voluntary but that circumstances surrounding Cst Adair's whereabouts between the bodily substances demand and the urine sample are unclear. This led the judge to find that statements within this period should be excluded.

SEARCH AUTHORIZED BY LAW

Tests outside those the officer is trained on and enunciated by statute and regulation cannot be performed.

R v McLachlan, [2015] OJ No 6984 (Ct J) (Weighing the person)
PC Gonsalez observed McLachlan driving her vehicle 90 to 95 km/h in an 80 km/h zone. He pulled the vehicle over and discovered that the plate did not match the vehicle. McLachlan was unable to roll down her window and was asked to step out of the vehicle. When the door opened, PC Gonsalez smelled a strong odour of alcohol coming from the vehicle, and then on McLachlan's breath when she had exited the vehicle. PC Gonsalez made a demand for an ASD sample, which McLachlan failed on her sixth attempt. PC Gonsalez arrested McLachlan, explained her right to counsel and caution, and made a breath demand. PC Burlow conducted the breath test and was aware that, due to the time delay, expert evidence from a toxicologist would be required, along with a record of McLachlan's weight. McLachlan refused to be weighed but complied, without consent, after PC Burlow insisted.

The defence argued that McLachlan's section 8 right was violated by obtaining her weight and that it should be excluded under section 24(2). Additionally, the defence suggested that bolus drinking was a possibility in this situation because of the availability of alcohol in residences and businesses in the area in which PC Gonsalez first spotted McLachlan's vehicle. While the defence argued that there is no authority for non-voluntary weighing, the Crown argued that this was part of the search incident to arrest. The judge noted that the purpose of weighing McLachlan was not to identify her but to assist the Crown in getting an expert opinion for trial. The judge found that this was a breach of her section 8 right. In the section 24(2) analysis the judge noted that the policy PC Burlow was following was not authorized in law and that forcing McLachlan to provide evidence against herself was a serious impact on her interests that the *Charter* protects. The judge excluded the evidence of McLachlan's weight under section 24(2) and she was not convicted of impaired driving.

R c Grand-Louis, 2014 QCCQ 9411 (Non-standard field sobriety tests)

Grand-Louis was charged with impaired driving and refusing to comply with a breath demand. Grand-Louis made a motion to exclude evidence under section 24(2) based on an alleged violation of his section 9 right. Officer McComber received a call regarding a hit and run with a parked vehicle and the results of his investigation led him to suspect that Grand-Louis was the driver involved in the accident. Officer McComber received a call, informing him that Grand-Louis was drunk and behind the wheel of a white Ford. When the officer pulled Grand-Louis's vehicle over he noted that Grand-Louis had glossy red eyes, that his breath smelled of alcohol, and that there were glass and scuff marks on the bumper of the truck. Officer McComber asked Grand-Louis to perform a sobriety test involving twelve steps heel-to-toe in a straight line. McComber was not trained to administer the test but concluded that Grand-Louis failed because he swayed from side to side with each step during the test. McComber testified that the failed test was important to his reasonable and probable grounds to arrest Grand-Louis. The test conducted by Officer McComber was not one provided for by regulation. The judge found that Officer McComber's demand was legal because it was performed at the site of detention, with minimal inconvenience to Grand-Louis, and did not put the safety of Grand-Louis at risk. Further, the judge acknowledged that McComber subjectively believed he had reasonable grounds, but that this belief was not objectively reasonable. Therefore, the judge found that the detention of Grand-Louis was in violation of his section 9 right.

R v Hebert, 2014 ABPC 246 (Taking to hospital to get "checked out," including blood)

Hebert was at a restaurant when a witness, Oursien, saw her walking into tables and counters. Oursien, an Emergency Medical Technician, was concerned that Hebert was impaired or intoxicated so when Hebert got into her car, he called the RCMP and followed her. He noted that her driving was normal until she got onto the highway. She was swerving in her lane until being pulled over by the police. Constables Vaughn and Chan noted that Hebert alternated from calm to crying and her pupils were very constricted. When asked if she was on drugs and if she could show them to the officers, Hebert produced three prescription bottles with pills. Cst Vaughn arrested Hebert for impaired driving, took her to the police cruiser, and read her warning and right to counsel. Hebert asked to speak with a lawyer. Believing that it was required, Cst Vaughn made a blood demand and Hebert agreed to provide a sample. Cst Vaughn had never done a blood demand and called dispatch to speak to a DRE. No DRE was available, so Cst Vaughn spoke to his training officer and senior officers who were unable to tell him if taking blood was the correct decision. Cst Chan searched the vehicle and found another bottle of prescription drugs. The constables then took Hebert to the RCMP detachment where she was in the lawyer room for 45 minutes. Cst Vaughn found Hebert nodding off with her cell phone in her hand and she informed him that she was waiting for a call back from her lawyer. Vaughn told Hebert they were going to the hospital but to take her cell phone for when her lawyer called back. A blood sample was taken at the hospital and her lawyer did not call back while they were there.

The judge found that the constables did not follow the proper procedure in making the blood demand because they did not require Hebert to undergo physical coordination tests to determine if she should be evaluated by a DRE. The constables did not have the right to detain her at that point to obtain a blood sample. The judge found that Hebert should have been released when the constables learned that a DRE evaluation could not be performed "as soon as practicable" and that she could have been released to her mother because her mother had also followed her from the restaurant. Further, the judge noted that the constable read the incorrect blood demand. For these reasons the judge concluded that Hebert's section 9 right was violated. Cst Chan's search was not in violation of Hebert's *Charter* rights because it was incidental to the lawful arrest for impaired driving caused by drugs. The judge found that the constables breached Hebert's section 10(b) rights by failing to inform her that she had a right to reasonable opportunity to speak to counsel and by failing to wait to take her to the hospital until she had this opportunity. Further, the judge noted that 48 minutes to 1 hour is a reasonable time to wait for counsel to return Hebert's call. The examination by the physician at the hospital was a violation of Hebert's section 8 right as she was not taken there for treatment but for gathering evidence against her. The judge found that the fact that Hebert complied with the unlawful blood demand before receiving advice from counsel does not amount to consent or was not legally informed consent. The judge found the *Charter* breaches to be very serious and, in considering the *Grant* factors, found that all evidence gathered by police after one hour at the roadside should be excluded. The pill bottles Hebert gave to the constables were not produced at trial and there was not admissible evidence regarding what type of pills were in the bottles. The judge drew the inference from the testimony of the pharmacist that the pills in the bottle were the ones from the prescription Hebert had filled earlier that day, including Zopliclone, Oxycodone, and Lorazepam. The judge did not accept the inference that Hebert had taken these drugs before driving because two of them are sleep aids and cause drowsiness, which she was not exhibiting at the roadside, according to the constables. Further, the judge was not satisfied beyond a reasonable doubt that Hebert's ability to drive was impaired by drugs based on her driving pattern before being pulled over. The judge found that the Crown did not prove the *actus reus* or *mens rea* of dangerous driving. Finally, the judge held that if the exclusion of evidence under section 24(2) was incorrect that there should be a judicial stay under section 24(1).

R v Campbell, 2015 ONCJ 127 (SFST where officer not trained)

Campbell was charged with impaired and refuse, and argued that his *Charter* sections 8, 9, and 10(a) rights were violated. Cst Payne observed a vehicle travelling over 100 km/h in a 50 km/h zone. The vehicle stopped abruptly and did not move to the side of the road when Cst Payne's vehicle arrived. Campbell was the driver of the vehicle and Cst Payne observed signs of intoxication and noted a strong odour of alcohol coming from the vehicle as well as poor motor skills and glassy eyes. When Cst Payne asked about alcohol consumption and noted the smell of alcohol coming from Campbell's breath, Campbell denied having any alcohol and said he would prove this by blowing into a machine. Cst Payne discovered that Campbell was a suspended driver. Cst Payne then asked Campbell to go to the rear of the vehicle to perform a physical test of his balance. Cst Payne arrested Campbell for impaired operation following the test. The intoxilyzer technician had independent grounds to make a breath demand and Campbell spoke to counsel before the demand was made but refused to comply.

The judge found that Cst Payne had grounds to stop the vehicle due to its high rate of speed. Regarding the alleged breach of section 10(a), the judge found that Campbell was sufficiently aware of the scope of the investigation based on Cst Payne's line of questioning. The judge found that Cst Payne had a subjective belief that he had grounds to arrest Campbell but questions whether they are objectively sustainable. Cst Payne did not formally intend to demand compliance with section 254(2)(a) and did not have experience or training to administer the physical coordination tests. For these reasons the judge found that the results of the test had no probative value and should be excluded. Cst Payne's reasonable and probable grounds were based on the results from the physical test. Further, Cst Payne could not recall whether he had an ASD in his vehicle that night and said that if Campbell had refused to perform the physical test, he would have made an ASD demand. Based on this, the judge found that Cst Payne would not have believed to have reasonable and probable grounds without the physical test. The judge found a breach of sections 8 and 9.

Campbell applied for the exclusion of the observations when he was walking around to the back of the vehicle, the observations of the physical test, and the statements made to prove the refuse charge. The judge assessed the nexus between the evidence and the *Charter*-infringing conduct, as required by *Grant*. The judge found that Campbell would have had to get out of the vehicle because he was a suspended driver. Further, the judge found that, although Cst Payne's subjective belief of reasonable grounds could not be separated from the observations of the physical tests, objectively there were numerous grounds that would support the subjective belief. This mitigates the seriousness of the breach of sections 8 and 9 and, because the nature of the physical test was not demeaning or capricious, this favours inclusion of the evidence. The judge found, however, a serious infringement on Campbell's sections 8 and 9 interests. The judge excluded the observations of the physical coordination test because it was not performed in compliance with statutory regulations and excluded the observation of behaviour after getting out of the vehicle but before the tests because the main purpose of getting out of the vehicle was to perform the test. The judge admitted the statements made to the intoxilyzer technician. The judge found a breach of sections 8 and 9 because Cst Payne did not have reasonable and probable grounds for arrest and therefore Campbell was acquitted of the impaired driving count. Campbell was convicted of refusing to provide a breath sample.

REMEDY UNDER *CHARTER* SECTION 24(2)

Different considerations must exist in cases involving SFST and DRE testing. This relates to the lesser availability of officers properly trained at these two levels when compared to the ready availability of alcohol-screening devices and approved instruments. As a result of this, it will necessarily take longer in most cases to locate an officer able to conduct the necessary testing. The query then is whether this excuses longer delays as it is reasonable that police forces balance their limited dollars by having fewer of these officers available or whether the individual's rights take priority as they are the ones facing longer detentions where agencies have made such decisions, which makes such delays a systemic issue and thus more serious under the *Grant* analysis. Truly, it will be for the judiciary to weigh individual and societal rights in each case to determine the impact of such decisions.

R v Tonelli, 2011 ONCJ 542
Charter section 24(2) analysis will be different in cases where urine or blood is taken as compared to breath in alcohol cases (see the section on ASAP earlier in this chapter for a more thorough review).

R v Hase, [2013] OJ No 6420 (Ct J)
The test for exclusion under section 24(2) differs in drug-impaired driving cases. Urine tests require watching the accused provide the sample to ensure continuity and avoid contamination by things in the police

station. This will increase the impact on the individual when measured in a *Grant* analysis:

> The drug recognition examination scheme [*sic*] is in my view a significantly intrusive process. It takes a considerable amount of time. It involves a great deal of physical participation on the part of an accused person, and it leads to a great deal of personal health information being disclosed, to the police. This is particularly so where urine samples for analysis are demanded. If one compares, for example, an intoxilyzer demand, the intoxilyzer process requires a minimal sample of breath that is analyzed for one substance only, and is rather transient in nature. Urine, on the other hand, must be sent to a lab, must be tested, is tested for a wide range of substances, and is in that sense considerably less transient a sample.
>
> Accordingly, if evidence obtained by this process is to be constitutionally acceptable, it must be obtained in strict compliance with all of the rules and regulations that are applicable (paras 22–23).

R v Antosh, 2013 SKPC 81

Where an accused is arrested for another offence, such as possession of a substance, but the officer begins questioning for other offences such as impaired driving, then the lack of caution will be a serious breach justifying exclusion.

CHAPTER 8

Bill C-46 and the Amendments to the *Criminal Code*

Bill C-46, *An Act to amend the Criminal Code (offences relating to conveyances) and to make consequential amendments to other Acts,* passed the House of Commons on 31 October 2017. While certain changes are likely to occur to the exact wording of the bill, there is a legislative desire to see this bill passed coincident to the legislation that is to legalize marijuana in Canada. The changes to the *Criminal Code* affect both alcohol- and drug-impaired driving and set up the legislative scheme for testing, as well as a number of evidential burdens that will be shifted to the accused to disprove in order to maintain innocence if certain preconditions are met by the state. Part 1 of the bill makes a number of changes but is immediately repealed by Part 2 and so will not be reviewed in any depth. However, the changes made in Part 2 that touch on drug-impaired driving will be reviewed section by section in this chapter.

The definition section retains, generally, the definition of *analyst* and *approved container* as those to be designated by the Attorney General. However, some new definitions arise and others should be read and understood:

> 320.11 "approved drug screening equipment" means equipment that is designed to ascertain the presence of a drug in a person's body and that is approved by the Attorney General of Canada under paragraph 320.39(b) (*matériel de détection des drogues approuvé*)

Although the exact equipment has not been designated, it is likely to include the kind of equipment reviewed relating to drug screening devices in Chapter 3.

> "evaluating officer" means a peace officer who has the qualifications prescribed by regulation that are required in order to act as an evaluating officer (*agent évaluateur*)

It is anticipated that such designations will remain the same as those required of evaluating officers currently.

> "qualified technician" means . . . (b) in respect of blood samples, a person who is, or a person who is a member of a class of persons that is, designated by the Attorney General under subparagraph 320.4(b)(i) (*technicien qualifié*)

While paralleling the current definition, this is likely to become of increased importance with the necessity of blood testing to prove *per se* limits in drug-impaired driving cases.

A new preamble-esque section, 320.12, is added. Of importance specifically is the recognition that driving is a privilege subject to sobriety and the importance of deterring persons from operating conveyances while impaired by a drug. However, it goes further and statutorily states that

> (d) an evaluation conducted by an evaluating officer is a reliable method of determining whether a person's ability to operate a conveyance is impaired by a drug or by a combination of alcohol and a drug.

This should be of concern as it seems to legislate that something is reliable rather than relying on the backing of science and the ability of a trier-of-fact, usually a judge, to properly assess the weight that should be attached to such testimony. An assertion that something is reliable when its subjective nature and interpretive application have been commented on by appellate courts should be of concern to both the Crown who seeks to act as a minister for justice and defence counsel arguing on behalf of their clients.

> 320.14 (1) Everyone commits an offence who
>
> (a) operates a conveyance while the person's ability to operate it is impaired to any degree by alcohol or a drug or by a combination of alcohol and a drug;

. . .

(c) subject to subsection (6), has, within two hours after ceasing to operate a conveyance, a blood drug concentration that is equal to or exceeds the blood drug concentration for the drug that is prescribed by regulation; or

(d) subject to subsection (7), has, within two hours after ceasing to operate a conveyance, a blood alcohol concentration and a blood drug concentration that is equal to or exceeds the blood alcohol concentration and the blood drug concentration for the drug as prescribed by regulation for instances where alcohol and that drug are combined.

. . .

Operation—low blood drug concentration

(4) Subject to subsection (6), everyone commits an offence who has, within two hours after ceasing to operate a conveyance, a blood drug concentration that is equal to or exceeds the blood drug concentration for the drug that is prescribed by regulation and that is less than the concentration prescribed for the purposes of paragraph (1)(c).

These sections preserve the offence of driving while impaired by drug while also creating the offences involving *per se* limits, both of drugs and a combination of alcohol and a drug. What is of greatest note in this section is the proscription of having a blood level of a particular drug "within two hours after ceasing to operate a conveyance," which will be examined later in this chapter with the exceptions.

Exception—drugs

(6) No person commits an offence under paragraph (1)(c) or subsection (4) if

(a) they consumed the drug after ceasing to operate the conveyance; and

(b) after ceasing to operate the conveyance, they had no reasonable expectation that they would be required to provide a sample of a bodily substance.

Exception—combination of alcohol and drug

(7) No person commits an offence under paragraph (1)(d) if

(a) they consumed the drug or the alcohol or both after ceasing to operate the conveyance;

(b) after ceasing to operate the conveyance, they had no reasonable expectation that they would be required to provide a sample of a bodily substance; and
(c) their alcohol consumption is consistent with their blood alcohol concentration as determined in accordance with subsection 320.31(1) or (2) and with their having had, at the time when they were operating the conveyance, a blood alcohol concentration less than the blood alcohol concentration established under paragraph 320.38(c).

The exception that an individual consumed the drug (and alcohol as the case may be) after driving is essential to protect innocent drivers who return home and consume a substance after ceasing to drive and thus not being a danger whatsoever to the public. However, the additional requirement that there be no reasonable expectation of a requirement to provide a sample is of particular note in this exception. With no statutory definition, it will be up to the courts to define this nebulous term. One can imagine examples that clearly fall on either side of this requirement, but also examples involving facts that straddle the line will undoubtedly arise. The individual who sees lights at the end of their street but pulls into their driveway, thus not driving through a RIDE program, may equally have been required to reasonably expect to have to provide a sample having seen the RIDE program or may not as their trip did not take them through such a program. An interpretation where any individual who consumed drugs prior to driving may be as open to the trier-of-fact as an interpretation so narrow as to capture almost no one.

Failure or refusal to comply with demand continues as an offence, now found in section 320.15.

Punishment is contained in section 320.19 for impaired operation and exceeding the *per se* limit of drug or drug and alcohol combination and sets minimum penalties where the Crown proceeds by way of summary conviction of $1000 for a first offence, 30 days jail for a second offence, and 120 days for a third offence and a maximum of two years less a day jail. Should the Crown proceed by indictment then there are similar minimums and there is a maximum sentence of ten years. Refusing to comply with a demand carries a minimum $2000 fine for a first offence and follows the same elevations for subsequent offences. For the offence under section 320.14(4) of being over the lower *per se* limit for a drug the punishment is only by way of summary conviction with a maximum fine of $1000.

Elevated penalties, including higher maximums, are allowed in cases involving bodily harm or death having been caused. Other aggravating circumstances for sentencing include if multiple individuals are injured or killed, if the offender was racing, if a person under the age of sixteen years was a passenger, if the driver was being paid (taxi or Uber), if the motor vehicle being operated was large, or if the driver was not permitted to operate the conveyance.

> 320.23 (1) The court may, with the consent of the prosecutor and the offender, and after considering the interests of justice, delay sentencing of an offender who has been found guilty of an offence under subsection 320.14(1) or 320.15(1) to allow the offender to attend a treatment program approved by the province in which the offender resides. If the court delays sentencing, it shall make an order prohibiting the offender from operating, before sentencing, the type of conveyance in question, in which case subsections 320.24(6) to (9) apply.
>
> *Exception to minimum punishment*
>
> (2) If the offender successfully completes the treatment program, the court is not required to impose the minimum punishment under section 320.19 or to make a prohibition order under section 320.24, but it shall not direct a discharge under section 730.

The preceding section carves out an exception to the minimum penalties so long as both prosecutor and accused agree. This creates strong power for the prosecutor and a tool which may be wielded broadly. Whether individual Crowns are granted the power to make such decisions themselves or whether policy will be driven from a higher level remains to be seen. Certainly, it will be a tool more likely to be utilized by the prosecution in cases where the offender pleads guilty, thus deterring the accused from exercising their right to a trial. The utility of such a tool will be somewhat diluted in first-time offences since the mandatory prohibition on driving pending the completion of the program will deter some first-time offenders from participating in such a program because of the availability of ignition interlock immediately with no waiting period, which will be reviewed with section 324.24(10), below in this chapter. An ignition interlock machine installed in a vehicle requires a person to blow into it prior to starting the car. If the person has a Blood Alcohol Count above a prescribed rate then the car will not start. It requires a person also to blow into it at random intervals in order to keep the car running. This elimination of the three-month, six-month, and twelve-month mandatory period of prohibition prior to entering into an ignition interlock program that currently exists will likely lead to further uptake on such programs because a person may be able to drive immediately after a finding of guilt, depending on the availability of such programs in their province. Also important to note in this section is the elimination of the possibility of a discharge by participating in such rehabilitative programs. Given the shift in some provinces to essentially decriminalize such behaviour, this will be an interesting social tension to observe in the coming years.

> 320.24 (1) If an offender is found guilty of an offence under subsection 320.14(1) or 320.15(1), the court that sentences the offender shall, in addition to any other punishment that may be imposed for that offence, make an order prohibiting the offender from operating the type of conveyance in question during a period to be determined in accordance with subsection (2).

It is expected that "type of conveyance" will act similarly to existing legislation limiting the prohibition to the class of conveyance, i.e., motor vehicle or vessel or aircraft or railway equipment and not merely to a more limited reading such as car or truck or motorcycle, though this remains to be seen.

Similar to existing provisions where no bodily harm or death occurs, the prohibition period, in addition to any period of custody, is for a first offence one to three years, for a second offence two to ten years, and for each subsequent offence at least three years with no maximum. However, for the low *per se* drug levels the prohibition order is not mandatory and shall be for not more than one year. Incidents involving bodily harm or death do not carry mandatory prohibition orders but do have much wider ranges as to the maximum prohibition allowed.

> 320.24 (10) A person may not be registered in an alcohol ignition interlock device program referred to in subsection 320.18(2) until the expiry of:

(a) in the case of a first offence, a period, if any, that may be fixed by order of the court;
(b) in the case of a second offence, a period of three months after the day on which the sentence is imposed or any longer period that may be fixed by order of the court; and
(c) in the case of a subsequent offence, a period of six months after the day on which the sentence is imposed or any longer period that may be fixed by order of the court.

This section technically speaks to when a person is no longer prohibited under the *Criminal Code* rather than the impact of such participation on a prohibition order thus being written differently than the existing section 259(1.1) though it is expected to operate in much the same manner. Importantly, for first offences the court has the power to allow an individual to register in an alcohol ignition interlock device program immediately if they so wish. As well, the limitations for second and third offences are lowered to three and six months from the existing six and twelve months.

Investigative Matters

Testing for presence of alcohol or drug

320.27 (1) If a peace officer has reasonable grounds to suspect that a person has alcohol or a drug in their body and that the person has, within the preceding three hours, operated a conveyance, the peace officer may, by demand, require the person to comply with the requirements of either or both of paragraphs (a) and (b) in the case of alcohol or with the requirements of either or both of paragraphs (a) and (c) in the case of a drug:
(a) to immediately perform the physical coordination tests prescribed by regulation and to accompany the peace officer for that purpose;

. . .

(c) to immediately provide the samples of a bodily substance that, in the peace officer's opinion, are necessary to enable a proper analysis to be made by means of approved drug screening equipment and to accompany the peace officer for that purpose.

This section deals with "roadside" testing. The wording in this section clarifies that where a peace officer has reasonable suspicion to believe that an accused is operating a conveyance with a drug in their system, the officer can demand that the individual comply with the SFST or a drug screening equipment test or both. The section requires that such testing occur "immediately." The interpretation of this is likely to be similar to that of the prior "forthwith" requirement. What will be interesting is whether such changes no longer allow for the detention of an individual awaiting screening equipment, should the officer not have it with them or not have the training to conduct the SFST. The immediacy requirement suggests that an officer may be better served by making a demand for both if they are unsure whether screening equipment or a trained SFST officer will arrive first as the demand should also be made immediately one would presume, similar to existing requirements.

> 320.27(2) If a peace officer has reasonable grounds to believe that a person has operated a conveyance while the person's ability to operate it was impaired to any degree by a drug or by a combination of alcohol and a drug, or has committed an offence under paragraph 320.14(1)(c) or (d) or subsection 320.14(4), the peace officer may, by demand, made as soon as practicable, require the person to comply with the requirements of either or both of paragraphs (a) and (b):
>
> (a) to submit, as soon as practicable, to an evaluation conducted by an evaluating officer to determine whether the person's ability to operate a conveyance is impaired by a drug or by a combination of alcohol and a drug, and to accompany the peace officer for that purpose; or
>
> (b) to provide, as soon as practicable, the samples of blood that, in the opinion of the qualified medical practitioner or qualified technician taking the samples, are necessary to enable a proper analysis to be made to determine the person's blood drug concentration, or the person's blood drug concentration and blood alcohol concentration, as the case may be, and to accompany the peace officer for that purpose.

This section emulates the existing ability of an officer to demand that an individual comply with DRE testing. It also allows a demand for samples of blood, noting the plural, as deemed necessary by a medical practitioner or technician to enable an analysis. These demands can be made whether the officer believes that the individual before them is impaired or over the legal limit similar to the requirement for breath tests in alcohol-impaired driving. The ability to demand such things in the absence of impairment will undoubtedly be based on similar failure on approved drug screening equipment (**ADSE**) in the same vein as alcohol breath sample demands. The impact of the more intrusive nature of blood sampling is almost certainly going to make an impact in assessing *Charter* breaches, especially around in the section 24(2) analysis.

Section 320.27(3) allows for a breath demand by an evaluating officer should they have reasonable grounds to suspect alcohol to be present in the person's body. The demand must be made as soon as practicable but requires the use of an approved instrument rather than an approved screening device. This is a method where an arresting officer may not have a belief of alcohol being involved but instead drugs; yet an evaluating officer suspects alcohol and the breath sample is taken on the standard of reasonable suspicion rather than reasonable and probable grounds. This is similar to the provision currently in force.

> 320.27 (4) If, on completion of the evaluation, the evaluating officer has reasonable grounds to believe that one or more of the types of drugs set out in subsection (5)—or that a combination of alcohol and one or more of those types of drugs—is impairing the person's ability to operate a conveyance, the evaluating officer shall identify the type or types of drugs in question and may, by demand made as soon as practicable, require the person to provide, as soon as practicable,
>
> (a) a sample of oral fluid or urine that, in the evaluating officer's opinion, is necessary to enable a proper analysis to be made to ascertain the presence in the person's body of one or more of the types of drugs set out in subsection (5); or
>
> (b) the samples of blood that, in the opinion of the qualified medical practitioner or qualified technician taking the samples, are necessary to enable a proper analysis to be made to ascertain the presence in the person's body of one or more of the types of drugs set out in subsection (5) or to determine the person's blood drug concentration for one or more of those types of drugs.

Subsection 4 allows for the DRE officer who believes the accused to be impaired by a particular class or classes of drug(s) to make a demand for a bodily sample—oral fluid, urine, or blood. The reference to class or classes of drug(s) is new. Statutory interpretation suggests that Parliament would not include surplus language without purpose. Whether this reference means that testing can only be done for drugs in the class or classes which the DRE officer calls or whether it continues to allow for testing for a wider variety of drugs remains to be seen. If this limits the blood testing to the classes of drugs which the DRE officer calls, it may consequently limit the methods of testing that are allowed on the sample taken by a laboratory. This may miss certain drugs that were not in the class or classes called or may encourage DRE officers to call multiple classes of drugs to ensure testing. As well, it may be problematic for certain classes of drugs that lend themselves to multiple classes based on dosage and tolerance, including THC, the active ingredient in marijuana. If this limitation was not intended, then it begs the question why this language was included. Ultimately, it will be up to courts to properly determine the interpretation of this additional language. Section 320.3 may be instructive in this regard.

The types of drugs listed in section 320.27(5) mirror the classes of drugs noted in the DRE program—namely, a depressant, an inhalant, a dissociative anaesthetic, cannabis, a stimulant, a hallucinogen, or a narcotic analgesic.

Section 320.27(6) limits the taking of blood to where a qualified medical practitioner or qualified technician is satisfied that doing so would not endanger a person's health. Subsection 7 requires that samples be taken into approved containers and sealed. Subsection 8 requires a sample to be retained for testing by the defence if requested. Subsection 9 states that an analysis is not affected if subsection 7 or 8 is not complied with, thus making subsections 7 and 8 a best practice rather than a requirement.

The release of the sample retained for defence testing is governed by subsection 10, which requires the release of the sample on a summary application to a court of criminal jurisdiction made within six months of the samples being taken. The court may attach terms if it deems it necessary to ensure the safeguarding of the sample.

Section 320.29 allows police to apply for a warrant or telewarrant to obtain blood samples and to require a qualified medical practitioner or qualified technician to take such samples if the officer has reasonable grounds to believe that the suspect was operating a conveyance that was involved in an incident involving bodily harm or death, including to the suspect, within the preceding 8 hours and that the suspect has alcohol or a drug in their body. Further to the officer's beliefs, a medical practitioner must be of the opinion that the suspect cannot consent to the taking of blood because of their medical issues and that taking blood would not endanger the suspect's health. The warrant is only valid so long as the medical practitioner's opinion remains the same. Therefore, if the accused becomes conscious and able to consent, then police must use a different method. The officer must provide a copy of the warrant as soon as practicable to the person from whom the samples are taken. A second sample is to be taken, retained, and released on application in the same method as with a blood demand made by a DRE officer.

> 320.3 Samples of a person's blood that are taken for the purposes of this part may be analyzed to determine the person's blood alcohol concentration or blood drug concentration, or both.

While it is seemingly obvious that samples will be analyzed, this section seems more inclusive regarding the testing allowed on a blood sample to any blood drug concentration rather than limiting the testing to a particular class as perhaps suggested in section 320.27(4).

> 320.31(2) The result of an analysis made by an analyst of a sample of a person's blood is proof of their blood alcohol concentration or their blood drug concentration, as the case may be, at the time when the sample was taken in the absence of evidence tending to show that the analysis was performed improperly.

The impact of this section is a presumption of accuracy being applied to the analysis of a sample. What it does not create is a presumption of identity relating the readings at the time of the sample being taken, to the concentration in a person's body at the time of operating a motor vehicle. This is, of course, very important when considering crimes involving *per se* limits as some further evidence will be required in order to prove an illegal level of the drug in a person's system at the time of operating a conveyance. Basically, the link between the two pieces of evidence, the level and the driving, never cross, unless something more is called.

Considering that many drugs do not have a straight line elimination rate like alcohol, but instead require individualized testing, this makes sense, though it will be of little help to a prosecutor seeking a conviction.

> 320.31 (3) Evidence of the following does not constitute evidence tending to show that an analysis of a sample of a person's blood was performed improperly:
> (a) the amount of alcohol or a drug that they consumed;
> (b) the rate at which the alcohol or the drug would have been absorbed or eliminated by their body; or
> (c) a calculation based on the evidence referred to in paragraphs (a) and (b) of what their blood alcohol concentration or blood drug concentration would have been at the time the sample was taken.

The foregoing eliminates evidence being called in the manner that it previously had been in alcohol-related cases pre-2008 in a "Carter" defence. Instead, actual evidence about the testing procedure will need to be called or challenged. For this reason, obtaining all relevant disclosure will be imperative to confirm the manner in which the bodily substance was tested and any frailties with the testing procedure that arise. Determining what method was used and how that method was put into practice will be key for a proper examination of the evidence to the contrary, which may be relevant. That being said, it may be of little import to bring such evidence to the contrary where no presumption of identity exists, and the prosecution will require the evidence of a toxicologist to relate back readings to establish *per se* limits. Toxicologists typically have the knowledge necessary to be qualified as experts in the effects of a drug as well and can provide some evidence that may raise a doubt about the impact of a drug at a particular level, especially at a level consistent with treatment.

> 320.31 (5) An evaluating officer's opinion relating to the impairment, by a type of drug that they identified, or by a combination of alcohol and that type of drug, of a person's ability to operate a conveyance is admissible in evidence without qualifying the evaluating officer as an expert.

This simply codifies the Supreme Court's decision in *Bingley*.

> 320.31 (6) If the analysis of a sample provided under subsection 320.28(4) demonstrates that the person has a drug in their body that is of a type that the evaluating officer has identified as impairing the person's ability to operate a conveyance, that drug — or, if the person has also consumed alcohol, the combination of alcohol and that drug — is presumed, in the absence of evidence to the contrary, to be the drug, or the combination of alcohol and that drug, that was present in the person's body at the time when the person operated the conveyance and, on proof of the person's impairment, to have been the cause of that impairment.

This creates a presumption at law that if the DRE officer calls a certain drug category in their opinion and that type of drug is found, in any amount, in the individual's body, that it is the cause of impairment. It allows for evidence to the contrary to be brought but this establishes a burden on the accused to show this. What this burden is and what could constitute evidence to the contrary is left wide open. While there are limitations on evidence to the contrary to establish whether analysis of a sample of blood was performed correctly, this limitation does not appear for this section. This creates an interesting situation where consumption pattern, rate of absorption and elimination and calculation based on this does not impact on the blood analysis results, such evidence may impact on the ability to challenge impairment. This presumption may encourage DRE officers to call multiple classes when in doubt as it creates an evidential shift whereby their opinion will be given a higher persuasive value than it is afforded by current legislation. This, in some ways, goes against the decision in *Bingley* that the opinion is admissible but subject to an assignment of weight by the trier-of-fact, given the inherently subjective nature of DRE testing.

It is likely that this presumption will be challenged strongly by defence counsel. Similarly, a determination of the correct standard for evidence to the contrary will be required. At this point, a parallel can be drawn to prior forms of evidence to the contrary that required the defendant to raise a reasonable doubt as to the existence of factors. Alternatively, this may be considered similar to cases of bolus drinking that create an evidential burden but not a persuasive burden for the defendant to put the issue in play. A point of interpretation that will require necessary hearing will be whether the presumption in this section applies when the analysis shows presence of the drug at the time of analysis but not necessarily at the time of operation (see section 320.31(2)) or whether the presumption will require the coincident factors of operation of a conveyance with a present drug level rather than one then the other.

> 320.31 (7) The result of an analysis of a sample of a person's breath, blood, urine, sweat or other bodily substance that they were not required to provide under this Part may be admitted in evidence even if the person was not warned before they provided the sample that they were not required to do so or that the result of the analysis of the sample might be used in evidence.

This section indicates that police need not warn a person that they need not consent to the taking of a bodily sample. This seems to go against existing law with regard to consensual search and the requirement that such searches be informed.

> 320.31 (8) Unless a person is required to provide a sample of a bodily substance under this Part, evidence that they failed or refused to provide a sample for analysis or that a sample was not taken is not admissible and the failure, refusal or fact that a sample was not taken shall not be the subject of comment by any person in any proceedings under this Part.

On the one hand, this prevents the Crown from speculating on the failure to take a sample and what the result could have been but also prevents the defence from conjecturing as to the reasons why such a sample was not taken. In essence it codifies the zero sum effect of no evidence being no evidence.

> 320.31 (9) A statement made by a person to a peace officer, including a statement compelled under a provincial Act, is admissible in evidence for the purpose of justifying a demand made under section 320.27.

This broad admissibility of statements, including those made under compulsion, goes against the requirements that have been in existence for many years regarding the use of such compelled statements. Such compelled statements have not been admissible due to the impact that the use of such statements will have. The justification for the exclusion of compelled statements is strong. The state should not be able to rely on a statement that the individual would be punished for if they chose not to make it. This violates the principle against self-incrimination. There are policy reasons as well. The immunity afforded to compelled statements is because of the societal interest in seeing such statements taken. It may encourage individuals to not report accidents rather than risk self-incrimination. This could lead to results of individuals injured in accidents being left unreported and thus untreated due to a self-interest in not reporting, or else an accused providing a false statement in order to try to protect themself. "The prospect of unreliable confessions is very real given the serious consequences which the driver may feel will flow from telling the truth." Further, "[t]he possibility is real and serious that permitting the use of compelled accident reports within criminal proceedings might increase the likelihood of abusive conduct by the state. In taking accident reports from drivers, police would have a strong incentive or perhaps an unconscious inclination to overemphasize the extent of the statutory duty to report an accident under the Act, in order to obtain relevant information. The effect of such an overemphasis might be to circumvent or defeat a driver's s. 7 right to remain silent when under investigation for a criminal offence." [See *R v White*, 1999 CanLII 689 at paras 62 and 64 (SCC).] This section will likely be the subject of intense *Charter* scrutiny and litigation.

Section 320.21(10) allows courts to draw an adverse inference from the failure or refusal to comply with a demand, presumably aimed at an inference of impairment.

Section 320.32 deals with the certificate of an analyst, qualified medical practitioner, or qualified technician. It continues the existing system where the certificate is proof even without proof of the signature but continuing to require "reasonable notice of the intention to produce it" and a copy being provided. Application to require attendance for cross-examination continues to exist but is now required to be made in writing at least thirty days before the application is to be heard and such hearing must be at least thirty days before the trial, thus totalling at least sixty days. Certificates can include relating to prohibition orders.

> 320.36 (2) No person shall use, disclose or allow the disclosure of the results obtained under this part of any evaluation, physical coordination

> test or analysis of a bodily substance, except for the purpose of the administration or enforcement of a federal or provincial Act related to drugs and/or alcohol and/or to the operation of a motor vehicle, vessel, aircraft or railway equipment.
>
> (3) The results of an evaluation, test or analysis referred to in subsection (2) may be disclosed to the person to whom they relate, and may be disclosed to any other person if the results are made anonymous and the disclosure is made for statistical or research purposes.

This portion mirrors existing legislation. However, the existing legislation has been referenced in attempts to deny disclosure of prior evaluations conducted by a particular DRE officer in an attempt to determine through statistical analysis the ability of the DRE officer to properly conduct and interpret the testing regime. Crowns may wish to rely upon this section to limit the disclosure often requested needlessly in each case while the defence may wish to have an able knowledge of the exception to justify their request in order to properly justify their requests.

Most driving offences will now be included as designated offences for the purpose of Dangerous or Long-Term Offender applications pursuant to section 753 of the *Criminal Code*, including dangerous operation, operation while impaired or over the legal limit (though not including the lower drug *per se* limit), failing or refusing to comply with a demand, failure to stop after an accident, and flight from peace officer.

While not an amendment to the *Criminal Code*, Bill C-46, when it comes into force, requires more than just amendment of the *Code*. It also requires follow-up by the government. Specifically:

> 31.1 (1) Within three years after the day on which this section comes into force, the Minister of Justice and Attorney General of Canada must undertake a comprehensive review of the implementation and operation of the provisions enacted by this Act, and prepare a report setting out his or her conclusions and recommendations and including robust data sets collected by government and non-government agencies on the effectiveness of these provisions and the impacts resulting from them.
>
> (2) The Minister of Justice and Attorney General of Canada must cause a report on the review to be laid before each House of Parliament on any of the first 15 days on which that House is sitting after it is completed.

This is important as it requires the re-addressing of matters in the amendments and continued data collection on whether or not the amendments have had a desirable impact. It will be that much more important during those first three years that Crown and defence effectively litigate and put forward their positions so that any issues that do arise come to the attention of Parliament and changes are effected in order to encourage the ongoing evolution of these sections to enhance the justice system long term.

Upon passing, the legislation specifically applies retrospectively from the date the legislation comes into force. The legislation will come into force on the 180th day after the Act receives royal assent. This includes evidential and trial procedural elements. As per the *Charter*, the lesser of either sentencing provisions will take precedence.

CHAPTER 9

Provincial Legislation

With criminal law being governed federally in Canada, and driving and licensing issues being dealt with provincially, it is important to understand the interplay between these levels of government. In most cases, the initial detention, interaction, and investigation of impaired drivers begins as a result of provincially empowered actions by the police. As well, different provincial legislatures are taking different views as to the dangers imposed by drug-impaired driving. Although the tests for criminal culpability are standard across the country, factors such as lesser amounts of drugs in a driver's system, age of the driver, and what searches are allowed in pursuing regulatory charges differ from province to province. This chapter reviews the cogent parts of each province's legislation as it deals with drug-impaired driving.

BRITISH COLUMBIA

Currently, if an officer believes that a driver is affected by drugs, they may conduct a field sobriety test. A failure on this test is grounds to impose a 24-hour administrative suspension and continue with investigation of a criminal charge at their discretion.

British Columbia has not yet introduced any new legislation to deal with drug-impaired driving issues. Because BC has been dealing with alcohol-impaired driving via administrative penalties rather than the criminal justice system, it is expected that the legislature may decide to follow suit with regard to drug-impaired driving. Section 215 of the *Motor Vehicles Act* sets out the current state of the law, including 24-hour suspension of a driver's licence if the officer has grounds to believe the driver is impaired by drug.

The government has currently published the public survey results but not a plan for where they will go from here. The current law also allows police to subject both SFST and DRE testing where the officer suspects or has grounds to believe the accused is impaired by drug.

ALBERTA

Presently, there is an immediate ninety-day suspension for drivers charged with impaired driving or where there are grounds to lay a charge. This includes impaired by drug. As well, there is a continued suspension until the resolution of the criminal charge. Upon reinstatement there is a one-year interlock requirement.

Legislation

- Bill 26, An *Act to Control and Regulate Cannabis*;
- Adds cannabis impairment to *Traffic Safety Act*;
- Bill 29, *An Act to Reduce Cannabis and Alcohol-Impaired Driving*—passed 29 November 2017.

Driving Changes

- Zero tolerance for drivers in Graduated Driver's Licensing (GDL);
  - Zero tolerance for cannabis, alcohol, or combination of cannabis and alcohol and illegal drugs; any breach will lead to thirty-day suspension, seven-day vehicle seizure, and an extension of the GDL program for two years including at least one year of suspension-free driving;
- Any form of impairment leads to 24-hour suspension and vehicle seizure;
- Provincial sanctions for drivers with blood drug concentration, or blood drug and alcohol concentration, over the legal limit in regulations under *Criminal Code* or impairment by drug under the *Criminal Code*;

◇ Immediate licence suspension (ninety days), vehicle seizure (three days), remedial education, ignition interlock program (one year), possible further sanctions via Alberta Transportation Safety Board hearing.

SASKATCHEWAN

At the moment, the administrative consequences for impaired by drug are the same as for impaired by alcohol. The suspension of driving privileges mirrors what a court has ordered. There is, though, a 24-hour suspension available for those who fail or refuse the SFST beyond the consequences pursuant to a criminal conviction.

Legislation

- Bill 112, *Miscellaneous Vehicle and Driving Statutes (Cannabis Legislation) Amendment Act, 2017*—28 November 2018.

Driving Changes

- Zero tolerance for all "New Drivers" for drug-impaired driving with escalating sanctions beginning with sixty-day immediate suspension, three-day vehicle seizure, four demerit points, and remedial education;
- If driver is charged with one of the new *per se* offences under the *Criminal Code* they will face administrative consequences under the *Traffic Safety Act*, including immediate licence suspension until charges dealt with before the court, thirty-day vehicle seizure, remedial education, one- to five-year suspension if convicted depending on prior record (note: no interlock requirement if solely drug);
- If charged with drug-impaired operation, then thirty-day vehicle seizure, licence suspension until charges dealt with by court; if convicted then remedial education, interlock requirement further and one- to five-year suspension depending on prior record;
- See backgrounder chart for further information.

MANITOBA

The administrative sanctions for a conviction for impaired driving are the same whether that impairment is caused by alcohol or a drug. Drivers suspected of being under the influence of drugs can receive an immediate 24-hour roadside suspension. Upon conviction, impaired by drug charges are dealt with the same as impaired by alcohol with escalating sanctions including licence suspensions for minimums of one year, five years, ten years, and life for first through fourth offences respectively.

Legislation

- Bill 11, *Safe and Responsible Retailing of Cannabis Act (Liquor and Gaming Control Act* and *Manitoba Liquor and Lotteries Corporation Act Amended)*;
- Bill 25, *Cannabis Harm Prevention Act.*

Driving Changes

- Changes to *Highway Traffic Act* and *Drivers and Vehicles Act in Cannabis Harm Prevention Act*;
- Prohibits transportation of cannabis anywhere except in trunk and consumption of cannabis in a vehicle;
- Roadside suspension for 24 hours if officer has reasonable grounds to believe driver cannot safely operate vehicle because under influence of drug;
- Maintains same punishment for drug-impaired driving as alcohol-impaired driving.

ONTARIO

The current state of the law in Ontario regarding suspensions involving criminal charges for drug-impaired driving is to treat them the same as being over the legal limit with alcohol. This includes the initial roadside ninety-day suspension and seven-day vehicle impoundment. If convicted, there is a driver's licence suspension for one year, three years, or life for first, second, and third offences, respectively. As well, for first and second offences, there is an interlock device requirement for one and three years, respectively.

Legislation

- Bill 174, *Cannabis, Smoke-Free Ontario and Road Safety Statute Law Amendment Act, 2017*, to repeal two Acts and to make amendments to the *Highway Traffic Act* respecting alcohol, drugs, and other matters.

Driving Changes

- Zero tolerance for any drug for young (twenty-one and under), novice (G1, G2, M1, M2), and commercial drivers with suspension for three to thirty days, depending on quantity, prior record, and which class the person falls under;
- Exception to zero tolerance for individuals with medical prescription for drug;
- Drug-impaired drivers who fail SFST would face monetary penalty, licence suspension, ignition interlock, and education program on top of *Criminal Code* penalties;
  - Summary of specific penalties on government website, online: www.mto.gov.on.ca/english/safety/impaired-driving.shtml#penalties.

QUEBEC

An officer who has reasonable grounds to believe an individual is impaired while driving, if such belief is confirmed by DRE tests, will immediately suspend the person's licence for 24 hours. There is no suspension for failure on SFST tests. There is a ninety-day suspension for refusal to perform tests. Upon conviction, a rehabilitative education program is also proscribed. Upon conviction an administrative suspension between one to three years for a first offence, three to five years for second or subsequent offences will apply, and this could be longer if bodily harm or death occurred or for failure to participate in rehabilitative programming.

Legislation

- Bill 157, *An Act to constitute the Société Québècoise du cannabis, to enact the Cannabis Regulation Act and to amend various highway safety-related provisions.*

Driving Changes

- Sanctions post-conviction are set as the same as alcohol-impaired driving;
- Roadside suspensions based on zero tolerance for drivers with drugs in system;
- Police can ask for saliva sample if suspect driving high and can suspend licence for ninety days if sample is positive;

- If ongoing addiction issues, then province can suspend driver's licence pending assessment or terms.

NEW BRUNSWICK

New Brunswick does not currently have an administrative suspension for individuals suspected of driving while impaired by drug or upon being charged. Upon conviction, the minimum penalty of twelve months' suspension will apply under the provincial administrative scheme.

Legislation

- Bill 16, *Cannabis Control Act*;
- Bill 17, *Cannabis Management Corporation Act*;
- Bill 18, *Cannabis Education and Awareness Fund Act*;
- Bill 19, *An Act to Amend the Motor Vehicle Act*—Royal Assent 20 December 2017;
- Bill 20, *An Act to Amend the New Brunswick Liquor Corporation Act*.

Driving Changes

- Create three-step test for drivers impaired by cannabis;
  - Could have licence suspended immediately;
- Step 1: use device measuring THC in saliva;
- Step 2: assessing impairment through test such as asking to walk in straight line;
- Possible step 3: blood test;
- Zero tolerance for new drivers and drivers younger than twenty-one via *per se* testing.

NOVA SCOTIA

As things stand, there are no administrative penalties or loss of licence for drug-impaired drivers in Nova Scotia. An individual charged may drive immediately, from an administrative standpoint, though doing so could risk a further *Criminal Code* charge if impairment remains.

Nova Scotia has announced that it plans to update its provincial legislation surrounding the legalization of marijuana, including its *Motor Vehicle Act*, but has not yet stated or published what changes it plans to make.

PRINCE EDWARD ISLAND

If a peace officer has reasonable and probable grounds to believe that a driver is impaired by drug then the officer can issue an immediate 24-hour driving suspension. If the accused fails SFST testing, then there is a seven-day suspension. There is a further ninety-day administrative driving prohibition effective seven days after the 24-hour roadside suspension is issued if charges are laid. Impoundment of the vehicle involved will occur if an impaired-driving charge is laid.

Prince Edward Island has announced that it expects to be releasing legislation dealing with the legalization of marijuana and its impact on driving in the winter of 2018 but as yet has not done so.

NEWFOUNDLAND AND LABRADOR

A person suspected of impairment by drug can be requested to surrender their licence (section 60.02 of the *Newfoundland and Labrador Highway Traffic Act*) for a period of seven days (section 60.03).

A conviction for driving while impaired by drug under section 253 of the *Criminal Code* carries a twelve-month driving suspension (section 65(1)). According to section 73.1(1), there is a mandatory use of the ignition interlock device for those convicted under sections 253, 254, and 255 of the *Criminal Code* for a period of twelve months for a first conviction.

The successful completion of an education program prior to reinstatement of driving privileges for alcohol- or drug-related offences is required (section 196(1)(u.1)). A person may be required to provide for screening tests to determine whether or not a driver is dependent upon alcohol or other drugs, and where necessary complete a rehabilitation program before a driver's licence will be reinstated (u.2).

Legislation

- Amend *Liquor Corporations Act*

Driving Changes

- Still working on framework for impaired driving—more legislation expected in 2018; as yet the nature of the changes have not been announced but are expected.

NUNAVUT

Section 116(2) of the *Motor Vehicles Act* allows an officer who believes, on reasonable and probable grounds, that a driver is adversely affected by alcohol or any drug to surrender their licence. According to subsection (4) the officer has discretion to suspend a person's licence from 4 to 24 hours.

A breath test may be voluntarily requested by the accused and if their level is below .06 then they are entitled to have their driver's licence returned to them. There is no further action taken if impaired by drug.

YUKON

Section 256 of the *Yukon Motor Vehicles Act* allows for a 24-hour suspension for suspected drug or alcohol impairment.

NORTHWEST TERRITORIES

A 24-hour suspension may be imposed on someone suspected of being impaired by drug.

CHAPTER 10

Common Concerns with Drug-Impaired Driving Cases

Given the relative novelty of drug-impaired driving cases or rather the manner in which they are currently being prosecuted, it is not surprising to find that many judicial officers, lawyers, and members of the public are struggling to understand them. Drug-impaired driving has existed alongside alcohol-impaired driving for decades. However, it has been recognized throughout that drug-impaired driving is particularly difficult to prosecute. With the introduction of DRE and SFST testing, it was hoped that such a difficult and complicated area of law might be simplified in some way. Unfortunately, it seems that the opposite effect has occurred. With the legalization of marijuana and the increasing prevalence of drugs, both medically prescribed and illicit, being present in society, it is important that triers-of-fact are properly educated as to the purpose and abilities in the current testing provided for by law. A drug recognition expert officer is given their expertise without the need for a *Mohan* voir dire. However, it is sometimes forgotten, especially where a jury is not present, that such a voir dire can serve to educate the trier-of-fact as to the use and weight that can be apportioned to the evidence before them. Just because one is not required does not mean that it may not still be a good idea to perform some function of reviewing the science behind the testing to better inform the trier-of-fact as to the usefulness of the evidence being provided. In short, there may be little that is required, as impairment may be obvious. However, in the cases where the impairment is not so obvious, then that is the perfect time for an experienced police officer, as the DRE officer is likely to be, to provide an opinion, just as any other layperson is allowed to, regarding the ability of the individual to operate a motor vehicle.

The best expert testimony tends to be educational rather than conclusive. A strong prosecutor can use the Socratic method in court to educate the trier-of-fact to come to the same conclusion that they have—namely, that the individual charged was impaired to operate a motor vehicle and that that impairment was the result of consumption of a drug. The opinion of any officer or any individual will be tested by the defence and is usually strongest when it admits its frailties alongside, pointing out the reasons why it is credible and reliable.

The legal system is not famous for its ability to adapt quickly to emerging technologies and testing procedures. However, that is exactly what is being forced upon it through changes in legislation. As a result, prosecutors need to be able to educate judges and defence counsel to have the knowledge to deal with the questions that arise.

Unlike alcohol-impaired driving cases, there is no presumption of accuracy in drug-impaired driving cases. As the Ontario Court of Appeal noted in *R v Bingley* [2015 ONCA 439 at para 49, aff'd 2017 SCC 12], although the expertise and admissibility of the opinion of a DRE officer is presumed under the *Criminal Code*, the weight to be given to such evidence is not. The results of this are twofold. Firstly, the evidence of the officer may be open to challenge through a number of ways which are reviewed throughout this book. Medical, psychological, outside factors, and other issues all may give explanations that otherwise negate the expert's opinion. Secondly, although an officer may note all of these issues at the time of testing, there is no read-back or presumption of identity that the results they noted as present when the testing was performed were necessarily there at the time of driving. Simply put, just because a person looks drunk now does not mean they were drunk then. Conversely, there will be cases involving fast-acting drugs, such as inhalants, that may show no effect at the time of testing but nevertheless were present at the time of driving. The prosecution is in an unenviable position in such cases and needs to provide as many links as possible between the evidence of impairment noted by witnesses at the scene or an arresting officer to the evidence of the officer performing other tests. It will become more and more important to note similarities in observations throughout an investigation and it will be expected that defence counsel will seize upon any differences. It will be for the trier-of-fact to determine the significance of any such differences and what weight should be attached to them. Whether the differences result from the changing concentrations of the drug in an accused's body or whether they are explained in a different way or even whether they are unexplainable will have a strong effect on the ability of the prosecution to prove its case.

Currently, urine testing is the most common form of chemical analysis to determine exposure of an individual to drugs. The weaknesses in urine testing are reviewed in Chapter 3, but suffice to say that the mere ability to present whether or not an individual has been exposed to a particular drug or substance but not when, to what quantity, or whether a present amount is in the individual system, is extremely limited. As the prevalence of drugs, and particularly prescription drugs, increases in our society, it is more and more possible that exposure to a drug can occur in methods that are either non-impairing or non-intentional. A study by Angela Rodayan mentioned in Chapter 13 shows that trace amounts of prescription medications have been found in treated wastewater and even drinking water. These studies are not from far afield but have been undertaken in Ontario in municipal water systems there. While it is unlikely that such environmental exposure is significant enough to cause a positive urine test, it is not beyond the realm of possibility. Factors to consider in mounting a proper defence depend on the individual tested, the water treatment systems they rely upon, and exposure elsewhere in the environment, including their workplace. Conversely, the prosecution needs to be ready to explain the significant unlikelihood of such exposure having an impact on an individual. Presuming that consumption of a drug that causes impairment is voluntary, then the onus to raise such a doubt falls upon the defence and can be significant where such environmental exposure will necessarily be somewhat speculative.

As well, impairment by drug can be caused by the interaction of a drug and other contributing factors in the human body. However, some impairment must be caused by a drug. It is not enough to say that the drug had some effect but that the effect caused impairment of the ability to operate a motor vehicle. Effect is important. For this reason, it is important to understand the different ways to describe drug interaction with other human behaviour and conditions.

The three main methods of explaining impairment in combination are **additive**, **synergistic**, and **antagonistic**. Additive impairment is where the impairment caused by one factor adds to impairment caused by another factor. Simply, 1 + 1 equals 2. If an individual is partially impaired by drug and partially impaired by something else, then those two events can cause impairment of the ability to operate a motor vehicle that is sufficient to ground a conviction. Synergistic interaction is where the effect is greater than the sum of its parts. The mathematical equation here would be 1 + 1 equals more than 2. This is often the case where individuals consume different kinds of drugs and the interaction is greater than the expected effect of either drug by itself. It is for this reason that polydrug use can be of greatest concern because of the unknown impact that it can often have on any particular individual. Antagonistic effect occurs when the sum effect is less than the sum of the parts, or 1 + 1 equals less than 2. This may again occur in certain polydrug or multiple-drug combinations. The effects of one drug counteract the effects of another, leaving a state of impairment or lack thereof to a lesser state than if either drug had been taken on its own. Due to the great number of drugs in existence and the varying degrees to which they affect particular individuals, cases involving multi-drug use are often the most complex. The signs noted by investigators and lay witnesses may contradict the expected result of a particular drug or drug class because of interacting or conflicting effects of particular drugs. As impairment by drug only requires that the drug was a contributing factor in causing impairment, the prosecution needs only to be able to rely on evidence that shows the drug noted was indeed a contributing factor.

Understanding and being able to explain the different ways in which a drug can contribute to impairment can help to explain to the trier-of-fact the manner in which it contributed to the impairment of the ability to operate a motor vehicle. Where the drug plays no impact or contributing relationship to the ability to operate a motor vehicle, then a conviction will not be founded. Therefore, prosecution and defence must be able to explain contributing factors and how that contribution leads to impairment along with either another substance, another outside force like tiredness, or some other action in the human body.

CHAPTER 11

Into the Future

In the area of impaired driving, new views are emerging constantly. For example, years ago it was unthinkable that requiring passengers to wear seatbelts could be considered as important as zero tolerance for drinking and driving, but now it is. As time goes by, the experience of driving will continue to change and the law regarding impaired driving will change with it. Technology, public perception of the offence, and treatment under the law are in a state of constant evolution.

For alcohol-impaired driving, the US National Highway Traffic Safety Administration (NHTSA) and the Automotive Coalition for Traffic Safety (ACTS) have partnered on the Driver Alcohol Detection System for Safety (DADSS). Begun in 2008, this endeavour seeks to produce a viable technology to screen drivers quickly for alcohol, and immobilize vehicles where the driver has a BAC above a set range (defaulted to over 80 mgs of alcohol in 100 ml of blood but available to be lowered by the user).

AUTOMATED SYSTEMS FOR DETECTING IMPAIRMENT

Currently, two separate detection methods are being considered: first, a breath-based system, and second, a touch-based system. The breath system would use distant/offset spectrometry to remotely measure alcohol in the driver's breath, whereas the touch-based system would use tissue spectrometry through physical contact of the skin to the device.

Both systems have advantages and disadvantages. Obviously, a touch-based system would require the driver to be in contact with a sensor on an ongoing basis. This sort of a system may require multiple sensors to be installed into a steering wheel and require constant or repeated touching by the driver to ensure that the vehicle is not put in motion by a sober driver only to be taken over by a drinking driver. A remote breath-based system may be vulnerable to other passengers in the car and their breath alcohol circulating in the vehicle. Although these vulnerabilities can be managed through proper planning, the final system may require a blend of both systems to ensure the best outcomes.

The DADSS program sets high goals, including measurably high outcomes, with relation to reliability, accuracy and precision, and speed of measurement. Currently in Stage 2 trials, DADSS is investigating the preceding two detection methods in a manner similar to interlock but faster and less intrusive. The system will be held to a Six Sigma quality with regard to reliability, meaning it must be accurate to the sixth standard deviation—a very high-quality efficiency standard. With regard to accuracy and precision, the requirements to avoid false positives and false negatives have been limited to allowing only the smallest percentage of errors, into the third and fourth decimal place, meaning from 1⁄10th of a percentage point to 3⁄100th of a percentage point depending on the BAC being measured. Most important to consumers though will be the requirement for speed of measurement. While current systems, such as ignition interlock devices, often require 30 seconds or more to obtain and analyze a test, the DADSS system has a turnaround of 325 milliseconds, roughly the time it takes to turn on the car. While a drunk driver would still be able to start a car for limited purposes, i.e., to use the heat to stay warm in the winter, they would be locked out of putting the car in motion.

The mandate of the DADSS program is to create a voluntary system that vehicle manufacturers can choose to install. It is specifically not meant as a mandatory safety requirement. However, it is likely that, should such a system prove viable, lobby groups such as MADD (Mothers Against Drunk Driving) will push for its installation. Canada, and even more specifically Ontario, is a relatively small market for vehicle sales compared to the US. Although a large sector of auto manufacturing exists in Ontario, the models produced tend to be identical to American models to allow for cross-border sales. This means that many technologies, such as backup cameras, which have become mandated in the US, are required on Canadian vehicles by default rather than design.

Although rarely an innovator, Canada is often an early adopter. It is likely that the lead in requiring installation of technology such as DADSS will be taken elsewhere and adopted in Canada as a result and not as a prime mover. One needs look no further than current ignition interlock legislation to see that Ontario leaves the approval of such systems to other jurisdictions—namely, the US through NHTSA. However, once adopted elsewhere, Canada often will follow quickly to impose stringent laws if it can provide safer roads.

The impact of US laws is significant in the Canadian market. The technology adopted there will become commonplace here soon after. This is quite evident in motor vehicle safety law. New technologies will be vetted and approved by the federal regulator Transport Canada. Although the provincial governments in Canada deal with regulating roads and drivers, the safety equipment in vehicles is federally controlled. Although much of the lobbying by groups such as Arrive Alive and MADD has recently focussed on provincial legislatures, a sea change in technology like this will require pressure on the federal government.

This sort of technology is in the soon-to-be implemented stage. While it is focussed on dealing with alcohol-related impairment, there is no reason to believe the technology will not be adapted to deal with drug-impaired driving. With the impending legalization of marijuana, there will be a push by public safety groups, especially those with a focus on impaired driving, to develop and fund new technologies to prevent impaired driving, be it by drug or alcohol. Alcohol has been the most commonly found drug in impaired driving and thus harm reduction focuses on it. However, with implementation of systems such as DADSS, there is a significant likelihood that the leading cause of harm will soon be overtaken by other factors such as drug impairment.

With this rise, there can be an expected shift of focus to technologies to deal with the dangers presented. Canada, with an aging population, has a special interest in seeing such technologies developed. A large portion of the general population is under the treatment of some form of medication. Many of these can have impairing effects if used improperly, either intentionally or not.

NEW DRUGS

We need look no further than the schedules to the *Controlled Drugs and Substances Act* to realize the vast number of drugs that are classified as illegal. Even greater numbers exist that are not covered by these schedules but instead are controlled prescription medications in our society. Pharmacology seeks to create a vast array of different chemical structures to try to hone in on the best possible chemical to achieve a particular effect. Treatment of particular symptoms in an individual while limiting side effects is the goal. Similarly, illegal drug manufacturers often produce new forms of drugs in order to skirt the classification of them under *Controlled Drugs and Substances*. In essence, both legal and illegal producers are attempting to do the same thing for vastly different reasons. The result is that new drugs that are variations on chemical structures which have already been identified are created each day. Significant work is required to identify and classify these new chemicals properly as they become known. An example of this is crystal methamphetamine. It was created in an attempt to make a drug using regular available substances. Similarly, there were different variations of particular cannabinoids that disappeared quickly once they were listed in the schedule to the Act. It takes time to develop the ability to test for these new drugs. It is sometimes difficult to properly identify these new drugs with the existing chemical analysis utilized in drug-impaired driving investigations, which is aimed at detecting existing drugs and not new ones.

As well, the ability to understand the effects of these new drugs sufficiently to prove to the criminal standard is particularly difficult for prosecutors. With the impact of drug interaction, mixing one drug with another in the human body can be even more difficult to know or understand given the state of flux that the human body is often in. Different people metabolize drugs in different ways and certainly are affected in different ways, depending on the dosage of each drug or drugs in their interaction. For these reasons, it is important for prosecutors to work closely with forensic testing to understand the limitations of chemical testing and the intricacies involved in it. As well, it means that continued work will need to be done by front-line agencies to always be adaptable to new situations as they present themselves. New drugs are often created to fill a particular market need, legal or illegal. Similar chemical structures often have similar effects on the human body but whether there is sufficient testing to determine the exact effect will be key in providing the needed tools to ground a conviction. Conversely, it is important for defence counsel to understand that while similar drugs do often have similar impact, they are not always the same. As a result, it will be important to continue to challenge the evidence put before the court to ensure that the presumption of innocence is maintained. The most common current drugs remain well known to current criminal law practitioners, both prosecution and defence, and will do so for some time. That is not to say that courts may not be presented with novel drugs and novel scenarios of impairment that need to be tested through the court process as time goes by.

SELF-DRIVING CARS

The dynamic of federal and provincial heads of power in Canada leads to an open future with regard to issues relating to self-driving cars. While federal powers regulate the criminal sphere and safety regulations relating to cars, the provinces hold power in enforcing licensing and driving issues. New vehicle safety measures require approval through the federal department Transport Canada. As well, the department often dictates to car manufacturers which safety measures are mandatory in the installation of vehicles. However, the province may also require certain equipment and holds the final power for penalizing non-compliance by the end user, i.e., the driver. In the case of self-driving cars, the interplay of these jurisdictional issues will need to be resolved. Self-driving cars by necessity impact both the concept of safety equipment and design along with driver licensing and regulation. For example, Ontario Regulation 305/15 creates the framework within which automated vehicles, or self-driving cars, can seek to operate in Ontario. This province has created a ten-year pilot project to allow companies to seek approval to test vehicles with differing levels of automation. It requires the company to be either the manufacturer of the vehicle and authorized under the federal *Motor Vehicle Safety Act (Canada)* to apply a national safety mark to its vehicles under the federal statute, or in the business of converting non-automated vehicles into automated vehicles and have satisfied the provincial registrar of motor vehicles that they have the expertise to properly undertake such conversions (section 7).

The regulation requires the ability of the driver in the vehicle to immediately assume control of the vehicle should the need arise (section 12). This is in direct opposition to the opinion of companies such as Google which feel that the safer manner of proceeding is to create a car where the user cannot interfere with the automated system. In Canada a driver must not only have the ability to take over operation at a moment's notice but is also under a duty to do so should the automation not act properly (section 13). The occupant of the driver's seat is deemed to be the driver, whether or not the automated systems are engaged (section 1). This is important because it makes the occupant liable for any traffic violations that occur. This does not limit and may even extend the liability of a person in the driver's seat who is impaired.

Under the *Criminal Code*, a person who is in the driver's seat of a motor vehicle is deemed in care or control of the motor vehicle and, if impaired, over the legal limit, or refusing to provide a sample, is guilty of an offence. While this is a rebuttable presumption, it is often a high bar to clear. The regulation for automated vehicles would seem to continue and perhaps even expand this concept. At least until the law is reconsidered, there will be no use of automated vehicles to drive home an intoxicated person, at least not without criminal liability continuing to attach. While an impaired person may never intend to actually control the vehicle, they will be deemed to be the driver and liable. Even sleeping in your automated vehicle may increase your likelihood of criminal conviction if impaired, given this deeming section. The ease with which the vehicle may be put in motion through limited physical interaction also heightens responsibility even though the automation will be responsible for the driving, barring an emergency.

Self-driving cars in Canada will face particular issues that exist only in certain locations in America. Canada faces an intersection of a small relative population in contrast to a huge geography. Self-driving cars rely on known roads and mapping. While this will work in many of the larger cities, there is a significant length of roads outside. Further to this, Canadian drivers often face problematic weather conditions for which current self-driving algorithms cannot properly compensate. The idea of black ice is difficult for many humans to understand and compensate for and, simply put, self-driving cars will require significant improvements to both sensor and reaction systems before they are ready to deal with a Canadian winter.

It will be increasingly difficult for the police to prosecute certain offences because a person will be able to blame the self-drive mode. There will need to be some way in which to determine what mode the vehicle was in at a particular moment. This also crosses into offences such as drinking and driving. It does not take much imagination to think of someone using the self-drive mode to get them home safely from a bar after drinking. However, the law as it currently stands criminalizes such a person as they are in "care or control" of the motor vehicle. This law exists to prevent danger from a number of actions such as accidentally putting the vehicle in motion while impaired, and causing danger. Changes will be needed to praise the person who decides not to drive drunk rather than punish them. Some sort of lock-out mechanism to avoid manual override by a drunk occupant will be essential to programming around this legal quagmire.

With the rise of automated and semi-automated driving technologies in Canada, the ability of the police to detect impairment by drugs will be greatly diminished as poor driving is unlikely to be noted. That being said, from a pure safety perspective, the lack of poor driving is what the law seeks to prevent. Thus, the lack of detection may be offset by the lack of danger where automation prevents the risk from impaired drivers.

SFST AND BOATING

Given the increased concern regarding drug-impaired driving that is currently gripping lawmakers, it will only be a matter of time before issues of drug-impaired driving also apply to other modes of transportation. Already, modified SFST are being developed. In certain areas of the US, these SFST are already in use. Given the more dynamic environment that typically accompanies boating, especially recreational boating, where the room to perform standard existing SFST does not exist, other methods must be utilized. The HGN test forms the backbone of the marine SFST battery though the VGN test is also prescribed.

Along with these tests, three others are added. The first is the Finger-to-Nose test, which mirrors the same task but exists in the DRE battery. Two new tests are then utilized. First, is the Palm-Pat test. This requires the subject to put one hand in front of them palm up. The other hand is then put palm down on top of that hand. The top hand is then rotated back-and-forth patting the bottom hand with the back and palm of the upper hand. The bottom hand does not move. The subject counts each pat aloud one-two, one-two. The subject is to start slow but gradually increase speed until a rapid pace is reached. Police may prompt the subject to increase the speed if they feel it is appropriate, i.e., if they are going too slow. The test is to continue for 10 to 15 seconds. Any failure to follow instructions constitutes an indicator. Two or more indicators constitute a fail on the test.

The third task is the Hand Coordination test. The subject is to make a fist with both hands. The left fist thumb is to be placed against the sternum. The right fist thumb side is to be placed against the fleshy side of the left fist. The officer is to demonstrate and then ask the subject to stay in that position until told to begin. The subject is then instructed to count from 1 to 4 placing one fist in front of the other in a step-like fashion. The officer is to demonstrate. The individual is instructed to memorize the position of their fist after counting to 4. They are going to clap three times. They need not count the claps. They are then to return their fist to the memorized position. The officer demonstrates. The subject is then to count from 5 to 8 and move their fists in the reverse order of the rotation previously used while counting from 1 to 4. The officer is to demonstrate this. They are then to return their hands open and palm down to their lap. The officer confirms acknowledgment and then instructs the individual to begin.

For failure on this test, three or more clues must be noted. Any failure to follow instructions is a clue. This ranges from starting too early to forgetting to count to forgetting to change direction when moving fists.

Similar to the standard SFST battery, these tests are validated with regard to alcohol consumption beyond 80 mg of alcohol in 100 ml of blood. That being said, it is likely that they too will be applied to drug-impaired driving at some point.

LEGISLATIVE CHANGES

As we look to the future, it is important to consider the law in different jurisdictions across the country. Currently, British Columbia is an innovator and their strategy, essentially to decriminalize impaired driving, must be considered in relation to the growing issues of drug-impaired driving. By imposing immediate, administrative suspensions as well as rehabilitative programs through their ministry, they are taking a different tact to deal with the strife caused by impaired driving. For example, BC mandates first-time offenders, generally, to be dealt with through a provincial administrative forum whereby a person loses driving privileges immediately and cannot seek reinstatement of them until they pay a reinstatement fee ($1000), take an educational course, and install interlock, and then no sooner than three months after the stop. Certainly, the moral culpability of an individual driving while under the influence of a drug varies wildly based upon the state of facts of each particular case. Every impaired driver is a potential killer, but not every killer is a murderer. When one considers individuals under the influence of a prescription medication, then the moral culpability tends toward the regulatory sphere on the spectrum of blameworthiness. An adult giving in to their disease might also be differently characterized than an individual consuming a drug recreationally, knowing its impairing effect.

Given the reduction in harm that has accompanied the changes made in British Columbia, and the assessment of the true goals of criminalizing drug-impaired driving, these outcomes need to be examined. If the goal is to punish moral blameworthiness, then the criminal justice system is appropriate. However, if prevention or education is the purpose behind the testing, then the regulatory scheme may be more appropriate. Of course, it is always to be balanced against the individual's rights to properly address the allegations against them. That being said, the lesser consequences of the regulatory scheme do justify the lesser ability to challenge opinion, punishment, and actions by the state.

The cost of the criminalization of drug-impaired driving will be great. Because of this, enforcement agencies are already assessing the expected costs in the hundreds of millions of dollars. The cost of saliva testing is currently much greater than that of breath testing. The increased intrusion on the liberty of the individual for the longer testing for drug-impaired driving is of concern. The complications and inevitable challenges made in criminal court will drive the cost of enforcement up even further. As a result, cost as much as any other concern may force drug-impaired driving from the criminal speaker to the regulatory.

It will also be interesting to note how the judiciary deal with the issue of impaired driving where some jurisdictions have essentially decriminalized it and others have not. Generally, criminal actions across the country should be dealt with similarly. Where the same actions are being dealt with differently in certain jurisdictions it may lead to a different view among judicial officers where one strategy or punishment is available in one jurisdiction and not another.

There is no doubt that drug-impaired driving will remain criminal in Canada for many years to come. However, the general enforcement and dealings with this sort of matter may be through other regimes in the near future. Alberta has already begun the adoption of a regulatory scheme similar to British Columbia's and it is likely that other provinces and territories will follow suit in the near future. Nonetheless, lawyers need to be able to have a strong grounding in the principles that underlie drug-impaired driving regardless of the manner in which they will be dealt with by the state. The onus may shift but the importance of ensuring that accurate, scientifically based, reliable mechanisms are in place to assess drug-impaired driving will fall to lawyers litigating issues in whatever environment they find themselves.

ETHICAL ISSUES

There are particular ethical issues somewhat unique to drug-impaired driving cases. Presenting a defence involving a proper assessment of the issues or prosecuting in a manner consistent with the public interest may be different in these cases than in most others.

Both sides are required to meet their duties as applicable to their own job. However, the prosecution is in a particularly unique situation in assessing the value of moving ahead on a charge where a medical defence may be present. The proper evaluation of the issue may require reference to experts or simply to be put before the judge to determine.

It is important to recall that even the presence of a medical issue may not fully explain the actions of an accused in a particular case. As well, the interaction of a medical condition, the drugs used to treat that condition, and any other factors may need to be assessed contextually with all the other evidence to provide a proper assessment of the case. As a result of Canada's open-court system it may be required that an individual has personal information released in a very public setting. However, no mechanism exists to prevent such publication given the importance of the open-court system.

As further ethical issues arise, the assessment of disclosure requests will evolve. It is in this vein that it is important that the defence counsel realize the use to which they may seek to put disclosure provided. There are occasions where defence counsel may unscrupulously request items of disclosure in a mere attempt to determine that the Crown can produce them. It is important for defence counsel to be making proper use of disclosure and to review each case on its merits. It is the few which give the many a bad name in these cases. However, the obligation on the Crown to provide all disclosure that is not clearly irrelevant is a high onus. Therefore, defence should be reviewing all the disclosure provided both to provide their client with the best defence and in the form of academic honesty to better justify the request itself. Rather than merely putting the Crown to the test of providing a list of items, it is important for the defence to properly review them, as this will provide the strongest defence for any defendant and ensure that any conviction is properly grounded. It is for this reason that the Crown should seek to provide that disclosure to ensure that convictions are properly founded.

Prosecutorial discretion allows for review of each case on its merits but also an assessment of the public interest in pursuing such a prosecution alongside the reasonable prospect of conviction. Cases should not proceed where there is no reasonable prospect of conviction but also need to be assessed clearly when determining the public interest in the pursuit of the prosecution. Given the varying degrees of moral culpability involved in the wide range of cases involving drug-impaired driving, it is important for the prosecution to be very much alive to the public interest in prosecuting such matters. Certainly, most matters will justify prosecution on the public interest standard. However, there will be matters where the moral culpability of an accused in a drug-impaired driving case may be so significantly low, given their health and medical issues, that the Crown should not proceed. Each Crown must be bound by their conscience but also by the prosecution manual with which they are provided. It is for this reason that defence may be required to seek out senior Crowns who have the discretion in such matters to properly deal with impaired drug cases.

A proper use of resolution privilege will be key to the ability of prosecution and defence to come to a meeting of the minds in order to try to resolve certain matters. As medical opinion and documentation may be required in such resolution meetings, it is important that both sides understand the use they may make of such information. Defence should be clear when providing information whether it is in hopes of a resolution and whether or not the client could be cross-examined on such information should a trial become necessary.

Another issue that occasionally arises in drug-impaired driving cases is the limited use for which disclosure provided to defence from the Crown can be used. Certain Crown offices require the disclosure provided be used only for the purposes of defence of a particular case. It is for that reason that it may be incumbent upon the defence to request similar disclosure in multiple cases even though they have already reviewed it in another case. This is particularly annoying to a Crown's office but is nonetheless necessary unless information is granted the freedom to be used across multiple cases. Of course, counsel cannot be expected to forget what they have learned in other cases. So it will be up to them to ensure that the knowledge they have gained is appropriately disseminated, either to other counsel or to other cases that they represent, in the proper manner, either by seeking an exception to a disclosure undertaking or seeking to not make such an undertaking at all.

CHAPTER 12

Useful Cases

R v Bingley, 2017 SCC 12

Bingley was observed driving erratically and hitting a car. Officers arrived and saw signs of impairment but Bingley passed the roadside screening for alcohol so they requested a sobriety test conducted by a DRE. Bingley failed this test and was arrested for driving while impaired by drug. The twelve-step Drug Recognition Evaluation was completed at the police station. Bingley admitted to using marijuana and taking two alprazolam in the last 12 hours and his urine showed cannabis, cocaine, and alprazolam. He was acquitted at his first trial which was overturned by the court of appeal and a new trial was ordered. At the second trial the court found that the admission of a DRE's evidence is not automatic and that a voir dire under *Mohan* was required. Bingley was acquitted because the trial judge found on voir dire that the evidence from the DRE was inadmissible as expert or lay opinion. The court of appeal ordered a new trial upon finding that such evidence was automatically admissible without a voir dire.

The issues at the Supreme Court were whether section 254(3.1) provides for automatic admissibility, whether the evidence would be admissible under the common law if not automatically admissible, and if it could be admissible as lay opinion if not expert. The Court found that section 254(3.1) does not provide for the automatic admissibility of a DRE's opinion evidence. As Bingley conceded all *Mohan* criteria were met except for special expertise, the issue is whether the DRE has special expertise. The

Court found that the DRE had knowledge and expertise outside of the trier-of-fact and that knowledge of the underlying science is not a pre-condition because the scope of a DRE's expertise is in the application of the twelve steps and not the scientific foundation of the test. The twelve steps are reliable based upon the statutory framework. The Court found that the trial judge erred in concluding that because the officer was not an expert in the scientific foundation of the test that none of the opinion evidence was admissible. As the Court found the DRE's evidence would be admissible as expert opinion, it did not consider whether it would be admissible as lay opinion. The dissent agreed that the DRE is an expert for the limited purpose of administering the twelve-step evaluation. The dissent disagreed, however, that Parliament determined the twelve-step evaluation was sufficiently reliable to be admitted and suggested that it was only endorsed by Parliament as an investigative tool. The dissent held that it should be open for a trial judge to refuse to admit such evidence. The appeal was dismissed and a new trial was ordered.

WEIGHT ISSUES WITH DRE EVIDENCE

R v Wernicke, 2013 BCPC 90

The weight to be given to a DRE officer's opinion is something which the trier-of-fact must assess. As an opinion, it must be based on proven fact and reasonable in the circumstances.

> 51 The evidence of Mr. Wayne Jeffery, one of the architects of the DRE protocol and the person who has trained almost all of the DRE officers in Canada, failed, in my view, to establish the reliability of the DRE evaluation as an indicator of impairment. Mr. Jeffery's evidence failed to establish any scientific basis for equating performance in divided attention tasks with the ability to operate a motor vehicle, beyond a bald assumption that impairment of ability to perform those tasks would show impairment of one's ability to operate a motor vehicle. He gave no evidence of any tests that had been done to confirm that hypothesis.
>
> . . .
>
> 53 When it was put to Mr. Jeffery on cross-examination that impaired coordination in performing divided attention tasks would not necessarily

mean that one's ability to operate a motor vehicle was impaired, Mr. Jeffery simply answered, "If a person had impaired coordination I wouldn't want him to drive."

54 I find this analysis to be simplistic and unscientific. In my view, Mr. Jeffery's evidence does not establish any foundation for the reliability of a DRE evaluation to determine impairment of a person's ability to operate a motor vehicle, beyond what could be determined by the standard field sobriety tests.

R v Nguyen, 2014 ONCJ 291

The application of *Bingley* allows for the opinion evidence of a DRE officer to be entered. The weight is something which must be decided by the trier-of-fact in the particular case. The officer's opinion should only be given with reference to the tests approved by Parliament and the opinion created for those results. The officer must not expound beyond their expertise and certainly not into the pharmacological effects of drugs absent a *Mohan* approval.

> In my opinion, the provisions regarding the evaluation of suspected drug impaired drivers were intended to provide a simple and efficient means to investigate and prosecute the offences. In some ways, the process was designed to track the breathalyzer provisions. That said, given the subjective nature of the testing and the opinion being offered, it will remain to be seen whether the reality of such investigations and prosecutions will be able to achieve that intention. It is obvious that an evaluating officer's opinion regarding impairment is qualitatively different than an Intoxilizer reading (para 16).

R v Oum, 2014 ONSC 5131

Admissibility is different than weight. Given the decision in *Bingley*, the trial judge had erred in not admitting the opinion evidence. Given the significant training which DRE officers undertake, their evidence should be admitted and considered in light of all the evidence. "The weight to be given to their opinion evidence is a question of discretion by the trier-of-fact and is a separate issue" (para 24).

R v Abbasi-Rad, 2016 ONCJ 542

It will be important for the prosecution to provide information to a trier-of-fact linking the results of the DRE testing to the ability to drive.

> 25 Beyond that though, there was little explanation about how the accused's performance on various DRE tests related to the issue of alleged impairment in the ability to drive. What does it mean if later during a test, one eye converges and the other doesn't? Something? Nothing?
>
> 26 Even with some of the physical motor tests it is not plain how the results relate to impairment at the time of driving. There was no evidence about the relationship, if any, between performance on the one-legged-stand test and the ability to drive. With no baseline as to how the average sober person performs and no baseline as to how this particular accused with his injuries performs sober as opposed to when he is in an impaired state, it is not plain what to make of the results.
>
> 27 Common sense inferences are available of course where the accused exhibits physical or mental errors performing simple tasks where the errors are not reasonably explained otherwise. Combined with other circumstances such as similar observations at the roadside, no intervening drug or alcohol consumption since arrest, evidence of prior drug use, reasonable inferences may be available regarding the physical and mental abilities required to drive safely. It is harder to know what to make of other DRE test errors, but all circumstances are considered here in assessing the overall case for impairment.
>
> 28 The impact of the few significant deficiencies observed in the DRE examination is much reduced in this case where the accused's prior injuries reasonably provide an alternate explanation. The accused's slow movements did not manifest in any observed driving deficiency and the defendant is correct that a number of circumstances indicate his ability to operate his vehicle was not impaired even to a slight degree at the time of operation.

R v Duhamel, 2011 ONCJ 365

To found a conviction it may be first necessary to educate the trier-of-fact as to the significance of passing and failing in certain ways on certain tests. Failure to do so may leave the trier-of-fact in a vacuum, wondering how to assess the weight and importance to be accorded to the results of particular tests. In this case, the accused performed well on some tests and poorly on others. The lack of a *per se* limit can affect a court's ability to assess or attribute weight to analysis of bodily substances beyond presence or absence. Innocent explanations for factors such as blood pressure and balance issues must also be assessed.

R v Manaigre, 2015 MBPC 56

While impaired individuals are more likely to fail the tests that make up the DRE, some sober people may also have trouble with the tests (para 81). Although a lack of driving issues is not determinative to show a lack of impairment, the signs of impairment noted on DRE tests are similarly not determinative of impairment. "The Accused in this case did well on several aspects of the tests and not as well on others. It is also difficult to know how a completely sober person would perform on several of these tests. The presumptive statement of the officer that sober people do not have difficulty with these tests is not helpful" (para 89).

R v Perillat, 2012 SKPC 135

Explaining the relationship between failures on particular tests and the ability to operate a motor vehicle will be important for the prosecution. Failing to do so will leave a trier-of-fact in a position where inferences may not be made.

> When doing the test at the police station, he said she swayed, had eyelid tremors and lifted her head up after 36 seconds. I find myself wondering if the differences in these two tests is significant and how these results relate to whether or not the accused was impaired at the time she was driving . . . . Despite having her hands out and missing some heel-to-toe steps, the accused walked a straight line away from the officer and back to him on both occasions. Again, I find myself asking whether this result is indicative of impairment and if so, how? . . . In any event, I would have appreciated some evidence as to how these observations related to the accused's ability to drive a motor vehicle (paras 31–33).

R v Antosh, 2013 SKPC 81

Wording does matter in impaired by drug cases. Because triers-of-fact may be less familiar with the impact of marijuana consumption when compared to alcohol consumption, issues such as "stoned" vs. "impaired" will arise.

> The present case involves alleged impairment by drugs, which is somewhat different from cases involving impairment by alcohol. In the latter cases the Court can in effect take judicial notice of the standard signs of impairment such as bloodshot eyes, flushed face, unsteadiness on feet and slurred speech. However, in a situation involving alleged impairment by drugs there are no standard symptoms. The fact that the accused's hands were shaking when trying to get his licence from his wallet, in the absence of expert evidence, does not give any indication of impairment by a drug. A more logical assumption, suggested by the investigating officer himself, was that the accused was nervous, as most people would be when placed under arrest. Likewise the lethargic speech of the accused is of little evidentiary value unless contrasted with the accused's speech on other occasions. With reference to the redness of the accused's eyes and the smallness of his pupils, there is no basis on which I can find that this is a symptom of impairment by a drug. I must also consider the fact that the officer did not observe any erratic driving by the accused or any other signs such as unsteadiness on feet, staggering or swaying which would clearly go to the accused's ability to operate a motor vehicle. Accordingly, even on an objective basis, I would find that the symptoms observed by the officer fell short of providing him with reasonable grounds to make a DRE demand (para 25).

R v Bugden, 2015 CanLII 27425 (NLPC)

The symptoms of alcohol impairment are well known. This is why a layperson can give opinion evidence with regard to the impairment by alcohol of another. However, it becomes more complicated where drugs are the impairing, or potentially impairing, factor.

> Unlike for alcohol impairment, there is no generally accepted list of indicia for drug impairment. Given the different effects that various types of drugs can have, this is not unexpected; however, there still must be sufficient indicia for an objective basis to exist to support a belief that a person is impaired by drugs before a DRE demand is given. Here, at best, there may have been indicia to suspect impaired operation of the motor vehicle. Unfortunately, Constable Alcock was not aware that a s. 254(2) demand would in such circumstance be available to demand that

> a person such as the accused perform physical coordination tests prescribed by regulation (para 41).

R v Sodyl, 2013 BCPC 213

The court can take judicial notice of the effects of various drugs. However, in doing so, those symptoms must be consistent with general knowledge or established by credible expert evidence. Where the symptoms are not so common as to fall into the general knowledge of an average trier-of-fact then expert evidence will be required.

> For instance, where a material factor relied upon does not easily fit into the category of indicators of impairment which have been considered in the established authorities, confirmatory evidence from a witness with the appropriate expertise is essential in order to enhance the reliability of those observations and place them in proper perspective.
>
> [20] Again, without wanting to venture into the arena of evidence that the court can properly take judicial notice of, anyone with a cursory knowledge of physiology would certainly question the assertion that opiates cause the pupils to become dilated (paras 19–20).

R v Hase, [2013] OJ No 6420 (Ct J)

The officer needs to relate the opinion that the accused is impaired to an effect on the ability to operate a motor vehicle. While it may be assumed, it should be expressed (para 21).

R v Phinney, 2012 NSPC 68

While not a DRE case, the issue of police expertise and the weight to be afforded to an opinion is something which a court must approach carefully. Police experts are rarely subjected to scrutiny outside of court in the way other scientific experts are. Issues with the ability to "test results, rates of error, peer review and general acceptance in a scientific community of the reliability of opinions gained by any particular scientific method" (para 21) must be considered. A good starting point for a court to determine the weight to be given to an expert includes:

- Has the expert been qualified before and how many times and at what levels of court?

- Does the opinion come from quantifiable research conducted or developed for the purpose solely of testifying in the case before the court?
- Has the expert adequately accounted for alternate explanations?
- Has the expert dealt with all relevant facts in coming to his opinion and has he given the facts proper weight in his analysis?
- Is there a sufficient degree of impartiality and objective analysis such as to give significant weight to his opinion? (para 22).

DIFFERENCES BETWEEN SFST *PEACE OFFICER* AND DRE *EVALUATING OFFICER*

R v Parada, 2016 SKCA 102

Parada was charged with impaired driving. Cst De Bruin was on patrol and observed a vehicle driving over the centre line, shoulder line, and back over the centre lane of the highway so he pulled the vehicle over. Parada was the driver and had trouble retrieving her licence. Cst De Bruin smelled alcohol and, when asked, Parada told him that she had had three beers. Cst De Bruin did not have an approved screening device at the time so he read Parada a demand for sobriety tests. He had Parada perform the Horizontal Gaze Nystagmus test, Walk-and-Turn test, and One-Leg-Stand test. From the results and Parada's driving, the constable formed the opinion that Parada committed an offence under section 253. A breath test was completed at the detachment less than one hour later. Parada was convicted of an over 80 charge and the summary conviction appeal judge dismissed her appeal.

The issue is whether the constable's evidence regarding the sobriety tests is expert testimony and would have triggered procedural obligations of notice from the Crown. The trial judge found this was not expert testimony and pointed to the distinction in the *Criminal Code* between *peace officer* and *evaluation officer* (evaluating officer must be certified drug recognition expert). Section 254(2) of the *Criminal Code* allows a peace officer to demand physical coordination tests as opposed to an evaluating officer and recognizes that peace officers must have another means of developing grounds to make breath demand. This case had a peace officer who conducted exact sobriety tests in the regulations. The court found that it would be contrary to the purpose of the 2008 *Criminal Code* amendments to require the Crown to qualify the arresting officer as an expert witness to explain the impaired driving investigation. The court found that *Bingley* demonstrates that the *Criminal Code* requires a DRE to make a determination regarding impairment. Further, testing officers must have a higher level of qualification and training than peace officers. The court explained that arresting officers are not required to have special training or knowledge to perform the sobriety test or to be qualified to testify to the results of the test because a DRE does not need to be qualified by a *Mohan* voir dire. Therefore, a *Mohan* voir dire was not required to qualify Cst De Bruin as an expert and the appeal was dismissed.

USE OF HOSPITAL RECORDS

R v Hatchard, 2016 BCCA 134

Hatchard was driving across the centre lane of the highway and collided with a car driving in the opposite direction. His blood sample showed therapeutic levels of methadone and potentially toxic levels of diazepam (Valium). He was charged with impaired causing bodily harm and dangerous driving causing bodily harm. The RCMP forensic toxicologist testified that the combination of methadone and Valium would impair his ability to operate a motor vehicle. Hatchard argued that he had not consumed Valium and that his blood must have been contaminated before being analyzed. The hospital record before his sample was taken showed that Hatchard admitted to taking Valium before driving. Hatchard said he did not remember making such a statement.

The issue is whether the trial judge erred in relying on the statements in the hospital records for the truth of their contents. There was no evidence of the *Ares v Venner* requirements and the statutory requirements for the business records exception were not established. The court accepted the Crown's argument that the hospital records were admitted as *prima facie* proof of the truth of their contents because the defence agreed to their admission (para 22). The court found the judge did not err, granted an extension of time to appeal, but dismissed the appeal. Hatchard's appeal of his sentence was dismissed in 2016 BCCA 388.

This highlights the importance to defence counsel to speak to their client. Statements against interest made to a person in authority may be excluded as being compelled or against a *Charter* right. However, statements made to other civilians, witnesses, or medical personnel are more likely to be included. For this reason, it also becomes important for the prosecution to seek out all possible witnesses and determine if any statements were made to them, which may aid in the prosecution of a case.

MENS REA

R v King, [1962] SCR 746

The seminal case regarding the *mens rea* component of impaired driving comes from *King*. It affirms that *mens rea* is an essential element that the Crown must prove but creates a rebuttal presumption where if the prosecution can prove impairment by drug then the onus shifts to the defence to show that the consumption of the drug was not voluntary or that the accused did not know, or have reasonable grounds to believe, that the drug could have an impairing effect. This issue becomes more heightened with the introduction of drugs, particularly marijuana, which may take forms that may not be immediately apparent to be drugs, such as "**edibles.**" Consider a person who ate a cookie or handful of gummy bears at a party and did not realize that they were consuming THC.

> The existence of *mens rea* as an essential ingredient of an offence and the method of proving the existence of that ingredient are two different things, and I am of opinion that when it has been proved that a driver was driving a motor vehicle while his ability to do so was impaired by alcohol or a drug, then a rebuttable presumption arises that his condition was voluntarily induced and that he is guilty of the offence created by s. 223 and must be convicted unless other evidence is adduced which raises a reasonable doubt as to whether he was, through no fault of his own, disabled when he undertook to drive and drove, from being able to appreciate and know that he was or might become impaired.
>
> If the driver's lack of appreciation when he undertook to drive was induced by voluntary consumption of alcohol or of a drug which he knew or had any reasonable ground for believing might cause him to be impaired, then he cannot, of course, avoid the consequences of the impairment which results by saying that he did not intend to get into

> such a condition, but if the impairment has been brought about without any act of his own will, then, in my view, the offence created by s. 223 cannot be said to have been committed (p 763).
>
> It seems to me that it can be taken as a matter of "common experience" that the consumption of alcohol may produce intoxication and, therefore, "impairment" in the sense in which that word is used in s. 223, and I think it is also to be similarly taken to be known that the use of narcotics may have the same effect, but if it appears that the impairment was produced as a result of using a drug in the form of medicine on a doctor's order or recommendation and that its effect was unknown to the patient, then the presumption is, in my view, rebutted (p 764).

R v Toews, [1985] SCJ No 48

The *mens rea* component is dealt with further in *Toews* at paragraph 7:

> The *mens rea* for driving while impaired is the intent to drive a motor vehicle after the voluntary consumption of alcohol or a drug. The *actus reus* is the act of driving where the voluntary consumption of alcohol or a drug has impaired the ability to drive. Similarly, the *mens rea* for having care or control of a motor vehicle is the intent to assume care or control after the voluntary consumption of alcohol or a drug. The *actus reus* is the act of assumption of care or control when the voluntary consumption of alcohol or a drug has impaired the ability to drive. In proving its case, the Crown must establish the presence of impairment by evidence in the usual way and the element of care or control may be established either by reliance upon the presumption in s. 237(1), where it is applicable, or by showing actual care or control without reliance upon the presumption.

While the intention to put the vehicle in motion is not the *mens rea* component that the Crown need prove, it may contribute to an assessment of the *mens rea* component. The voluntary consumption of an impairing substance is therefore part of both the mental and physical components of the crime.

R v Barrett, 2012 NLCA 12

Barrett was driving the wrong way down a one-way street when he hit and scraped another vehicle going the opposite direction, struck a parked car, then got out of the car and started walking down the street. He was stopped by the police but could not speak due to a recent throat and mouth surgery and was on medication for the resulting pain. He was acquitted at trial for refusing to provide a blood sample, impaired driving, and failing to stop at the scene of an accident. The issues on appeal included whether the judge erred in directing a verdict of acquittal on the refusal charges, determining that Barrett did not have the requisite *mens rea* for the impaired offence, or determining that Barrett did not have the requisite *mens rea* for failing to stop at the scene of an accident. The trial judge directed a verdict of acquittal on two charges of refuse to provide a blood sample because there was no evidence from a qualified medical practitioner who was satisfied Barrett's life or health would not be endangered. Barrett was not able to provide a breath sample due to his medical condition. Barrett agreed to the demand when it was read to him by the officer. When asked by a nurse at the hospital if he consented to his blood being taken, Barrett refused. The court found that the trial judge erred in directing a verdict of acquittal because it was premature to do so as the Crown had evidence regarding the essential elements of the offence. The court ordered a new trial on these counts.

Barrett testified that he had tried to have a mouthful of beer but spilled it on his shirt, resulting in the smell detected by the officers. He also ingested the drug Tramacet as prescribed after his surgery but exceeded the prescribed dosage. The court did not interfere with the trial judge's finding that impairment must have been a result of the medication. The trial judge found that, while the prescription included a warning not to exceed the dosage, it did not include the potential effect that exceeding the dosage could have on Barrett. For this reason, the trial judge concluded that exceeding the dosage was not reckless in the criminal law sense. The court dismissed the appeal of the trial judge's acquittal of driving while impaired.

R v Domb, 2011 ONCJ 756

The *actus reus* is to be in doubt where the prosecution fails to prove that the impairment was as a result of the voluntary consumption of a drug or alcohol. Where the prosecution can prove that any part of the impairment was caused by consumption of alcohol or a drug, then the question shifts to whether the accused knew or ought to have known of its impairing effect and it goes to the *mens rea* of the offence.

With regard to an individual who has been on a particular medication for a significant time which has not earlier impaired their ability to drive, the court must not speculate as to reasons for this. The question of subjective intent, taking "medications on his doctor's orders and ... unaware of any ill effects they might have on his driving that day" (para 88) grounds a proper acquittal.

R v Blayone, [2012] OJ No 2191 (Ct J)

The accused was required to have blood tests taken. He disclosed a needle phobia and was prescribed an anti-anxiety medication. The doctor prescribed five pills of Ativan at 5 mg each. There was some confusion over the fact that the accused was to take one pill at 5 mg rather than five pills. The accused voluntarily took five pills which caused the impairment to drive in fact.

> Given the potential danger to the community, is it reckless to not make any proactive inquiries before deciding to drive home after the procedure or is it reasonable to rely on the health care practitioners to bring such worry to the attention of the patient? Frankly, I see equally convincing arguments for both propositions. The danger to the community that goes with the driving privileges that each of us enjoys can certainly justify the expectation that any driver should be proactive in finding out any side effects of medication that they've been prescribed. On the other hand, from the perspective of any individual driver dealing with a medical practitioner, I see a very strong argument can be made that one would anticipate that, without a warning, that there was no concern with respect to that medication.
>
> In such circumstances, I believe any doubt should be resolved in favour of the defendant (paras 36–37).

R v Hoskins, 2013 ONSC 5989

Individuals are generally expected to understand the nature and consequences of taking a medication. Where a warning about possibly impairing effects has been given, the accused cannot escape liability where they took an unacceptable risk.

R v Weening, 2013 ONCJ 408

The judge in this case found that the accused was well aware of the effects of his usual dose, even if he had resumed taking it after a period of abstinence. However, the judge found that the accused took twice his regular dose. In determining the *mens rea* issue, the issue of accidental impairment was led. “In order to rebut the presumption all there has to be is evidence that raises a reasonable doubt about his knowledge or appreciation of the effects of the drugs consumed and his awareness about his condition while driving. To require proof of a state of non-insane automatism while driving would be to effectively shift the onus to Mr. Weening. And a decision about the defendant’s awareness should be entirely based on the evidence rather than my personal opinion about what he may or may not have been cognizant” (para 24).

R v McGrath, 2013 ONCJ 528

The Crown need not prove voluntary consumption. Voluntariness of proved intoxication is a rebuttable inference. Absent evidence to the contrary, it can be presumed. The defendant must raise the issue of involuntary intoxication and that intoxication was not realized prior to driving. In this case, the prosecution of the impaired-driving offence was at risk if the *mens rea* component of the offence was affected. The question for a trier-of-fact in a case of this sort is whether the accused can point to evidence to successfully rebut this presumption. Where the accused cannot recall the hours prior to the offence, then the court should have trouble believing such a witness in an attempt to rebut the presumption.

SFST MUST ONLY BE USED FOR ITS STATED PURPOSE

R v Yeh, 2009 SKCA 112

Officers saw Yeh drifting from side to side in the lane while driving. They pulled him over, didn’t smell alcohol or drugs, but his skin had a greyish tone and his hands were shaking. Yeh produced his licence and registration and didn’t have any problems answering questions. Officers thought Yeh was “acting strangely” and were concerned that he might be using narcotics. RCMP Cst Wilson (with SFST training but not trained as a drug recognition expert) came and asked Yeh to look at him and open his hands. Yeh's eyes were pink and his hands were shaking. When asked about the last time he used alcohol Yeh said it had been a long time ago. The officer then asked when he had last used a narcotic and Yeh replied by repeating the question and saying, "A long time ago." Cst Wilson asked him to get out of the car but didn't tell him that he was going to conduct sobriety tests or that participation was voluntary. Wilson administered the "Romberg balance test" but did not read the standard police warning beforehand. Yeh had tremors in his arms, demonstrated rapid eye movement, and had slightly enlarged pupils. Cst Wilson concluded Yeh had used cannabis marijuana in the previous 2 to 4 hours but Yeh told Cst Wilson it had been two days earlier. Wilson also concluded that it was more than likely that Yeh was in possession of a narcotic. He told Yeh he was being detained and advised of right to counsel and standard police warning. Yeh did not want to contact counsel. Cst Wilson continued to perform impairment tests on Yeh while a dog was deployed by another constable. The dog did not detect any odour of drugs on Yeh but did from his vehicle. He was charged with possession for purposes of trafficking and being in possession of proceeds of crime.

The trial judge determined that Yeh's section 10(a) and (b) rights had been violated because he had been detained beginning with the initial stop but had not been informed of the reason until later. Also, the trial judge found that his section 8 right had been violated because Cst Wilson had no reasonable grounds to believe Yeh was in possession of narcotics. In finding this, the trial judge also determined that Cst Wilson's lack of expertise meant his opinion regarding Yeh's impairment and drug use were meritless (para 37). The trial judge excluded the evidence based on section 24(2) and found Yeh not guilty. The court of appeal considered Wilson's assessment of Yeh's behaviour with respect to Wilson's training and experience. The SFST course Wilson completed did not include training regarding how long a drug may last in a person's system, nor did it involve recognizing effects of different kinds of drugs. The court of appeal found that Wilson's reading from an unnamed publication regarding drug consumption did not give meaningful weight to his opinion about when Yeh consumed marijuana. The suspicion that Yeh had consumed marijuana in the last 4 hours was not accompanied by a smell of marijuana or any other evidence of drug use in Yeh's car;

therefore the court of appeal found that the dog search violated Yeh's section 8 right and sustained the trial judge's decision to exclude the evidence under section 24(2).

RELATING BACK (PRESUMPTION OF IDENTITY)

R v Jansen, 2010 ONCJ 74

The accused was in a single motor vehicle accident. His speech was slurred and he was talking in a very slow, deliberate manner. His eyes were droopy and half closed. A DRE examination was conducted after arrest at the police station and the DRE Officer indicated the accused was impaired by a CNS depressant. A urine test confirmed the presence of aminoclonazepam. The issue of being able to relate back the impairment noted on the DRE testing was raised. It was acknowledged that the urine test could not determine the quantity of drug or when it was ingested.

> The hurdle for the Crown in these cases is to relate back the findings of the evaluation, and the subsequent chemical analysis, to the time of the driving. In alcohol impairment cases, we frequently see the use of the breath tests mandated by the *Code* for which there are the statutory presumptions of accuracy and identity. The enactment of these presumptions by Parliament was based upon careful consideration of the science of breath alcohol testing, and of absorption and elimination rates as it relates to alcohol. In the case of drugs, the Crown does not have the benefit of the statutory presumptions, and must by cogent evidence relate back the findings of its expert evidence, and the consequent analysis, to the time of driving. In this case, the delay between the time of driving to the time of the evaluation and the urine sample being taken was 2 hours or greater (para 61).

The court acknowledged that there will be cases where the "prominence and severity of symptoms exhibited at the time of arrest" (para 63) lead to an inescapable inference that the accused was impaired.

R v Perillat, 2012 SKPC 135

The time between driving and testing is significant in assessing the weight to be given results of DRE testing. "Finally, it is significant that the accused was stopped at 12:05 a.m. but the Drug Recognition Evaluation was not completed until 1:45 a.m. There is no evidence correlating the test results back to the time of driving" (para 35). The lack of a read-back may be fatal to some prosecutions.

R v Dejesus, 2014 ONCJ 489

The onus on the prosecution in a criminal charge is a high one.

> In my view, it is probable given the manner of driving and the indicia of impairment observed by P.C. Silva and P.C. Mugford at the scene and later by P.C. Reimer during his Drug Recognition Evaluation, that Mr. Dejesus' ability to drive was impaired by a drug or drugs. Of course, proof on a balance of probabilities does not amount to proof beyond a reasonable doubt. The mere presence of drugs in the accused's system with the potential to cause driving ability impairment is some evidence but not sufficient evidence in this case to found a conviction. Dr. Mayers' testimony and report make it clear that urine findings cannot be used to determine the effects, including impairment, of a drug on an individual at a given time since they do not necessarily mean that at the time of the incident there was a blood concentration of a drug or drug effects. Here the police decided not to have a blood sample taken from Mr. Dejesus. A blood sample has the potential to determinatively reveal that the accused's impairment was caused by the ingestion of an identified drug or drugs. A urine sample does not. The evidence does not establish that any identified drugs in the accused's system were in sufficient quantities to impair his ability to drive (para 10).

R v Card, [2012] OJ No 6331 (Ct J)

While the presumptions of accuracy and identity apply to alcohol testing, they do not in the case of drugs.

> Accordingly, it must by cogent evidence relate back the findings of its expert evidence and the consequent analysis to the time of driving. That evidence is not here. So the sorts of evidence that I would be looking for would be: how much of the drug was found in her system, what was the absorption rate, what might have influenced the rate of absorption, what was the elimination rate of the drug from the body's system. Was the state of science of drug testing such that the results could be reliably

> related back to the time of the alleged offence? Was the state of the science investigation such that the presence of the drug in any quantity, or an ascertainable quantity, would lead one to the inescapable conclusion that the defendant's ability to drive, at the time she was found in the car, to have been impaired by the drug? (para 14).

R v Hawkins, [2015] OJ No 3446 (Ct J)
Judicial notice with regard to the symptoms of medications must be undertaken carefully. The effects of most drugs will not be in the common knowledge of an average trier-of-fact. "I cannot take judicial notice that clonazepam, lithium, or a combination of both, or a combination of one or both with some alcohol, would impair one's ability to operate a motor vehicle. Furthermore, there is no evidence of the quantity and dosage of the medication that she took at 11:30 a.m. and its retention period in the body" (para 27).

R v Klatt, [2014] OJ No 2302 (Ct J)
A judge should not take judicial notice of a brand name of a drug equating to a different name for a drug being found in an accused's body. Proving the *actus reus* of the offence will require more than impairment and the presence of a drug. There must be a link between these two pieces of evidence in order to ground a conviction. "It is simply not sufficient for the Crown to say her ability to drive surely seems impaired and then expect the court to jump to the conclusion that it must be caused by certain drugs in her system, just because her urine sample shows the drugs present in her system. There must be evidence that assists the trier-of-fact in relating the drugs in her system to the impairment" (para 29). See also *R v Duck* (7 March 2013), Peterborough, Information No 9980122334 (Ont Ct J), Beninger J.

R v Thompson, 2015 ONCJ 705
Where the accused performed well on portions of the DRE testing they must be given credit for this. While evidence of impairment post-driving can be considered in an assessment of the question of impairment at the time of driving, the lack of relation between a urine test and a concentration at the time of driving provides little evidence.

> The police and the Crown have a very difficult challenge when it comes to drivers who are charged with impaired driving especially where the impairment is alleged to be by a drug. There can be no doubt that driving a motor vehicle when one's ability to do so is impaired by a drug is every bit as dangerous as driving while impaired by alcohol. However, while I am sympathetic to the challenge faced by police, the defendant before this court is charged with a criminal offence which must be proved beyond a reasonable doubt (para 78).

ADMINISTRATIVE TRIBUNALS

JRS (Re), 2013 ABTSB 182

Administrative licence tribunals have lesser standards relating to the evidence required to justify the actions taken than the test of proof beyond a reasonable doubt in criminal cases. While toxicological evidence stated "no direct inference can be made with respect to degree of impairment or the time of drug use based on these findings alone" (para 35), the board found, on a balance of probabilities, that the appellant had driven a motor vehicle, having consumed a drug in such a quantity as to impair their ability to drive within the preceding 3 hours.

The board agreed that it could be guided by principles of criminal law but that in all the circumstances, impairment was proven on balance.

Giorio v Wilson, 2014 BCSC 786

Appeal of an administrative 24-hour driving licence suspension was not allowed after the 24 hours had run, due to the wording of the section. As a result, administrative entries on a provincial driving registry may not be appealable to have them removed.

Bandi v Gustard, 2016 BCSC 920

In grounding an administrative suspension, proof of compliance with the statute is required. The test for review is reasonableness. "A decision is unreasonable when it fails to display justification, transparency and intelligibility within the decision making process. Or, as Johnston J. stated in *Giorio v. Wilson*, 2014 BCSC 786 (CanLII) at para 33, when its result does not fall 'within a range of possible, acceptable outcomes which are defensible in respect of the facts and law'" (para 8). The officer who issued the suspension was not trained to administer either SFST or DRE and thus the decision to issue a suspension was not reasonable. The conclusion that there was a reasonable probability that the appellant's ability to drive was affected by marijuana lacked grounding and was overturned.

INNOCENT EXPLANATION AND POSITIVE RESULTS ON TESTING

R v Duplessis, 2012 NBQB 139
The trier-of-fact is entitled, and indeed required, to consider innocent explanations put forth by an accused to explain their behaviour and poor results in DRE testing. If the trier-of-fact finds this evidence credible, then they are required to provide an explanation as to why this evidence does not undercut the Crown evidence or give rise to a reasonable doubt.

R v Henry, 2014 ONSC 4115
Decisions as to guilt must be founded on all evidence. Lack of a drug in a urine test is not necessarily proof that an individual has not consumed drugs. An admission as to consumption of an impairing substance, in this case marijuana, can provide support that grounds a conviction even where no drugs are found in the bodily sample. "Having regard to the erratic driving behavior, again, the evidence of the investigating officer who observed the erratic driving behavior, the evidence of the drug recognition expert and the intensive tests undertaken under the twelve step protocol, the manifest systems of impairment by marijuana, the admission of the accused that he had consumed marijuana, and even considering that the toxicology report, while not supporting the prosecution's case, does not negate it, I find the Crown has proved the impaired charge on the criminal standard of proof beyond a reasonable doubt" (para 36, quoting the trial judge).

The appeal court found that the trial judge applied the relevant legal principles to the facts before the court and the inferences that could be logically drawn from them.

R v Padda, 2015 ONCJ 77

Where an accused performed well on SFST tests, in this case at the station post-arrest, the good performance must be accorded evidential weight just as poor performance would be. Issues with regard to language barriers or understanding may impact on the ability of an individual to perform physical testing. Without full understanding of the instructions, some issues can be expected and not attributed to impairment. In this case the accused did not speak English and mimicked the actions of the testing officer rather than following the spoken instructions. The court found that this was not a fail but instead was explained.

R v Sanclimenti, [2010] OJ No 5917 (Ct J)

Signs of impairment consistent with fatigue, as much as impairment by a drug, must be linked to the drug to lead to conviction. Should the prosecution fail to link the drug at the time of driving to the ability to impair a motor vehicle, they will fail to secure a conviction.

R v Jamieson, 2015 ONSC 4291

A lack of alcohol should not lead to a presumption that an accused is affected by drugs. Some sign of drug use, through admission, paraphernalia, or some other evidence, must ground a belief that an accused is affected by a drug and not merely by being in an accident, fatigue, or some other non-criminal explanation.

R v Greenwood, 2010 ONSC 912

The prosecution needs to prove that there was impairment of the ability to operate a motor vehicle and that this was caused by the consumption of a drug. It is essential that the prosecution prove that the impairment was, at least, partially caused by the drug, at least beyond *de minimis.* Other contributing factors to impairment can coincide but at least some portion of the impairment must be caused by a drug. In this case, many of the indicia of impairment were consistent with the use of THC and it was open for the trial judge to ground a conviction.

R v Young, [2013] NJ No 455 (Prov Ct)
While impairment of the ability to operate a motor vehicle was proven and the accused had admitted to consumption of Percocet, the link between the two was not established. Elimination of alcohol as a cause of impairment does not mean that the impairment was therefore caused by a drug. A lack of DRE testing or other expert opinion evidence linking the particular drug consumed to the signs of impairment noted led to an acquittal.

R v Petterson, 2015 BCPC 169
Expert medical opinion to provide an explanation as to symptoms observed by police is not necessary. Where the accused provides a "self-diagnosis" and the court accepts that this was a possible cause of poor performance on DRE testing, this will raise a defence. The lack of toxicological evidence, as to presence or absence, as well as effect, was proffered.

R v Evans, 2015 ONCJ 374
Positive results on the DRE testing must count positively toward the innocence of an accused. The results of the DRE test in this case

> establishes that the accused's ability to drive was not impaired to the slightest degree. The finger-to-nose was "perfect." The heel-to-toe was "perfect." His ability to establish time was "close to perfect." His pulse was normal. He was polite and co-operative. His balance was good. His speech was fine. The only issue raised by Constable MacInnes was that he noted some involuntary jerking of the eye movement while doing the Horizontal Gaze Nystagmus and that, on the Convergence Test, while his left eye converged, his right eye did a "loop." There was also a slow reaction by his pupils to light and his muscles (I do not know which muscle) was said to be "flaccid" (para 13).

R v Cartier, 2015 ONCJ 731
Where there is no indication of alcohol consumption, this does not mean that drugs are the reasonable conclusion to explain impairment. Where an accident had occurred and this may explain certain signs of impairment, then the officer must consider these innocent explanations prior to making an arrest. Failure to do so makes the officer's decision not

objectively reasonable. This will effect grounds as well as proof beyond a reasonable doubt (see para 26). SFST testing post-arrest was conducted but such tests are only for screening purposes and a demand is not justified where the accused has already been placed under arrest.

R v Khalaf, 2015 ONCJ 519
The DRE officer's opinion is admissible evidence but is not determinative. It requires more, especially in a case where the officer had to carefully weigh and consider his findings where some test results were outside the normal range while others were not. The fact that drugs may be detected in the urine a significant time after impairing effects have long since passed is important.

R c Jobin, [2002] JQ no 575 (CA)
Drug-impaired driving requires a link between a drug taken and the symptoms noted. Fatigue, stress, and physical or mental disability are not criminalized. While impairment is an essential element of the offence, so too is its cause by alcohol, drugs, or both. Mere impairment without the linkage to the drug taken is not enough.

R v Thompson (21 January 2013) Toronto, Courtroom A (Ont Ct J), Libman J
Where a medicinal drug prescribed by a doctor was alleged to have caused impairment, it was necessary for the Crown to lead scientific or medical testimony with regard to the drug's effect on the human body" (p 15 of transcript).

REFUSAL

R v Smith, 2015 ABPC 214
Where there was no evidence or explanation for the impairment noted by an officer and the accused is found with drugs on him, a conviction may be founded. The "fading attention span" of an accused and inability, perhaps due to impairment, to participate in the DRE testing led to an acquittal on the refusal to submit to demand charge. Convictions on both impaired and refuse may be difficult where an individual is so affected by drug as to be unable to comprehend the requirements of the test due to their impairment by that drug.

R v Dunlop, 2011 NSPC 30

The confusion over whether questions asked during the DRE examination are required can lead to issues with voluntariness. Refusal to answer such questions does not constitute a refusal.

Demanding that a person comply with a process or be charged with refusal, and then including an interrogation in that process, renders replies to the interrogation involuntary and contrary to the right against self incrimination. Use of the results of such an interrogation to advance criminal proceedings against an accused is akin to using a statutorily compelled report as evidence on a criminal charge, against the person who gave the report (para 9).

CHAPTER 13

Studies to Know: Further Readings

DOWNEY, LUKE A ET AL. "The Effects of Cannabis and Alcohol on Simulated Driving: Influences of Dose and Experience" (2013) 50 *Accident Analysis and Prevention* 879–86, online: dx.doi.org/10.1016/j.aap.2012.07.016.

This study reviews the effects of cannabis as well as the additive and synergistic effects of cannabis and alcohol on the ability to operate a motor vehicle. It confirms that cannabis can impair the ability to drive. Of particular interest is the finding that consumption of like amounts of cannabis can lead to different levels of THC in the blood depending on outside factors, in this case the consumption of alcohol. This is important to note given the imposition of *per se* limits since consumption of cannabis alone may lead to one blood level whereas consumption of the same amount of cannabis mixed with alcohol tends to lead to a higher blood concentration as well as a much greater level of impairment.

The study utilized double-blind, placebo-controlled trials. It focussed on individuals aged between twenty-one and thirty-five years old. It involved differing parameters, including no THC, low THC, and high THC consumption crossed with no alcohol, low alcohol (40 mgs alcohol/100 ml of blood administered, 30 mgs of alcohol/100 ml of blood present when tested) and high alcohol (60 mgs alcohol/100 ml of blood administered, 50 mgs of alcohol/100 ml of blood present when tested). A driving simulator was utilized to mimic driving conditions and look for driving impairment and signalling impairment.

The study specifically deals with the issue of whether a person is a regular or occasional cannabis consumer and this variable's impact on impairment. It noted that individuals who were regular users of cannabis tended to have a greater impairment than non-regular users, which was in contrast to expectations. As opposed to learning how to drive after smoking, individuals actually became worse with experience. It is almost as if individuals who do not have experience with consumption of cannabis are more careful in their driving than those who consume more often.

This study used a sample of eighty individuals, thirty-one female and forty-nine male. This small sample size provides a useful starting point but also emphasizes the need for more studies of its kind in order to better assess the impact of cannabis consumption on the ability to drive a motor vehicle safely.

At page 7 of the study it states: "It should also be noted that the degree of impairment in the overall driving and signalling measures was subtle, and that some of the individual driving simulator variables were relatively unaffected by the various THC/alcohol conditions."

The conclusion of the study is that consumption of cannabis, especially when mixed with alcohol and even when alcohol consumption is at an otherwise "legal" range, is a significant danger. However, it also illustrates that many indicia or signs of impairment are not affected negatively by cannabis consumption. For example, collision risk was lowest for low THC and alcohol mix during daytime situations while the highest collision risk was the same mixture during nighttime simulation. THC seemed to have an impact on the ability of drivers to maintain their lane with a much higher incidence but so too was there a positive correlation to THC consumption without alcohol and the ability to react to emergencies generally. Clearly, a larger sample size will be needed to draw better data.

SILBER, BEATA Y ET AL. "The Effect of *d*,l-methamphetamine on Simulated Driving Performance" (2012) 219:4 *Psychopharmacology* 1081–87, online: DOI 10.1007/s00213-011-2437-7.

This study reviews the impact of the use of methamphetamine on the ability to operate a motor vehicle. The study showed that there was no significant effect on the ability to operate a motor vehicle in the simulated driving environment by the use of methamphetamine.

Methamphetamine is one of the most commonly abused stimulants among drivers. It allows longer and sustained periods of driving. It is often abused by professional commercial drivers. It is classed in the DRE program as a CNS stimulant.

The study used twenty participants, equally ten of each gender, aged between twenty-one and twenty-four years of age. A double-blind, placebo-controlled design was used. Participants were given a dose of d,l-methamphetamine or placebo, then required to use a driving simulator.

Some indicators of impairment were more prevalent in those administered methamphetamine while others were not. For example, collision risk increased slightly, as did incorrect signalling at intersections. However, reaction time was positively affected as was the ability to deal with advanced situation collisions.

The conclusion of the study was that the use of methamphetamine did not significantly impair the ability to operate a motor vehicle. However, it did show some impact, both positive and negative, which could be argued as affecting the ability to drive.

The study identified limitations present in the study. Particularly of concern is that ethical considerations prevent the dosing of participants in a study beyond a certain limit. As a result, individuals may be impaired by a higher dose of methamphetamine but such studies cannot be undertaken ethically at this time. The problem this will pose for prosecutors is that the lack of such studies may reduce the ability to ground a conviction where methamphetamine is the only drug found in the system of the accused.

Further, the small sample size of participants limits the ability to extrapolate the data to the general population. The authors decided that while some deficits in the ability to operate a motor vehicle were noted following consumption, such deficits were not statistically significant.

PORATH-WALLER, AMY J & DOUGLAS J BEIRNESS. "Simplifying the Process for Identifying Drug Combinations by Drug Recognition Experts" (2010) 11:5 *Traffic Injury Prevention* 453–59.

The objective of the study was "to statistically identify the set of drug-related cues from Drug Evaluation and Classification (DEC) evaluations that significantly predict the categories of drugs used by suspected drug-impaired drivers (Abstract)." This study assessed the accuracy of DRE experts in classifying the substance(s) taken by participants. The results had shown that combinations of drugs created challenges for DREs to classify. In addition the evidence suggests that officers have a high rate of incorrectly classifying drug use when there were no drugs involved.

Drug use among drivers cannot be reliably detected or measured in breath; as a result blood, urine, or oral fluid is required. The Drug Evaluation and Classification (DEC) program was created in the 1970s in the US to assist the police in identifying drug-impaired drivers. A review of this program found the DEC's overall accuracy in DEC evaluations of suspected impaired drivers to be in excess of 80 percent (see Beirness et al, 2007). A more recent study in Canada reported an overall accuracy rate of 95 percent (see Beirness, Beasley, & LeCavalier, 2013). This shows that while accurate, the program is not perfect, noting that some drug classes are more difficult to detect than others. This is especially the case when drugs are mixed with alcohol or other drugs. It has also been noted that DREs were making their opinion based on one or two pivotal signs or symptoms while ignoring others (Shinar and Schechtman, 2005).

The current study found various tests to be more efficient at identifying various combinations of drugs than others. The worst classification rate was the combination of CNS stimulants and cannabis drug combination, at 52.4 percent. It was also found that the no-drug cases were resulting in a 56.4 percent classification rate.

> Eleven clinical indicators from the DEC evaluations significantly enhanced the prediction of drugs used by suspected drug-impaired drivers, including condition of the eyes, lack of convergence, rebound dilation, reaction to light, mean pulse rate, presence of visible injection sites, performance on the Horizontal Gaze Nystagmus Test, pupil size in darkness, performance on the One-Leg Stand Test, muscle tone, and performance on the Walk-and-Turn Test (p 1).

Using these eleven indicators, an overall classification rate of 75 percent across the three drug combinations was found (CNS stimulants with cannabis, CNS stimulants with narcotic analgesics, cannabis with alcohol). However, this did not take into account the classification rate of no-drug cases.

PORATH-WALLER, AMY J, DOUGLAS J BEIRNESS, & ERIN E BEASLEY. "Toward a More Parsimonious Approach to Drug Recognition Expert Evaluations" (2009) 10:6 *Traffic Injury Prevention* 513-18.

This study set out "to statistically identify the set of drug-related cues from Drug Evaluation and Classification (DEC) evaluations that significantly predict the substance used by suspected drug-impaired drivers" (p 1). This study focussed on the identification of a particular substance in a participant and did not address situations in which a combination of drugs was used. The study found a relatively high success rate in identifying the class of drugs taken with an overall accuracy of 81 percent.

Using the set of twelve signs and symptoms obtained from the DEC evaluation they were able to identify the drug used with a high degree of accuracy. The classification rate for these three drug categories was 83.7 percent for CNS stimulants, 90.9 percent for narcotics analgesics, and 72 percent for cannabis. Similar to the previous study, various signs and symptoms were more indicative of certain drug use than others.

"Nine clinical indicators from the DEC evaluations significantly enhanced the prediction of drug category, including pulse rate, condition of the eyes and eyelids, lack of convergence, hippus, reaction to light, rebound dilation, systolic blood pressure, and the presence of injection sites" (p 1). Using these nine indicators an overall classification of 81 percent over these three drug categories was found.

Unlike the previous study, this analysis does not focus on drug use combinations, reducing the applicability to general practice where drug combinations are common. This study also was limited in relation to the classification of drug categories not present in the study due to insufficient evidence being available.

BEIRNESS, DOUGLAS J, ERIN BEASLEY, & JACQUES LECAVALIER. "The Accuracy and Reliability of Evaluations by Drug Recognition Experts in Canada" (2009) 42:1 *Canadian Society of Forensic Science Journal* 75–79.

This study looked at the accuracy with which DREs in Canada could properly identify the drug(s) ingested by persons believed to be driving while impaired by drug. The study compared drug classification accuracy by comparing the opinion of the DRE experts with the toxicology reports. The second study involved having DREs examining pre-selected evaluation reports. The results showed a relatively high classification of success rate, with various variables such as the type of drug used and the suspect's admissions playing an important role. Inter-rater reliability among DRE was lower than expected, showing issues with re-test reliability.

Study 1: The study used 1,349 DRE evaluations; however, many of the evaluations were done on known or suspected drug users from the community. The DRE opinion and toxicological report in regard to drug classes matched 92.1 percent of the time. The DRE predicted correctly that no drug was present in 80 percent of the cases (nine cases where no drug was present but a DRE believed there was). The study found the miss rate (DRE judging a person to be drug-free when they are not) was considerably higher when the drug used is a depressant. Further study to assist in classifying different drug types will be needed. The suspects' own admissions of drug use may have affected the validity of the study.

Study 2: Seventy-five random police officers who were certified as DREs were asked to review DEC cases where all identifying information was removed as well as toxicological reports, witness statements, etc. Twenty-three cases were used containing six of the seven drug categories used in the DEC program. The results showed inter-rater agreement among officers varied according to the drug category. Among cases involving only a single drug category, CNS stimulants and inhalants had the lowest agreement (51.3 percent and 61.5 percent, respectively). When more than one drug was involved, the study concluded that the raters were correct if at least one of the two drug classes was identified. Three cases involved no drug or were dismissed for medical reasons. Out of these three cases the agreement rate ranged from a low 30.8 percent to 100 percent. This study only gave DREs the objective test results and observations of the subjects as recorded by the original DRE evaluation. Overall inter-rater reliability was 74 percent, suggesting that other variables not permitted in this study are necessary to improve drug classification accuracy.

BEIRNESS, DOUGLAS J, JACQUES LECAVALIER, & DEANNA SINGHAL. "Evaluation of the Drug Evaluation and Classification Program: A Critical Review of the Evidence" (2007) 8:4 *Traffic Injury Prevention* 368–76.

Evaluation studies included laboratory studies (volunteers ingesting drugs) and field studies in order to determine the accuracy of DREs in identifying the drug responsible for the symptoms. Overall, this review found that drug classification accuracy left much to be desired, with most studies showing a lack of drug classification accuracy. This accuracy was also clearly dependent on the type of drug used, with certain drugs much more easily identifiable than others.

LABORATORY STUDIES

BIGELOW, GE ET AL. *Identifying Types of Drug Intoxication: Laboratory Evaluation of the Subject-Examination Procedure*, DOT HS 806 753 (Washington, DC: National Highway Traffic Safety Administration, Washington, 1985).

The study found 53.5 percent of all individuals who were given an active drug were correctly identified. The DEC procedure correctly identified 74.5 percent of individuals who were not under the influence of drug. Of the cases in which participants were given a placebo, the DRE correctly identified 95 percent of participants as not under the influence. The false alarm rate (indicated a drug was present when it was not) indicated that 25.5 percent were identified as being under the influence of drug when they were not. Low dosage participants also resulted in higher miss rates (46.5 percent). Stimulants were shown to have the lowest rate of correct identification (20 percent).

HEISHMAN, STEPHEN J, EDWARD G SINGLETON, & DENNIS J CROUCH. (1996) "Laboratory Validation Study of Drug Evaluation and Classification Program: Ethanol, Cocaine, and Marijuana" (1996) 20 *Journal of Analytical Toxicology* 468–83.

This study involved analyzing participants with various doses of ethanol, cocaine, and marijuana. It found that accuracy in identifying these drugs was low. Cocaine was found to be the most difficult to identify with only a 29.6 percent accuracy rate.

HEISHMAN, STEPHEN J, EDWARD G SINGLETON, & DENNIS J CROUCH. "Laboratory Validation Study of Drug Evaluation and Classification Program: Alprazolam, d-amphetamine, Codeine, and Marijuana" (1998) 22:6 *Journal of Analytical Toxicology* 503–14.

This study involved administering standard doses of alprazolam (a CNS depressant), d-amphetamine (a CNS stimulant), codeine (a narcotic analgesic), or marijuana. The study found that DREs correctly identified that drugs were used; however, there was only 32 percent accuracy in identifying the type of drug used. None of the substances was identified reliably; however, the doses were relatively modest.

SHINAR, DAVID, & EDNA SCHECHTMAN. "Drug Identification Performance on the Basis of Observable Signs and Symptoms" (2005) 37 *Accident Analysis and Prevention* 843–51.

This study re-examined the previous study. The high false alarm rate (57 percent) may have been a result of the officer's belief that all participants had ingested drugs.

FIELD STUDIES

This portion of the review compared DREs identification in the field with toxicological tests to determine accuracy (non-controlled study).

COMPTON, RICHARD P. *Field Evaluation of the Los Angeles Police Department Drug Detection Program* (Washington, DC: National Highway Traffic Safety Administration, 1986).

Difficulty occurred in identifying cannabis (59.7 percent positively identified).

PREUSSER, DF, RG ULMER, & CW PREUSSER. *Evaluation of the Impact of the Drug Evaluation and Classification Program on Enforcement and Adjudication*, DOT HS 808 058 (Washington, DC: National Highway Traffic Safety Administration,1992).

This is one of the largest field studies to date (1,842 cases evaluated). Lab tests confirmed the named drug by the DRE in 64.1 percent of cases.

KERRIGAN, SARAH. *Drug Toxicology for Prosecutors: Targeting Hardcore Impaired Drivers* (Alexandria, VA: American Prosecutors Research Institute, 2004).

This article is designed to provide prosecutors with a primer on prosecuting drug-impaired driving, including the basics of drug toxicology, drug pharmacology, and testing in the US. This study is a good basic review of information that every prosecutor and defence lawyer should know when dealing with a drug-impaired driving case. This study starts by going over basic statistics in relation to drug use while driving. It notes that the extent to which drugs impair driving is often difficult to measure. Many drugs have not been properly studied, making it more difficult to determine their effect on the ability to drive safe. Currently the available evidence has not been used to properly correlate the amount of a substance in one's blood to a corresponding driving impairment: "Drug-related DWI is inherently more complex than alcohol-related DWI. Furthermore, the effect of alcohol on the body and on driving has been well characterized over several decades. Most people are familiar with the effects of alcohol and its ability to impair driving. However, that is not always true for other drugs" (p 5). This recognizes that laypersons, including police, may have difficulty in identifying impairment by a drug or drugs.

Difficulties often arise in drug detection; different drugs have different windows in which they can be detected in bodily samples. Marijuana metabolite stays in urine for a longer period of time, making urine testing unreliable to determine if they had used the drug before driving. Finding a light concentration of THC in the blood, however, may be consistent with recent use of that drug. The study continues by explaining the typical effects of common drugs and how it is further complicated by drugs with multiple symptom characteristics. While the straight line elimination of alcohol at a given rate over a given time (10–20 mgs/100 ml blood per hour) is widely understood, other drugs do not react so simply: "When a drug is metabolized in a non-linear fashion, it is generally not possible to extrapolate backwards from some known drug concentration to some earlier time and concentration. This is true for the majority of drugs, including cocaine, methamphetamine or THC" (p 16).

Pharmacokinetics looks at how the human body recognizes a drug and how that drug is metabolized. This includes the absorption rate, distribution of the drug, and the elimination of that drug from the body. For the majority of drugs, including cocaine, methamphetamine, or THC, it is not possible to determine the concentration of the drug at a previous time. Even if a certain concentration is known at a particular time, due to the non-linear metabolism of these drugs, backtracking cannot be accurately calculated to when the drug was administered:

> With the exception of ethanol, there is so far no widely accepted correlation between the drug concentration in blood and a corresponding level of driving impairment among the scientific community. What is more, factors such as tolerance can have a profound effect on the pharmacodynamics response in an individual. A quantity of cocaine sufficient to produce a mild 'buzz' in a chronic user could be acutely cardiotoxic in a naïve (inexperienced) user, resulting in coma and death (p 19).

Further, the same drug concentration may affect a person differently depending on where they are in the absorption and elimination phase. This is called hysteresis. Drugs may have a different effect unrelated to blood concentration as some create higher blood concentrations while being absorbed but lower blood concentrations while taking effect.

A significant review of ways in which drugs can impair driving is provided at pages 21 to 25, and understanding these impacts can aid in building the proper case needed to prove, beyond a reasonable doubt, the impairment of an individual. Understanding what factors can become impaired opens the ability to prove which were impaired in the particular case. Conversely, defence counsel should know these factors in order to raise doubt about them.

The simplified explanation of concepts in this paper provides useful courtroom examples for explaining complex tests to triers-of-fact. An example of this is:

> A helpful and widely used analogy for the GC-MS method is the following: inside the GC oven is a long, thin, coiled column; think of this column as a racetrack with different types of vehicles (drugs) traveling around it. Some cars are small and fast (methamphetamine), others big and slow (alprazolam); the road conditions (internal coating of the column) also dictate which cars travel faster—cars with special tires might perform better

in the snow, etc. As the cars travel around the track at different speeds they become separated and ultimately each crosses the finish line (the MS detector) and generates a unique "**retention time.**" At the finish line, each car is involved in a serious collision and is essentially blown apart by the MS; this generates pieces (molecular fragments) of the car, such as a bumper, hood, headlight, etc. These pieces are then compared with other cars of the same make, model and year (drug standards)—which allows for a near perfect overlay of car parts (unique drug fragmentation patterns) and finish times (retention times) for a positive drug identification. The GC-MS identification is based fundamentally upon how drugs are "put together" or arranged chemically, including molecular attractions which ultimately dictates how a molecule or drug will fragment or "blow up" (pp 41–42).

The paper explains how laboratories cannot test for every known drug and so DRE opinions may differ from toxicological reports for this reason. While this is a useful explanation, it may not be enough to diffuse doubts in the mind of the trier-of-fact. Nonetheless, it is a useful explanation.

Questions for toxicologists to determine the extent of their experience and knowledge are highlighted in the paper (p 45) and expanded in an appendix. For example:

- What type of toxicologist are you?
- Are you familiar with the field of performance toxicology and in particular, the effects of drugs on driving?
- How did you gain this familiarity?
- What specialized training have you received in this area?
- Are you familiar with drug testing methodology and interpretation of the results?
- How many times have you been qualified as an expert witness on the effects of drugs on driving and in what courts?

PORATH-WALLER, AMY J, & DOUGLAS J BEIRNESS. "An Examination of the Validity of the Standardized Field Sobriety Test in Detecting Drug Impairment Using Data from the Drug Evaluation and Classification Program" (2014) 15:2 *Traffic Injury Prevention* 125–31.

Objective: "[T]to assess the validity of the 3 components of the Standardized Field Sobriety Test (SFST), including the Horizontal Gaze Nystagmus

(HGN), One Leg Stand (OLS), and Walk and Turn (WAT) tests, in identifying impairment among suspected drug-impaired drivers using data recorded during drug evaluation and classification (DEC) evaluations (Abstract)." The drugs included in the study were CNS stimulants, CNS depressants, narcotic analgesics, and cannabis. The study found that each of the three tests was more or less helpful depending on the drug ingested. The results show that each test is insufficient on its own to classify the drug used.

The DEC has employed a much wider range of tests and measurements to identify drug impairment; however, the SFST is still viewed as the general test for impairment, regardless of the responsible substance. A study in 2012 found that d-methamphetamine did not impair performance on the SFST test, although MDMA did (Downey et al, 2012). Another study found that the SFST properly identified THC consumption in drivers with an accuracy of 76 percent (Papafotiou et al, 2005).

Data from DEC evaluations on the three tests that comprise the SFST were analyzed with the four drug categories.

HORIZONTAL GAZE NYSTAGMUS TEST

The inclusion of the three signs from this test resulted in a correct classification rate of 94.6 percent for CNS stimulants, 70.1 percent for CNS depressants, 0 percent for narcotic analgesics, and 1 percent for cannabis.

ONE-LEG-STAND TEST

Based on the four signs from this test the correct classification rate was 59.9 percent for CNS stimulants, 55.4 percent for cannabis, 10.6 percent for narcotic analgesics and no CNS depressant was correctly classified. Subjects in all categories were significantly more likely to sway while balancing or to use their arms to balance.

WALK-AND-TURN TEST

Based on the seven signs from this test the correct classification rate was 72.2 percent for CNS stimulants, 39.7 percent for cannabis, 9 percent for CNS depressants, and 3.5 percent for narcotic analgesics.

The results of this study show that certain symptoms from various drugs are more easily detected depending on the type of test used. Certain tests from the SFST are shown to be unreliable with certain drug classes, while being highly useful with other drug classes. However certain classes, such as narcotic analgesics, are difficult to identify with any of the three tests.

COMPTON, RICHARD P, & AMY BERNING. "Drug and Alcohol Crash Risk" (Traffic Safety Facts Research Note, Report No DOT HS 812 117) (2015) National Highway Safety Administration.

This article goes into detail in regard to the lack of knowledge and study consistency with respect to crash rates for those driving while under the influence of marijuana. This study found that the presence of THC in one's system caused little change to one's risk of being in a vehicular incident when factors such as age, ethnicity, and alcohol use are factored in:

> This study of crash risk found a statistically significant increase in unadjusted crash risk for drivers who tested positive for use of illegal drugs (1.21 times), and THC specifically (1.25 times). However, analyses incorporating adjustments for age, gender, ethnicity, and alcohol concentration level did not show a significant increase in levels of crash risk associated with the presence of drugs. This finding indicates that these other variables (age, gender, ethnicity, and alcohol use) were highly correlated with drug use and account for much of the increased risk associated with the use of illegal drugs and with THC (p 8).

The effect of drug impairment on driving performance and the likelihood of being in an incident are not fully understood. Although studies in relation to driving while under the influence of marijuana are prevalent, they do little to assist in predicting real world crash risks. Certain studies rely on urine tests that tested positive for marijuana; however, this creates the issue of whether the drug was present at the time of driving.

The National Highway Traffic Safety Administration (NHTSA) conducted the largest and most comprehensive study to address alcohol and drug crash risk in the United States. Research teams responded to crashes 24 hours a day, 7 days a week, over a 20-month period in Virginia Beach. The test found that crash-involved drivers had illegal drugs in their system with a rate of 10.4 percent, while 8.8 percent of control drivers (not in accidents) tested positive for illegal drugs. At first glance it appears that the presence of THC increased the risk of crashing by 25 percent; however, this risk reduced dramatically after inputting factors such as demographic variables, age, and gender. After taking the other factors into account it was found that there was nearly no increased risk for a person with THC in their system to be involved in a crash.

In conclusion, this study shows the difficulty of obtaining concrete data when analyzing the effects of marijuana on driving performance. This can be largely attributed to the current methods in place when testing for drugs and the large range of individual responses to various doses of these drugs.

RUBENZER, STEVEN J. "The Standardized Field Sobriety Tests: A Review of Scientific and Legal Issues" (2008) 32 *Law and Human Behaviour* 293–313.

This article discusses the issues in relation to the National Highway and Traffic Safety Administration's (NHTSA) Standardized Field Sobriety Tests and the growing concern that these tests are being used in areas other than blood alcohol consideration, for which they were not designed (i.e., impairment by alcohol or a drug rather than an alcohol *per se* limit). The author continues to question the perception of officers in using these techniques, as human errors are prevalent in the statistics. There is also a varying degree of inter-rater reliability in regard to classification rates. This means different officers get different results where they should not. This review found that studies used to assess the SFSTs should be viewed critically, understanding that the results are often portrayed in an over-optimistic manner. Other factors such as officer observations should be considered when addressing the validity of these roadside tests.

Recent research has noticeably provided misleading evidence. One study by Citek et al (2003) found false positive rates as high as 56 percent while using the Horizontal Gaze Nystagmus (HGN) test. The study noted this as acceptable; rationalizing that this is only one of possibly many pieces of evidence of impairment (p 298). The article continues by addressing concerns of police officers who are incorrectly viewed as competent witnesses in fields in which they are not. Police officers testifying to HGN test reliability is one critical area of issue.

Overall, it has been shown that the accuracy and reliability of individual sobriety tests should not be taken at face value as one should recognize "that such numbers are likely overly optimistic for the tests used as stand-alone measures" (p 302). In many studies it was the observations of the officers that determined classification accuracy, arguably validating the officer's judgments and not the SFST tests. In all of the SFST tests there appears to be vast inter-rater differences. In Citek et al (2003) different officers immediately retested subjects which resulted in inter-rater reliability figures from .59 to .71 for HGN tests. "The various reliability figures reported range from low to clearly unacceptable for tests that provide the basis for arrest and, often, evidence of impairment in legal proceedings (Rubenzer, p 303)." In determining impairment the SFST has been widely accepted despite various other factors such as medical conditions, fatigue, and fear not having been studied in relation to their contributing effects.

DIXON, PHILIP R, TONY CLARK, & BRIAN TIPLADY. "Evaluation of a Roadside Impairment Test Device Using Alcohol" (2009) 41:3 *Accident Analysis and Prevention* 412–18.

This study compared the portable impairment test device known as the Roadside Impairment Testing Apparatus (RITA) with the Field Impairment Test (FIT) that is used by roadside police in the UK. The FIT corresponds roughly to the SFST, though the FIT does not include the HGN test but instead an examination of the pupils and also adds the Romberg Balance Test and the Finger-to-Nose Test. This study found that RITA was more efficient at classifying alcohol impairment. Most notable was the failure of the FIT in determining impairment in suspects over the age of forty, resulting in considerably high false positive rates.

In 2002 development of RITA began, with the aim of creating a device "capable of giving an objective and quantitative measure of impairment due to drugs (Dixon et al, 2009, p 412)." The RITA is a computer-based set of six tests for impairment. For a similar example, see the DRUID app available on most phones or tablets.

This study used sixty male and sixty-two female volunteers across extensive age ranges. The participants were given doses of alcohol with an aim of reaching 90 mg/100 ml. The participants were tested at different time intervals after consumption of alcohol or a placebo. The intention was to use this alcohol impairment test to determine how they would carry over to impairment to drug in the future.

The results of the study included numerous findings. Arguably the most important finding was that FIT had a higher false positive rate than RITA, and that this difference was most notable in subjects over the age of forty. The use of FIT to assess older drivers raised concerns as the false positive rate was 67 percent for those who ingested a placebo who were over forty, whereas it was 27 percent for those under the age of forty. The difference that age had on performance was less noticeable using the RITA. Finally, the study found both tests to have flaws in relation to accuracy, especially FIT, recognizing that further research was needed.

The fact that FIT utilizes more of the divided-attention tests from the DRE testing than the SFST brings the issue of reliance on the usefulness of the particular tests into question when evaluating the weight to be assigned to failures, especially relating to individuals over forty years of age. Given Canada's aging population, this will be especially important when examining both SFST and DRE results in anyone in this age group.

BURNS, MARCELLINE. "The Robustness of the Horizontal Gaze Nystagmus Test" (Los Angeles: Southern California Research Institute, 2007).

This American study looked at the use of the HGN test that is used in field sobriety tests. Three experiments were conducted that looked at the validity of the HGN tests when the testing procedures were varied in specific situations. The first experiment included variations in stimulus speed and variation, as well as the distance of the stimulus from the suspect's face in a laboratory setting. The second experiment was conducted in training workshops and involved varying the participants' position during the test (standing, sitting, or lying down). The third experiment involved examining the results of the HGN test used on participants who had only one functioning eye. The study found little change in the accuracy of the HGN test when these mild variances were made.

EXPERIMENT 1 (STIMULUS VARIATION)

Stimulus Speed: When the stimulus was moved at a speed of 1 second instead of 2—the study found more signs were reported when the stimulus moved at a duration of 2 seconds as opposed to 1 second. The more common error exhibited in the quicker moving stimulus was false negatives, which were deemed less concerning than false positives for law enforcement. However, false positives occurred in 2⁄36 of all tests or roughly 5 percent of the time. As false positives are only possible where readings are under the screening limit of 50 mgs of alcohol in 100 ml of blood, the true false positive rate would be 2⁄9 or just over 20 percent as compared to 1⁄9 or about 10 percent of false positives when done properly.

Stimulus Elevation: The results of the different heights used did not produce drastically different outcomes according to the study, being 2⁄10 false positives.

Distance from Face: The results actually indicated that a distance of 25 cm (10 in) from the person's face as opposed to the standard 12–15 in was more useful for sign recognition by the officers. False positives occurred in 6⁄14 when too close, 6⁄14 when too far, and 7⁄14 when done right. This high rate of false positives in all cases should be concerning.

EXPERIMENT 2 (PARTICIPANT POSITION)

This study found that seating, standing, or supine positions had little to no effect on the detection of impairment.

EXPERIMENT 3 (IMPAIRED EYE TESTS)

Only seven individuals could be obtained for this experiment because of the distinct eye impairment requested for the study. This experiment "yielded a small but statistically significant difference between functioning and non-functioning eyes that is attributable to fewer HGN signs in non-functioning eyes" (p 33). However, due to the sample size, further follow-up research is needed.

The results of the experiments demonstrated the validity of the HGN test and the consistency of the test when minor variations were used. However, it does highlight the need to follow the standardization and only with minor variation.

HETLAND, AMANDA, & DAVID B CARR. "Medications and Impaired Driving: A Review of the Literature" (2014) 48:4 *Annals of Pharmacotherapy* 494–506, online: doi: 10.1177/1060028014520882.

This review looked at thirty studies between 1973 and 2013 that studied various medications and their association with driving impairment. The purpose of the review was to gain a better understanding of the effects of medications on one's ability to drive, in order to enlighten physicians of the potentially driver-impairing (PDI) medications. This study found that many medications caused substantial deprivations to one's ability to drive; however, the extent of these detriments will require further study given the limits of studying crashes retrospectively.

Certain classes of medications proved useful in identifying medications that increased crash risks for patients using them or cognitive impairments. In a study by LeRoy and Morse, barbiturates were found to increase the likelihood of being in a crash by 7.5 times when compared to a person not taking that kind of medication. Other studies found medications such as benzodiazepines double the risk of a car crash and can "cause measurable impairments in cognitive and motor functioning as well" (p 2). An important consideration to take into account is the varying degree in which the body eliminates these kinds of medications. Certain medications like midazolam have a half-life of 1 to 5 hours, whereas diazepam can take 30 to 60 hours to reach 50 percent.

Selective Serotonin Reuptake Inhibitors (SSRIs), citalopram or fluozetine, which are commonly prescribed to those with depression, also carry a slight increased risk of being in a motor vehicle crash, and the risk increases with higher doses. In addition, Second-Generation depressants such as venlafaxine and duloxetine "have been associated with a 78 percent increase in crash rate" (p 7). It is also important to take into account the potential impairment when first taking these medications.

Nonsteroidal Anti-inflammatory Drugs (NSAIDs) such as ibuprofen and naproxen have also been associated with a 58 percent increased crash risk (p 7).

In addition to the preceding medications, further types of drugs have been identified as having a detrimental effect on patients' ability to drive. These include Antiepileptics, Antipsychotics, Skeletal Muscle Relaxants, Hypoglycemic Agents, etc. It is important to take into account the limits of the data identified in this review. The studies used are largely based on retrospective vehicle crash claims and so further studies on real-time impairments will be needed to further understand and identify PDIs.

The article summarizes: "Driving impairment was observed with medication use in numerous studies. These medications may create stress, frustration, and inconvenience when they seemingly control whether a patient can safely operate a vehicle. Although this article discusses several deleterious effects of medication use, positive outcomes should not be underestimated. Medications improve or stabilize many medical conditions, which may also enhance the ability to drive" (pp 10–11).

RODAYAN, ANGELA ET AL. "Linking Drugs of Abuse in Wastewater to Contamination of Surface and Drinking Water" (2015) 35:4 *Environmental Toxicololgy and Chemistry* 843–49, online: dx.doi.org/10.1002/etc.3085.

This study monitored an urban watershed that is heavily impacted by discharges of municipal wastewater to determine the extent of drug contaminants in the water. The concentrations of seventeen drugs of abuse were tested for at a water treatment plant, both upstream and downstream. In addition, the water in a drinking water treatment plant (DWTP) was tested. This study took place in the Grand River in southern Ontario. The study found low levels of various illegal drugs at various testing sites. Certain drugs made it through the DWTP, while other drugs were shown to degrade before reaching this location.

Cocaine and benzoylecgonine (B) were detected at all monitoring locations. There was not a significant decrease in cocaine and B after going through the DWTP. Amphetamines were also detected in the water, with ephedrine being the highest detected amphetamine. However, this is likely due to its high use in non-illegal treatment and the large amount excreted from the body. It was shown that levels of ephedrine decreased with river distance, suggesting possible degradation of the compound. At the DWTP, amphetamine and methamphetamines were not detected in treated or untreated water. Fentanyl was detected in all samples, while levels of oxycodone were low. Levels of fentanyl decreased further downstream.

"The results of the present study demonstrate for the first time that drugs of abuse are present in Canadian surface waters impacted by wastewater discharges" (p 6). This study showed that certain drugs of abuse are contaminating drinking water at low doses, while others are degrading before reaching the DWTP. The potential for non-impairing levels of certain drugs, or even impairing levels, to be present in urine or blood testing through non-intentional consumption is possible, though unlikely.

BURNS, MARCELLINE, & ELLEN ANDERSON. "A Colorado Validation Study of the Standardized Field Sobriety Test (SFST) Battery" (Aspen, CO: Colorado Department of Transportation, 1995).

This is one of three studies which all SFST training reviews and the only one to include any adverse weather conditions such as snow.

This study found that officers successfully identified drivers with BAC levels above the legal limit at a correct arrest rate of 94 percent. The correct release rate was much lower at 64 percent; however, this is affected by inferences stemming from 20 percent of released drivers choosing to not give a sample. The study inferred that all drivers refusing to provide a sample were likely to fail.

During the study, officers only used the Walk-and-Turn, One-Leg-Stand, and HGN. By the end of the study, 305 records were completed. When officers decided to release a driver, the observer would then request a voluntary breath sample to determine the officer's accuracy. They would not be arrested if they failed the test; however, they would be required to take the provided transportation. In the end 20 percent of the drivers that were let go did not provide a breath sample, affecting the accuracy of the study in relation to correct/incorrect release. Due to the absence of this data it was inferred that the majority of those who refused to provide a sample after release were above the legal limit. Based on this assumption the findings were that:

- 94 percent correct arrest;
- 64 percent correct release; and
- 84 percent correct release/arrest overall.

It is interesting to note that drivers who were not appropriately dressed for the weather were more likely to be wrongfully released, the argument being that the officers went through the tests quickly out of concern for the driver's discomfort. Also, despite women being only 18 percent of the sample, they were 38 percent of the incorrect release and 25 percent of the incorrect arrests. This highlights subjective impact on the results of the SFST though typically to the subject's benefit.

WEATHER EFFECTS

Unfortunately, due to time constraints, data collection could not start until February. This limited the number of days in which the weather was bad. The study concluded that severe weather did not affect accuracy but the study failed to gain an appropriate sample size of reports in severe weather conditions, reducing the validity of one of the main areas sought to be addressed.

BURNS, MARCELLINE, & TERESA DIOQUINO. "A Florida Validation Study of the Standardized Field Sobriety Test (S.F.S.T.) Battery" (Washington, DC: National Highway Traffic Safety Administration, 1997).

This is one of three studies that all SFST training reviews. Similar to the study done in Colorado, this study aimed to assess the accuracy of officer's arrest and release decisions based on the SFSTs. The study found that officers using the three tests in the SFST (W&T, OLS, and HGN) were highly accurate when assessing whether to arrest a person for BAC over the limit or for releasing them.

This study was limited to those who were requested to perform the tests; those who drank but were not pulled over or those who did not appear to have drunk alcohol were not included in the study. On some roadside tests the officers used tests in addition to the SFSTs; these have been excluded from the primary analysis. Observers were present at 64 percent of all the stops. Similar to the previous study, there were suspects who were released by the officer, who did not consent to providing a breath sample to the observer for the study.

Between 1 June 1997 and 4 September of the same year 397 records were submitted for the study. The study found the highest percentage of arrests occurred during the beginning of the study and then declined as time passed, indicating that the officer's enthusiasm diminished over time. The mean BAC of the 206 arrested drivers was 0.150 percent, which is high. This subjective factor is of note. The mean BAC of 41 drivers who were correctly released was 0.31 percent. The mean BAC of the nine incorrectly released drivers was 0.115 percent. This is not including those who were released but refused to provide a sample, creating the inference that they were possibly above the legal limit. Despite the result being a suspended licence, 57 individuals refused to provide a specimen for BAC.

The results in this study in terms of correct or incorrect are based on BAC levels, and do not take into account the possibility or signs that the driver was impaired by other substances or conditions. The officers involved in the study made correct decisions to arrest 95 percent of the time. Out of the 197 arrested individuals, 9 were arrested incorrectly by having a BAC lower than 0.08 percent. Of the release decisions, 82 percent were correct. "In general, officers are more likely to err by releasing a driver who is impaired than by arresting one who is not" (p 21).

"During this study, men and women in roughly equal proportions admitted to the officers that they had consumed alcohol" (p 30). This could arguably assist the officers a great deal. Given the high mean BAC level of arrested drivers "an observed loss of car control was the most frequently reported reason the deputies made vehicle stops" (p 34). The biggest cues noted by the officers were failures to maintain a single lane and weaving within a lane. Given the already observed cues prior to stop, the need for and efficacy of the SFST when other signs of impairment are already noted limits the study somewhat.

BIGELOW, GEORGE E ET AL. *Identifying Types of Drug Intoxication: Laboratory Evaluation of a Subject-Examination Procedure*, Report No DOT HS 806 753 (Washington, DC: National Highway Traffic Safety Administration, 1985). Also known as the *Johns Hopkins DIE Validation Study.*

This study involved giving a specific drug dose to volunteer subjects who were then rated independently by four LAPD DREs. The results showed a correct drug classification rate of 91.7 percent.

Eight drug dose conditions were administered under double-blind conditions to eighty male volunteers, aged eighteen to thirty-five, who then received independent evaluations from the four DREs present in the study. The subjects were all males who reported using marijuana in the past year.

Two of the DREs involved were instructors of the DRE program; therefore, they had significantly greater training than standard DRE officers. The DREs were instructed to estimate drug classes even if they were not as confident as they would normally be in a field situation. They were told that no alcohol, PCP, or LSD was administered, that no combinations of drugs were used, and that some participants received a placebo. They were also told of the light drug use past of the participants. D-amphetamine, diazepam, and secobarbital were administered at a dose that was three to six times that of a recommended therapeutic dose. The doses were given at different time intervals.

"This laboratory simulation study does not represent a direct test of the validity of these or related behavioural examination procedures for detecting and identifying drug intoxication in field situations" (p 16). This study failed to take into account the possible inexperience that many of the participants in the study would have had with taking these drugs. This creates issues with validity as experienced users would likely have a higher tolerance. Further issues that would limit the ability to extrapolate this study sample to the general population include the fact that officers were informed to rule out poly-drug use, alcohol, and common hallucinogens. This meant that the DRE officers had fewer classes to choose from.

COMPTON, RICHARD P. *Field Evaluation of the Los Angeles Police Department Drug Detection Procedure*, Report No DOT HS 807 012 (Springfield, VA: National Technical Information Service, 1986). Also known as the *LAPD 173 NHTSA Technical Report.*

"There is no way to determine objectively whether the suspects were actually too 'impaired' to drive safely. The fact that drugs were found in a suspect's blood does not necessarily mean the suspect was too impaired to drive safely" (p 15).

A field study with real suspects was completed to validate the LAPD drug recognition program (what would later become the DRE tests) and to provide further support following the previous lab study. Blood samples were obtained from 86 percent of the suspects involved. Officers were correct 94 percent of the time when claiming that drugs, other than alcohol, were present. The officers were correctly able to identify at least one drug other than alcohol in 87 percent of the suspects. Most of the suspects had used multiple drugs. When a DRE identified a suspect as impaired by a specific drug, the drug was detected in the suspect's blood 79 percent of the time.

This study ran for approximately three months within the city of Los Angeles. Suspects were initially arrested by traffic officers who would conduct a field sobriety test. If it appeared that drugs were involved or if the suspect's BAC level was not consistent with their observed behaviour they would be transported to one of two jail facilities for DRE testing using the LAPD drug recognition procedure. If they were suspected of drug use, the DREs requested a blood sample. If they were deemed to not be under the influence they were released (not tested).

The study selected 25 DREs to participate, identified as having the highest seniority and skill. The DRE agents would use the same tests used in the previous study consisting of: an interview going over medical history; examined physiological symptoms; and a behavioural test (Romberg balance test, OLS, finger-to-nose, W&T). Blood samples were received from 173 of the 201 suspects believed to be under the influence of drugs.

The results show that the DREs are more accurate when the suspects had taken two different drugs as opposed to three or more types. DREs were able to determine one of the drugs used; however, the DREs' accuracy in identifying all the drugs taken decreased significantly with each added drug. DRE officers appeared to have the most difficulty in identifying the use of cocaine.

ADLER, EUGENE, & MARCELLINE BURNS. *Drug Recognition Expert (DRE) Validation Study: Final Report to Governor's Office of Highway Safety, State of Arizona* AZ DOT (Phoenix, AZ: Arizona Department of Public Safety, 1994). Also known as the *Arizona DRE Validation Study*.

Five hundred records from a DRE program were utilized. The purpose of the study was to compare the opinions of DREs with medical reports. Of the 500 cases, 253 specimens had two or more drugs, whereas 163 had only one drug. Of the arrestees, 16 refused to provide a specimen.

The DREs identified at least one drug in cases involving more than one drug, 91 percent of the time. DREs are less efficient at precisely identifying drugs used when more than one is involved. This is associated with certain drug cues overlapping with symptoms of other drugs. The false positives and misses of the DREs in the study equalled 16.5 percent.

The study took cases from a period of fifty-three months where there were no significant changes to DRE evaluations. These cases were taken from data entries dedicated to the Arizona project that were obtained from the Phoenix Police Department and the Arizona Department of Public Safety laboratory. If a person is not seen as impaired then they were released without testing. Certain key variables were used in the study including: eye signs, vital signs, time estimates, and arrestees' admissions.

Cocaine and marijuana were missed most frequently by DREs. "Importantly, unless a marijuana positive from the laboratory is corroborated with evidence of impairment at the time of the evaluation, it does not speak to the question of drug influence" (p 52). The DREs believed a drug was present forty-two times when no drug was found, approximately 8 percent of all tests. This study shows further research is needed to address classification errors when more than one drug is used.

HARTMAN, REBECCA L ET AL. "Drug Recognition Expert (DRE) Examination Characteristics of Cannabis Impairment" (2016) 92 *Accident Analysis and Prevention* 219–29.

The objective of this study was to evaluate toxicologically confirmed cannabis-only cases where DRE examinations successfully identified cannabis only. The purpose was to identify cannabis characteristics on cognitive and psychomotor function. The overall goal was aiming to identify the best overall cannabis-impairment indication. The study found "the most reliable impairment indicators included elevated pulse, dilated pupils, LOC, rebound dilation, and documented impairment in 2 of 4 psychophysical tasks" (p 9).

The study population was all of the cases in which THC was found and detailed notes on the DRE evaluation were available. Any cases involving other drugs or where the suspect admitted to cannabis use were excluded. Individuals older than sixty years were also excluded. The study was divided based on when the blood sample was taken (before, during, or after the evaluation).

Included in the investigation were 302 cannabis DRE cases, and 302 controls were obtained for comparison. In 72.3 percent of cases, the officer detected a cannabis odour. This study found that in order to obtain the most accurate results, blood samples should be taken as early as possible, and not after the DRE evaluation. Eye examinations provided valuable data for determining cannabis use, especially pupil dilation. LOC incidence was seven times higher than the control group.

Overall this study found the indicators in the DRE evaluations to be highly consistent when classifying marijuana use in suspected drivers. Due to the quick metabolism of THC it is important to obtain a blood sample as early as possible to confirm recent marijuana use. The DRE evaluations proved useful in determining the type of impairment following a failed SFST.

PAPAFOTIOU, KATHERINE, JAMES D CARTER, & CON STOUGH. "The Relationship between Performance on the Standardized Field Sobriety Tests, Driving Performance and the Level of Δ9-tetrahydrocannabinol (THC) in Blood" (2005) 155:2 *Forensic Science International* 172–78, online: doi.org/10.1016/j.forsciint.2004.11.009.

The aim of this study was to determine the level of impairment brought on by the consumption of THC, and the ability of officers to determine this type of impairment through the use of the SFST. The study found that driving performance was not significantly impaired 30 minutes after THC ingestion; however, driving performance was significantly impaired 80 minutes after THC consumption. Correct classification of drivers being impaired using the SFST was 65.8 percent for the lower dosage participants and 76.3 percent for the higher dosage participants.

Since THC can remain in the blood for several days this test is focussed on assessing officers' ability to determine whether an individual's driving behaviour is impaired following the consumption of a drug.

The study involved forty participants (fourteen females and twenty-six males) between twenty-one and thirty-five years who had previously smoked marijuana. THC was administered through marijuana cigarettes with THC dosages of 0 percent, 1.74 percent, or 2.93 percent. SFST were used and driving performance was measured using a driving simulator. Immediately after ingestion the levels of THC in the blood were 55 ng/ml with the low dose and 71 ng/ml with the high dose. By 125 minutes THC levels reduced to 2.4 ng/ml and 2.5 ng/ml.

Driving results 30 minutes in showed that driving was not significantly impaired when compared to the placebo group. When tested at 80 minutes, driving was observed to be significantly impaired, regardless of dose, not including the placebo dose. Those who were administered the low dosage were correctly classified as either impaired or not impaired at a rate of 71.8 percent at the 55-minute mark. Only 38.5 percent of those who were not impaired on the driving task were correctly identified as not impaired. With those administered a high dose of THC, only 15.4 percent of those who were not impaired on the driving task were correctly identified as not impaired. Of those who were impaired 92 percent were correctly identified as such.

It has been argued that the reason why the participants who passed the driving test failed the SFST was due to the SFST being a more sensitive test. "The findings of the present study are consistent with previous research in which it has been reported that driving ability is maximally impaired approximately 1 h after the beginning of smoking" (p 7), though this may be the time of highest drug blood concentration. "It should be considered that in real-world scenarios, the amount of false positives could be quite high if the SFSTs alone are used to determine if an individual is driving under the influence of drugs" (p 7).

BEIRNESS, DOUGLAS. *The Effects of Psychoactive Prescription Drugs on Driving* (Ottawa, ON: Canadian Centre on Substance Abuse, 2017).

A review of scientific journals and grey literature, such as technical reports, websites of particular organizations and groups (i.e., CAMH, NHTSA), internet searches, and the International Conference on Alcohol, Drugs and Traffic Safety, was undertaken using a number of different search terms. The goal was to review these with an eye to the likelihood and dangers associated with driving while influenced by drugs, specifically psychoactive ones.

An example of psychoactivity was the comparison between depressant drugs and stimulant drugs. While "depressant drugs slow the speed at which the brain receives, processes and responds to environmental information ... stimulant drugs speed up brain activity and can create a situation where decisions are made impulsively, greater risk is taken" (p 1). Thus, drugs of many varieties, even those with opposite effects, can have impairing effects though this impairment is created in potentially vastly different ways. In certain circumstances, "psychoactive prescription drugs can have a beneficial impact on health and well-being" (p 3), though "many prescription drugs, as well as a variety of over-the-counter (non-prescription) remedies, can also have adverse effects on a person's ability to operate a vehicle safely" (p 3).

Surprising to some, "41 percent of Canadians aged 6–79 had taken at least one medication prescribed to them in the two days prior" (p 4). Given the age range involved, this means that it is not merely the elderly or particularly ill who are medicated but a very significant minority of the population. While not all of these medications would be impairing, and some might even help avoid impairment, some of them will be.

Determining effect, and specifically the effect on a given complex task such as driving, is difficult.

> The pharmokinetics of drugs are considerably more complex than those for alcohol and can involve very different patterns of absorption and distribution, the production of active metabolites, and long and variable elimination rates .... Of particular relevance is an examination of the effects following initial use of the drug, as well as after a stable dose has been used for a period of time. This dual examination is required because tolerance to the acute effects of some drugs can develop with longer term use, minimizing or even eliminating some of the adverse effects on driving (p 7).

To put it simply, some drugs are impairing when first taken but not impairing once an individual acclimates to taking them. A neophyte may be impaired while a seasoned user may be unaffected from the standpoint of impairment. This is most noticeable with opioids:

> [I]n summary, therapeutic use of opioids by a naïve user, problematic opioid use even in a tolerant user, or combining opioids with other CNS depressant drugs or alcohol create a significant risk of driving impairment. Supervised chronic administration with a stable dose does not appear to create significant risk of impairment (p 10).

As mentioned, different drugs will have varying effects on separate individuals. Many will cause impairment. Some, such as non-benzodiazepine hypnotics (z-hypnotics) may cause impairment but may also influence issues of *mens rea* as they can cause activities such as sleep-driving, though this has only been reported anecdotally (p 9). While the intention to consume the drug rather than the intention to operate a motor vehicle is what is required in Canadian law, one wonders if such impact on intent issues may filter into the law more prevalently in drug-impaired driving cases.

Drugs in the amphetamine group:

> cause a lessening of fatigue, an increase in mental and motor activity, an elevation of mood, and a general feeling of well-being. However, their indiscriminate use in attempts to increase capacity for work or to overcome fatigue is undesirable and not necessarily effective. At high doses, amphetamines produce a euphoria that upon abrupt withdrawal of the drug reverts to severe depression and lethargy .... At low doses, stimulants can offset fatigue and delay the need for sleep (citation omitted). However, the administration of amphetamine does not compensate for the detrimental effects of sleep deprivation (citation omitted) .... These studies report that therapeutic doses of amphetamine or methylphenidate can improve driving performance and information processing, and reduce driving errors compared to that of untreated patients. However, 16 hours after administration of amphetamine, inattentive on-road driving errors increased, suggesting a possible rebound effect (citation omitted). In health volunteers, amphetamine improved various aspects of attention and suggested possible enhancements in tracking (citation omitted) ... compliant physician-supervised therapeutic use of methylphenidate or amphetamines can improve driver performance in individuals with ADHD (citation omitted). Inappropriate or problematic use of stimulants, including the use of amphetamines in an attempt to compensate for driver sleepiness, can result in impulsive, erratic behaviour, and can be followed by a period of depression and **dysphoria** that can have detrimental effects on driving (p 11).

Thus, the impact of drug use on the ability to operate a motor vehicle is mixed. "Although many studies reveal a statistically significant increase in risk, there are other studies that show the risk is no different than that associated with a driver who has consumed neither drugs nor alcohol" (p 19). There are simply too many drugs, dosage level, individual factors including tolerance, and kinds of driving to simply state that the consumption of a particular drug will have an impairing effect.

> The experimental research evidence leaves little doubt that psychoactive prescription drugs can adversely affect cognitive and motor functions involved in the operation of a motor vehicle .... Less evidence is available pertaining to the risks associated with the use of amphetamine and antihistamines .... Not all psychoactive prescription drugs with a category exhibit the same degree of adverse effects .... It is imperative to recognize that there are inherent differences between the medical use of psychoactive prescription drugs prescribed by a healthcare practitioner for the treatment of a medical condition and the use of psychoactive substances for other purposes. Whereas medical use of prescription drugs is widely viewed as necessary and beneficial, any other use is deemed potentially harmful and dangerous. One of the major factors involved is dose. Although medical use can involve high doses, non-medical use of prescription drugs is often associated with the use of doses higher than those typically prescribed to treat a medical condition (p 21).

Not all drug consumption hinders the ability to drive and some, rather than being merely neutral, may actually help the ability to drive.

> Further complicating the interpretation of the research is that in some cases the use of the appropriate psychoactive prescription drugs under the supervision of a healthcare practitioner might actually serve to improve the ability of a patient to operate a vehicle safely by helping to alleviate the effects of the disease (citation omitted) (p 22).

Where criminal justice should take this information is to be debated. This study recognizes that public safety is affected equally regardless of the drug causing impairment but goes on to also state that "while most would agree that arresting drivers impaired by alcohol or illicit drugs is appropriate and warranted, a gentler approach for dealing with drivers who are adversely affected by their prescription medication might find favour with many" (p 22) and "in the case of psychoactive prescription drugs, enforcement should perhaps take a secondary role and the primary response to prevent impaired driving should be prevention" (p 23).

LOGAN, BARRY, SHERRI KACINKO, & DOUGLAS BEIRNESS. *An Evaluation of Data from Drivers Arrested for Driving Under the Influence in Relation to* Per Se *Limits for Cannabis* (Washington, DC: AAA Foundation for Traffic Safety, May 2016).

With the upcoming legalization of cannabis products in Canada, this study is of particular note. However, its usefulness goes beyond that and provides information regarding fail rates on particular DRE tests with a control group that was not under the influence of any drugs.

> On the walk-and-turn test, 55.5 percent of drug free subjects were able to complete the test without errors while only 6.0 percent of the cannabis-positive subjects were able to do so. In the one-leg-stand test, 67.2 percent of drug- free subjects were able to complete the test with no errors, while only 24 percent of the cannabis-positive drivers were able to do so. On the finger-to-nose test 49.2 percent of the drug-free subjects performed the test without errors, compared to only 5.2 percent of the cannabis-positive subjects (p 1).

While a correlation exists between the inability to perform the tests, there is also a significant number of drug-free individuals who can similarly not perform the tests without error. The majority of drug free individuals could not perform the finger-to-nose test error free. Further, with relation to particular physical tests, the study notes:

> Over half (54.3 percent) of cannabis-positive arrested drivers had a pulse rate over 90 compared to just 14.7 percent of cannabis-negative drivers.... Whereas 23.6 percent of cannabis-negative drivers were found to have a systolic blood pressure above the average range (i.e., 120–140mmHg), 49 percent of cannabis-positive drivers had a systolic pressure in excess of this range (p 12).

Put clearly, this study recognizes that while failures on the DRE testing show that an individual is more likely to be impaired by cannabis where failure occurs, it is not definitive since many unimpaired individuals also fail such tests. Asking the trier-of-fact to consider how long they could stand on one leg, walk in a heel-to-toe manner, or accurately assess the passage of 30 seconds, especially when adding in age, environmental issues, or illness may be a tact taken by defence. Prosecutors must therefore explain the significance of such testing as a whole and couple it with other observations, especially any of actual driving, and toxicological testing to prove their case. The DRE tests should not be taken in isolation.

Specifically, this study looked at a *per se* limit of 5 ng of THC/ml of blood. It found:

> There is no evidence from the data collected, particularly from the subjects assessed through the DRE exam, that any objective threshold exists that established impairment, based on THC concentrations measured in specimens collected from cannabis-positive subjects placed under arrest for impaired driving. An association between the presence and degree of indicators of impairment or effect from cannabis use were evident when comparing data from cannabis-positive and cannabis-negative subjects. However, when examining differences in performance in these parameters between subjects with high (>5 ng/mL) and low (<5 ng/mL) THC concentrations, minimal differences were found .... Based on this analysis, a quantitative threshold for *per se* laws for THC following cannabis use cannot be scientifically supported (pp 2–3).

The study reviewed numerous DRE tests and found 602 that met the criteria for inclusion. The requirements, such as quantitative toxicological confirmation, complete evaluations and THC as the sole drugs being found, kept the numbers to this. A weakness that was identified by the authors is the time that elapses between the time of driving and the time of blood sampling. "In Colorado the average time from law enforcement dispatch to blood draw in cases of vehicular homicide and vehicular assault was 2.32 hours (SC +/– 1.31 hours) with a range of 0.83 to 8.0 hours, and a median of 2.0 hours" (p 11). This time between incident and testing is of concern because of the relative speed with which drug blood levels drop in cases of THC consumption.

> Following cannabis use, THC concentrations decrease rapidly as a result of metabolism and distribution into tissues including the brain, and blood THC concentrations drop rapidly. In occasional marijuana users, the maximum THC blood concentration was achieved an average of 0.5 hours after smoking and the THC concentration dropped below 5 ng/mL

> in 1–2 hours [20]. In frequent smokers the drop below 5 ng/mL occurred 3–4 hours after smoking (p 24).

This further undercuts whether a *per se* limit is supportable scientifically.

In deciding whether a 5 ng THC/ml of blood limit can be assessed through DRE tests, it was noted that "none of the indicators had sensitivity greater than 80 percent, and only eyelid tremors, finger-to-nose misses, walk-and-turn clues, and overall SFST impairment had specificity greater than 80 percent. Overall accuracy ranged between 51 and 64 percent" (p 19). This suggests that linking impairment to this particular *per se* limit is simply not achievable with these tests. While particular symptoms are noted as indicative of THC exposure on the DRE matrix, the best indicators include: "bloodshot eyes, reddened conjunctivae, droopy eyelids, inability to cross one's eyes, eyelid tremors, dilated pupils, rebound dilation, as well as elevated blood pressure and pulse" (p 24).

The reason why a *per se* limit for THC is especially difficult is that:

> For drugs like THC that are lipid-soluble and have a short distribution half-life, the drug is taken up rapidly into the brain and other fatty tissues where it concentrates while the concentration in the blood declines rapidly. Consequently, the blood concentration is not a useful surrogate for the effect experienced by the subject, especially as the time between ingestion and specimen collection increases beyond a few minutes (p 25).

While setting a *per se* limit seems like a useful exercise in order to deter individuals, the danger inherent to such a limit is that "experience has taught us that establishing a *per se* standard for impairment becomes viewed in the mind of much of the public as an 'illegal limit,' and there are in our experience few prosecutions of drivers with blood alcohol concentrations below the 0.08 *per se* limit" (p 26). The study notes that jurisdictions with *per se* limits need to stand ready to educate the public that a lower level is not necessarily a safe level.

The authors were unable to identify any information about how a drug *per se* limit impacts the rate or prosecution or outcome, including with regard to arrests, findings of guilt, or deaths prevented. The supporting notes also highlight that no states in the US have adopted *per se* limits with regard to oral fluid testing. This may be of some note where such testing may have an impact on provincial suspensions here in Canada, based on oral fluid fails.

BEIRNESS, DOUGLAS J, ERIN E BEASLEY, & PAUL BOASE. *Drug Use among Fatally Injured Drivers in Canada.* (Paper delivered at International Conference on Alcohol, Drugs and Traffic Safety, Brisbane, Australia, August 2013).

This study, restricted to fatally injured drivers, those who were deemed to be operating or in control of the vehicle who died and were tested for the presence of alcohol and/or drugs in the 6 hours after the crash found that testing often identified drugs that were not known to have psychotropic properties and unlikely to cause driving impairment. Of some interest is that different genders tended to be more likely to test positive for different types of drug, males for cannabis and stimulants, while females for depressants and opiates. As well, while alcohol was more frequently noted among young male drivers, including a mixture of alcohol and drugs, drug use was more common among female drivers.

Further, the study found that while alcohol use was more common than drugs among individuals aged eighteen to fifty-five, for both those under eighteen or over fifty-five, drugs were more likely to be noted than alcohol. As well, while alcohol was more prevalent on weekends, drug use was less common on weekends than on weekdays. Alcohol use tended to be seen in late night activity while drug-impaired driving fatalities "were more evenly distributed throughout all times of day" (p 5).

Drugs were found at a level comparable to alcohol in fatally injured drivers, with CNS depressants and cannabis being the most common types. A caution was noted by the authors that "whereas research has established thresholds for alcohol above which it can be confidently presumed that the driver was impaired, the same cannot be said of most drugs. Hence, the mere presence of the substance does not necessarily mean the driver was impaired. Further research is required to help understand the relationship between drug dose and various types of behavioural and cognitive impairments relevant to driving" (p 5).

An important conclusion of the study was:

> There remains a great deal to learn about driving after drug use. Although driving after drinking and driving after drug use appear to be related

> issues, the data suggest that they represent distinct social and behavioural phenomena.... [I]t cannot be assumed that the same techniques, policies, procedures and countermeasures that were developed and utilized effectively to combat drinking and driving can be readily adapted or transferred to deal with the drugs and driving issue. This highlights the need to develop unique prevention and enforcement strategies specific to the use of drugs by drivers (p 6).

BEIRNESS, DOUGLAS J, & AMY J PORATH-WALLER. *Clearing the Smoke on Cannabis: Cannabis Use and Driving—An Update* (Ottawa, ON: Canadian Centre on Substance Abuse, 2015).

This report provides support for many commonly asserted issues in drug-impaired driving with relation to cannabis. It notes:

> Cannabis use is not uncommon among drivers involved in collisions. In a study of seriously injured drivers admitted to a regional trauma unit in Toronto, 13.9% tested positive for cannabis [footnote omitted]. An examination of fatally injured drivers in Canada between 2000 and 2010 revealed that 16.6 percent of those tested were positive for cannabis (Beasley, Beirness, & Boase, 2013). Four out of ten fatally injured drivers who had used cannabis prior to the crash were between 16 and 24 years of age. It should be noted, however, that the data only indicate the presence of cannabis and do not necessarily address the issue of driver impairment (p 3).

This raises an important question in relation to risk management. Whether or not an individual is impaired by a drug, it seems that there is a correlation and possible increase in risk-taking behaviour when cannabis is consumed. "The incidence of driving after cannabis use, particularly among young Canadians, may be attributable in part to the fact that they do not necessarily perceive their driving ability to be adversely affected" (p 5).

"Cannabis also compromised the ability to handle unexpected events, such as a pedestrian darting out on the roadway. Combining cannabis with even small amounts of alcohol greatly increased the negative effects on driving skills (Downey et al, 2013; [footnote omitted])" (p 3).

Unlike alcohol, which has been so prevalent in society for so long, the dosage and effect of the ingestion of cannabis and its impact on the ability to operate a motor vehicle is less well known.

> Whereas some people may show substantial impairment after relatively small amounts of cannabis, others show only moderate effects after the same dose. These differences may be related to task skill, prior experience with cannabis, and the usual dose and frequency of cannabis use. These differences make it somewhat difficult to predict the extent to which a given amount of cannabis will have an impact on a particular individual (p 3).

Continuing in this vein: "Whereas most people are familiar with the usual signs and symptoms of alcohol use (e.g., odour of alcohol, bloodshot eyes, slurred speech, motor incoordination), the same is not true for cannabis" (p 4). This particular commentary is especially important when assessing whether or not a lay opinion is valid with regard to cannabis consumption. While the opinion of impairment by alcohol is well grounded in symptoms so notorious as to be in every trier-of-fact's understanding, the impacts of cannabis impairment, and by extension all other non-ethanol–related drugs, is not so well grounded. This applies equally to civilian witnesses as well as police officers. Without particular pharmacological or toxicological experience, there is no reason why an officer can provide an opinion that observed impairment is caused by a drug without some indicator that drug consumption has occurred or some greater than normal knowledge of the effects of a particular drug category. This will necessitate a review of reasonable suspicion and reasonable and probable grounds in drug-impaired driving arrests to determine whether the officer's decisions are reasonable in the circumstances where knowledge of the impact of particular drugs, rather than say a medical condition, are not known.

Moving forward, when assessing sentencing, it will be important to determine what efforts toward eliminating the risk of impairment by drug have been taken.

> Assessment and rehabilitation programs also play a role in an overall strategy. For those convicted of drug-impaired driving, the extent of

> their drug use should be assessed and, where warranted, treatment and rehabilitation programs made available to help ensure the behaviour does not recur or escalate. Together, these elements can be integrated to create a comprehensive and effective response to the issue of driving while impaired by cannabis (p 5).

BEIRNESS, DOUGLAS J, & D'ARCY R SMITH. "An Assessment of Oral Fluid Drug Screening Device" (2017) 50:2 *Canadian Society of Forensic Science Journal* 55–63, online: DOI: 10.1080/00085030.2017.1258212.

This report was created as part of a project to review oral fluid drug-screening devices to determine their usefulness in law enforcement settings, specifically in matters such as roadside or screening settings. It builds on work done in Europe on the DRUID (Driving Under the Influence of Drugs, alcohol and medicines) project. While the DRUID study did not recommend any devices as being adequate, it noted improvements, which continue, in this technology. To ensure access to a sufficient number of drug users, testing was done utilizing populations in Maricopa County, Arizona, and Jacksonville, Florida, which are also used for DECP (Drug Evaluation and Classification Program) training. Three devices were tested, the Alere DDS-2, the Drägar DrugTest 5000, and the Securetec DrugWipe 6S.

False alarm rates, which are individuals without a drug concentration being incorrectly identified as being over a set limit, are the most worrisome kind of result when justifying the warrantless search of an individual as in the case of roadside screening. With these three devices, false alarm rates varied based on the type of drug being tested for and the particular device being utilized. Generally, with regards to THC, a false alarm rate between 2.3 and 8.6 percent with an average of 4.5 percent was found. With cocaine the rate varied from 0 to 4.5 percent with an average of 0.7 percent; with amphetamine 1.5 to 7.5 percent with an average of 3.6 percent. Methamphetamine saw ranges of 1.3 to 8.4 percent with an average of 3.5 percent. Opioids varied from 4.1 to 11.2 percent with an average of 6.9 percent. Benzodiazepines ranged from 0.8 to 6.5 percent with an average of 2.4 percent. For all drug categories combined, the false alarm rate varied from 3.9 to 11.4 percent averaging 6.8 percent (see Table 2 at p 60 of the study). This means that approximately 7 percent of individuals who tested positive for a drug or class of drug on the screening device were later determined by laboratory analysis to not have that drug in their system. Further to this, approximately 13 percent of individuals who did have a drug in their system were not detected.

The use of these devices was especially questioned with regard to benzodiazepines and amphetamine. Before these devices will be of great use in the detection of such drivers, further refinement will be necessary. The results of 59.2 percent correct calls and 77.1 percent correct calls where individuals had a positive laboratory test for benzodiazepines and amphetamine respectively, means that significant numbers of individuals would slip through this screening net. "These results indicate that further work is required to improve the performance of the devices before the screening results for these latter two types of substances can be relied on in an enforcement setting" (p 61).

The study assesses that the 6.8 percent false alarm rate was low and recognizes the importance of encouraging the lowest possible rate here "to avoid imposing sanctions or additional testing procedures on individuals who have not ingested drugs. This is particularly important in jurisdictions that might ultimately use the results of the screening test to impose immediate administrative sanctions at roadside. To some extent, however, the false alarm rate can be reduced by establishing a higher detection threshold for the drugs. This would require a person to have a higher concentration of the drug in order to get a positive reading" (p 61).

The study concludes by encouraging the continued enhancement of these devices in order to better detect potentially impairing substances that are not well detected or not included in the oral fluid screening-device test panel (i.e., synthetic cannabinoids and dissociative anesthetics). Reliance on such oral fluid testing must not replace law enforcement's ability to discern impairment without these tests. If this were to happen, individuals could merely shift the type of drug they are using to avoid detection with such equipment.

CHAPTER 14

Sentencing

While the mandatory minimums relating to impaired driving apply equally to both drug-impaired and alcohol-impaired driving at the current time, the amendments that are expected to occur shortly will have some effect on this. The elimination of the availability of conditional discharges for such offences will give a greater number of accused an incentive to fight such charges. However, given the unavailability of curative discharges in some provinces and their poor uptake in other areas, this may have little effect overall.

What does change pursuant to the new amendments is the ability of a judge to impose a sentence less than the prescribed minimums, where participation in rehabilitative programming occurs. This can apply to either or both of the fine and the driving prohibition periods. Although the availability of alcohol interlock programs and the ability to enroll in them immediately after a plea may encourage many first-time alcohol-impaired drivers to plea at an early opportunity, the lack of such programs for drug-impaired drivers may encourage participation in a rehabilitative program to avoid a longer loss of licence. The impact of provincial suspensions and the availability of such programming province-to-province will have significant impact once the provincial and territorial governments have their say.

The imposition of a mandatory driving federally imposed criminal prohibition pending completion of such a program is offset to some degree by the provincially imposed mandatory suspensions most provinces currently impose for convictions for impaired driving. Should the provincial and territorial governments change their legislation to dovetail such suspensions with the prohibitions, and importantly reinstate where participating in an approved ignition interlock program ordered by a sentencing judge, then the allure of such programs may not come forward for drug-impaired driving.

The lack of a program similar to ignition interlock to detect drugs when driving and the actions of some provinces to disallow early reinstatement for drug-impaired driving will make the ability of a sentencing judge to reduce the mandatory prohibition that much more important.

The lower penalties and seeming availability of discharges for low-drug blood level offences will presumably lead to an important expansion of caselaw when such discharges are not contrary to the public interest.

The importance of rehabilitation in the case of individuals who suffer from addiction applies both to alcohol and to other drugs. However, the social stigma that prevents many from acknowledging an addiction to alcohol may not exist in certain drug users at the same prevalence, for example, users of medically prescribed drugs.

As well, there are individuals who are impaired or above a *per se* limit as a result of consuming prescription medication. Such individuals who acknowledge their struggles or have a valid medical reason for taking an impairing drug may be more likely to sway a judge and a prosecutor in accepting their entry into a rehabilitation program, and thus avoid the minimum sentences. The lower moral culpability of an accused who is impaired by a medication rather than an illicit substance or of an accused who suffers from a valid medically confirmed addiction weighs in favour of their entry into such a program, perhaps even where their driving is significantly worse than many alcohol-impaired drivers.

When considering the purpose and principles of sentencing enunciated in section 718 of the *Criminal Code*—namely, "to protect society and to contribute, along with crime prevention initiatives, to respect for the law and the maintenance of a just, peaceful and safe society by imposing just sanctions," it is easy to foresee how such rehabilitative programs will be useful in better protecting society through education and therefore crime prevention, than a jail sentence or fine can. As well, where moral culpability may be lower, such sanctions are more likely to promote responsibility and prevention of the harm done by impaired driving.

Although the decision to enter these programs must be equally agreed upon by both Crown and defence, lobby groups such as Mothers Against Drunk Driving encourage them because they act as behavioural modification strategies due to their effectiveness in eliminating the scourge of impaired driving.

The principle of restraint in sentencing, and the importance or proportionality, weigh in favour of different goals in the sentencing of drug-impaired drivers, especially in the early days of this new legislation. Although sentences should be like those imposed for similar offences, the issues unique to particular subsets of drug-impaired drivers will have to be considered. Also, the differing dangers of individuals based on the nature and quantity of the drug they had ingested as well as its prior influence on them may affect the length of a sentence, either increasing or decreasing it.

The continuing availability of conditional sentences in impaired-driving cases where the Crown does not file notice to seek an increased penalty must be examined to determine where and when such sentences may contribute to a safer and more just result in sentencing. The unavailability in cases involving serious personal injury remains.

With enhanced investigatory tools comes enhanced detection. Where an individual suffers from an ongoing addiction or abuse of drugs or a chronic medical condition that requires consumption of an impairing drug, the courts may be more willing to consider forfeiture of a motor vehicle in accordance with the principles of *Manning*. Where the danger of an individual getting behind the wheel is too great, the impact of an order of forfeiture may not be disproportionate where other issues, such as a lessening of the fine, are possible.

When dealing with cases involving bodily harm, the impact on the injured party is the same, whether the impairment was caused by alcohol, an illicit substance, or a prescription. To be blunt, the effect on the victim remains the same regardless of the cause of impairment. However, courts have imposed different sentences on individuals impaired by drug when compared to similar cases involving impairment by alcohol. In *R v Smith*, 2013 BCCA 173, the BC Court of Appeal affirmed the sentencing judge's emphasis on the importance to rehabilitate such offenders. It recognized the accused's issues in life and described her life as one of "tragedy and abuse, compounded by drug and alcohol addiction" (para 1). Because she was a very sympathetic and unique offender, with no criminal record, the analysis in determining the work that the accused did toward rehabilitation is useful. It notes the lesser moral blameworthiness for a person who took steps to deal with her issues but also a greater moral blameworthiness given her lack of prior steps to deal with her addictions. A sentence of two years followed by three years' probation and a ten-year prohibition was imposed. In this case, the accused was grossly impaired by crack cocaine and crossed the centre line, striking a motorcyclist and killing him.

In another case, *R v Hatchard*, 2016 BCCA 388, the BC Court of Appeal dealt with a sentence appeal where the accused had received a sentence of two years less a day, followed by two years' probation and a five-year driving prohibition. The court upheld this sentence. The accused was heavily sedated by methadone, Valium, and diazepam and struck an individual causing massive injuries, including a traumatic brain injury. The accused had two prior related convictions. His lack of insight justified a significant sentence. The court of appeal upheld the sentence imposed by the trial judge. This lack of insight will be of importance when assessing drug-impaired driving. The less the insight into the problems caused by their drug use, the greater the sentence will need to be.

These cases should be viewed in light of *R v Lacasse*, 2015 SCC 64 where the Supreme Court upheld a six-and-a-half-year sentence for alcohol-impaired driving causing death.

While many individuals convicted of drug-impaired driving carry the same moral blameworthiness as alcohol-impaired driving, there are reasons to vary the sentence, either increasing or decreasing it, depending strongly on the circumstances of the offender, their relation to the impairing drug, and the impact their actions had. Drug-impaired driving will not always be treated differently than alcohol-impaired driving, but the circumstances of the offender and their relation to the substance involved may impact matters in a wider range with drugs than alcohol.

APPENDIX

Possible Disclosure Materials

- Notes of arresting officer
- Wording demands
- Notes of DRE Officer, including handwritten and typed
- Face sheet of DRE Officer
- Any and all video—both at roadside and station, including of testing
- Results of any breath tests
- Copy of the matrix used
- Training manual for the DRE Officer
- Training manual for the SFST Officer
- Toxicology report
- Reviewing officer's sign-off for DRE officer
- Certificate of analysis of any drugs found
- Calibration records for instruments used (thermometers and sphygmomanometers)
- Rolling log of the DRE officer (log of all tests done, call made, and whether confirmed by toxicology—agree to delete identifying information)
- Review of pupilometer to determine accuracy
- Ability to attend location to view location of testing
- Raw data from any analysis, including charted results from GCMS or LCMS
- Affidavit of Continuity regarding any bodily sample
- Identification of kind of light used
- Identification of the timepiece used

- Designation of the DRE Officer
- CV of all experts including the DRE Officer and toxicologist
- Calibration of any instruments used to test bodily substances
- Retention time manual for the GCMS or LCMS instrument used
- Information regarding the standards used to check the linearity of any instrument used
- Batch testing results if batch testing of the bodily sample was undertaken
- Release and production of any retained bodily sample for independent testing
- Copy of the seal used on any bodily sample taken

Glossary

Accuracy: the proportion of true positive results (both negative and positive) in the tested group, i.e., (true positives + true negatives) divided by total number of tests. A test may be sensitive and specific but still not accurate. Accuracy means how close the measurement is to a known value—think of a target with shots all around the bull's-eye as accurate but not necessarily precise

Additive effect: where two or more drugs act together to have a total effect the same as the sum of their individual effects, i.e., 1 + 1 = 2

ADSE (Approved Drug Screening Equipment): one of a listed number of equipment for the testing for the presence of drugs in the human body prescribed by regulation made pursuant to the *Criminal Code* of Canada

AI (Approved Instrument): one of a listed number of instruments for the testing of breath to determine the quantity, if any, of alcohol in a person's blood as prescribed by regulation made pursuant to the *Criminal Code* of Canada, i.e., Intoxilyzer 5000C

Antagonistic effect: where two or more drugs act together to have an effect greater than the sum of their individual effects, i.e., 1 + 1 = 1

ASD (Approved Screening Device): one of a listed number of devices for the testing of breath to screen for the quantity, if any, of alcohol in a person's blood as prescribed by regulation made pursuant to the *Criminal Code* of Canada, i.e., Dräger Alcotest 7410 GLC

Ataxia: lacking the ability to voluntarily control and coordinate muscle action; typically includes swaying, unsteadiness on feet, and the like

Benzo: benzodiazepine, a class of psychoactive drugs, often used as a sleep aid or for treatment of anxiety; can be short or long acting; effects vary; one of the most widely prescribed forms of medication

bpm (beats per minute): used to quantify pulse

Conjunctiva: the white portion of the eye (typically noted as reddened or bloodshot)

CNS (Central Nervous System): the nerve tissues that control the activities of the body; the brain and spinal cord; as a result of these controlling the body, the impact of drugs on them is of particular concern to the DRE program

DECP (Drug Evaluation and Classification Program): the program that trains officers for and sets the standards of the DRE program

Diaphoresis: significant, typically excessive sweating

Diastolic blood pressure: when the heart is not pushing (the lower number)

DRE (Drug Recognition Evaluations): the twelve-step evaluation method used to determine whether an individual is impaired by drugs and classify what kind of drug they are impaired by

Dyskinesia: irregular or spasmodic movements, jerkiness

Dysphoria: being unwell or unhappy

Edibles: a method of consumption of marijuana or THC-laden food such as gummies, cookies, or other common foods laced with the drug

Elimination: the manner in which the body processes a substance such as a drug and eventually removes it from the body, and which can be zero order or first order. Zero-order elimination removes the substance at a linear, predictable rate, such as alcohol at 10–20 mgs/100 ml of blood per hour; first-order elimination is the removal in a non-linear manner that is difficult if not impossible to predict, such as THC or cocaine

FtN (Finger-to-Nose): one of the divided-attention tests pursuant to the DRE procedure

GCMS (Gas Chromatography Mass Spectrometry): a complex scientific process by which a urine sample is vaporized, then passed through a column that separates the constituent chemicals in the compound, identifies the chemicals, and ionizes each substance

HGN (Horizontal Gaze Nystagmus): one of the tests used in both SFST and DRE to check for involuntary jerking of the eyes when following a focal point on the horizontal plane

Hysteresis: that drug concentrations soon after a dose cause a greater effect than the same concentrations at a later time. Illustrates the complexity of drug action and that the relationship between drug concentration and effect are not necessarily directly linked

Insufflated: snorting, inhaling, or sniffing of a drug

LCMS (Liquid Chromatography Mass Spectrometry): see GCMS

Linearity: a mathematical function or relationship that allows prediction along the curve when multiple points on that curve are known. This allows extrapolation of accuracy where testing has occurred at points surrounding a result—think calibration at multiple points on a curve

LOC (lack of convergence): the inability to cross one's eyes

Malaise: feeling generally uncomfortable or uneasy, with the cause being challenging to classify

Matrix: a grid that is used to compare test results in order to come to a conclusion about the category of drug affecting a person

MDMA (ecstasy): a typically recreational drug with no medical or prescription uses; can cause empathy, euphoria, heightened sensations, as well as depression, fatigue, blurred vision, and other impairing effects

Metabolite: a substance that is produced in the body due to the breakdown of another substance; can be active (can cause impairment) or inactive (does not cause impairment), i.e., THC breaks down to hydroxy-THC (active) then carboxy-THC (inactive). Detection of THC or hydroxy-THC indicates the presence of a possibly impairing substance whereas the presence of carboxy-THC does not and only indicates prior exposure to THC

Miosis: constricted pupils

Mydriasis: dilated pupils

Ng: nanogram 1000000 ng = 1 mg

Nystagmus: the involuntary jerking of the eyes

OLS (One-Leg-Stand): one of the divided-attention tests pursuant to the DRE procedure

Precision: how close measurements are to each other; think of a target with all shots grouped in one part of the target but not necessarily the bull's-eye

Psychosis: loss of touch with reality; impairment to the point of interference with ability to think or emote

Ptosis: droopy eyelids

Pupilometer: a series of black circles or half-circles in half-millimetre-diameter increments used to measure pupil size by holding it next to a person's eye

Retention time: the time taken for a particular substance that has been broken out of a solution (a solute), to move through the chromatography column; more simply, how long it takes for the substance intended to be detected to move to a point where it is detected

Retention time with GCMS and LCMS testing: the manner in which the gas or liquid being tested breaks down; important because the use of a reagent for vaporization or liquefaction that has a retention time too close to the substance being tested for, may give a false positive

Sensitivity: the ratio of true positive assessments based on the number of positive assessments, i.e., if nine of ten positive assessments proved true, then it has a 0.9 or 90 percent sensitivity. This shows how good a test is at detecting what it is supposed to, i.e., drug present. If a drug test has low sensitivity, then too many people who have drugs in their system are not identified as such

SFST (Standardized Field Sobriety Test): a battery of three tests used as a screening method to determine whether to make an arrest for impaired driving

Somnolence: tiredness, sleepiness, or drowsiness

Specificity: the ratio of true negatives assessments based on the number of negative assessments, i.e., if four of five negative assessments were properly negative then it has a 0.8 or 80 percent specificity. This shows how good a test is at providing a correct negative call, i.e., drug not present. If a drug test has low specificity, then it incorrectly indicates people without drugs as having them in their system

Sphygmomanometer: blood pressure cuff

Synergistic effect: where two or more drugs act together to have an effect greater than the sum of their individual effects, i.e., 1 + 1 = 3

Systolic blood pressure: when the heart is pushing (the higher number)

THC (tetrahydrocannabinol): chemically (–)-trans-Δ^9-tetrahydrocannabinol, the main psychoactive ingredient in all cannabis

VGN (Vertical Gaze Nystagmus): one of the tests used in the DRE testing to check for involuntary eye jerking following a focal point in the vertical plane

W&T (Walk-and-Turn): one of the divided-attention tests pursuant to the DRE procedure

Table of Cases

Index

NOTE: Bold-faced locators indicate Glossary entries

About the Author

FOR THE PAST ELEVEN YEARS Nathan has been a criminal law practitioner who focuses on impaired-driving matters. Most recently he has taken on the additional role of standing agent for the Public Prosecution Service of Canada in Peterborough, prosecuting matters under the *Controlled Drugs and Substances Act* in addition to his private practice. Since 2012, he has produced the *Drug Recognition Exercise/Standardized Field Sobriety Testing Netletter* for practitioners, to keep them abreast of developments related to drug-impaired driving. He has developed and presented a day-long CPD course in consultation with DRE officers. In 2015, he was a panel member on the Law Society of Upper Canada's annual Drinking and Driving CPD and authored the paper provided to participants for the panel. Nathan has received training to conduct SFST and DRE training at seminars in Atlanta and New Orleans in 2014 and 2016, as well as completing the NCDD Mastering Scientific Evidence Course.

Printed and bound by CPI Group (UK) Ltd, Croydon, CR0 4YY

15/09/2026

14962401-0001